BERTIE AHERN

BERTIE AHERN

Taoiseach and Peacemaker

KEN WHELAN AND
EUGENE MASTERSON

BLACKWATER PRESS

First published in Eire in 1998 by
MAINSTREAM PUBLISHING COMPANY (EDINBURGH) LTD
7 Albany Street
Edinburgh EH1 3UG
in association with Blackwater Press

ISBN 1 84131 388 2

A catalogue record for this book is available from the British Library

Typeset in 11$^1/_2$ on 13$^1/_2$pt Galliard
Printed and bound in Eire by Microprint

Contents

ACKNOWLEDGEMENTS

In Edinburgh – our editor Andrea Fraile, editorial manager Judy Diamond and Mainstream directors Peter MacKenzie and Bill Campbell for their endurance; Marilyn Leichmann for being a friend and Irene for letting us in (!).

In Dublin – Kathleen Smith for further endurance above and beyond the call of duty, Donnacha Whelan and the Masterson family in Swords – Jim, Rosaleen, Barry, Sharon and Aoife.

Mairead Carey for being Mairead Carey. All the staff at *Ireland on Sunday*, particularly editor Liam Hayes, co-founder Cathal Dervan, managing director Ashley Balbirnie, chairman Paschal Taggart and colleagues Niamh O Connor, Niamh Hodgkins, Mary Kerrigan, Ciaran O'Tuama, Kathy Donaghy, Cathy Dillon, Claire Browne, Annmarie Durkan, Cormac Burke, Anthony Cawley, Simon Farrell, Domhnall Dervan, Dara de Faoite, Tom Mooney, Pat Chapman, Darach MacDonald, Jennifer Lee, Orla Cooney, Rachel Borrill, Fiona Ryan, Finnoula McCarthy, Rory Hafford, Aideen O'Sullivan, Marion Cullen, John Mooney, Ann Dermody, Brendan Liddy, Colm Coughlan, Mary McCabe, Kieran Carey, Oonagh McMahon and Christy and Karen Fox for all their constructive help and advice. And Michael Clifford for being so sycophantic! We would also like to thank aides of the Taoiseach, Sandra Cullagh, Cyprian Brady, Jackie Gallagher, Paddy Duffy, Tony Kett and Celia Larkin.

John O'Connor of Blackwater Press also deserves our thanks.

Others who helped out include Louise Kenny and Alex Connolly in the Department of Health, the staff at An Post's SDS depot in Kilbarrack, Mark Burke of Dublin's Naomh Padraig Celtic supporters club, *Hot Press* magazine.

This book would have been impossible to produce without the invaluable assistance of Barry O'Keefe of *The Irish Times*. Thanks, Barry. His colleagues, Jane Suiter and Padraig O'Morain also deserve our gratitude. Rafe Costigan deserves special thanks for help in proofreading and Paschal McKenna in Tuam and Kevin McDermot in Dublin for their support.

And a very big thank you to Bertie Ahern for his co-operation.

The photographs in this edition have been reproduced by kind permission of the following: Bertie Ahern; Maxwell's Picture Agency, Dublin; Joe O'Shaughnessy of the *Connacht Tribune*; Eamonn Farrell of Photocall Ireland!; Jim Walpole of the *Star*; Noel Gavin of All Pix; Dan Chung Reuters; and Reuters. Special thanks to David Dunne and James Clifford, also of the *Star*, for their photographic help.

Ken Whelan and Eugene Masterson,
Dublin, 23 October 1998

Chapter 1

'Round up the Usual Suspects'

When Garda Frank Fallon was gunned down on an April afternoon in 1970 in an apparent IRA bank robbery on Dublin's Arran Quay, the Special Branch made their routine call to the Ahern family in Drumcondra. Fallon was the first Garda murdered in the Republic for years and every one of the 'usual suspects' was rounded up for questioning. After a brief interrogation at the Ahern home on Church Avenue, the Branch departed, but one of their number had the wit to tell his superiors to take Con Ahern's name off the intelligence records which the Gardaí held on the IRA. The 66-year-old father of five adult children was hardly the most promising suspect for the crime.

The episode reflected a free admission by the authorities of the dearth of solid intelligence it held on the IRA at what was to be the start of another generation of violence on the island of Ireland.

Ever since Con Ahern came to Dublin to make his fortune in the '30s he was a routinely observed man and his family were accustomed to the attentions of the Special Branch. He had been a 'face' on de Valera's losing side in the Civil War and had remained so for most of his working life, at least in so far as his name was on the dusty ledgers at Garda headquarters. He lived his early life outside Kinsale and was a teenage runner for the 3rd Cork brigade of the IRA during the War of Independence. He remained with the Republicans when the Treaty negotiations were concluded. As Bertie Ahern recalls today, 'My father remained on that Republican list for a long time. When Garda Fallon was shot, we were visited as we had been on all the previous occasions. But they finally decided that at that stage, my father was too old. Both my father and mother were Republicans – hardline Republicans. My father would have continued his activities with Republican groups up until the '30s. He served all his stints and was proud of them all. He was in several prisons. Tom Barry was his commander in the IRA and until the day he died (in December 1990 at the age of 86) he had a huge respect for Barry.'

Con Ahern's role in the flying columns in the Munster region during the Troubles can be measured by the fact that the Free State security forces kept one Republican volunteer from each region in prison until the Civil War was deemed to be over. Con Ahern was the last Republican prisoner to go free. Like the combatants on both sides of the Civil War, he kept a permanent vow of silence from the 1920s about the war and never denied or elaborated upon his personal exploits during the civil upheaval. Neither did he credit or discredit the exploits of the other side.

'I knew all of those fellows my father was involved with. There were seven or eight of them, and all of them promised to tell me their stories before they died, but I was at all of their funerals and never heard those stories. They knew how to keep a secret,' Bertie remembers.

Like most of his generation whose families were involved in the Troubles, his inheritance was his parents' historical and political bias. The Ahern siblings would have been told that Con was in Cork jail the night Michael Collins was shot dead in West Cork and that the Republican prisoners there knelt down and said the Rosary when they heard the tragic news.

'Rather than being bitter that night, my father and his cellmates in Tin Town jail in the Curragh said the Rosary for Collins. It was an interesting insight from the Da because some would try to put it about that the Republicans would have been celebrating Collins's death,' he adds.

His mother Julia, who died shortly before the Good Friday Agreement was finally signed by her Taoiseach son, was from another Cork Republican family who lived outside Bantry. Her relations, Bertie's cousins, still run the family farm there to this day. She also came to Dublin in the '30s and worked as a children's nurse in a home on Holybank Road in Drumcondra. By chance, the nursing home was beside Con Ahern's digs and her future husband worked just across the road for the priests in All Hallows seminary. They courted in the

'30s, married in the '40s and raised their family in the '50s and '60s in the red-bricked, terraced house on Church Avenue which came with Con's farm manager's job at All Hallows.

The couple had five children: Maurice, the eldest, joined the Clonliffe harriers nearby and became a middle-distance athlete for Ireland, while Noel became a Fianna Fáil TD on the coat tails of his brother and, ironically, a spokesman for a late-century, Catholic, conservative Ireland. The two girls in the family, Kathleen and Eileen, lived quieter lives, with Kathleen marrying into farming stock in Co. Kildare and Eileen working at Dublin's Mater hospital. Bertie, the middle Ahern born at Dublin's Rotunda hospital on 12 September 1951, was destined to become the Taoiseach on his 20th year in politics.

The Republicanism of the Ahern household was understood and would have been reinforced by the visitations of the Special Branch. In any case, the local Fianna Fáil party machine always knew they could count on seven Ahern votes when all the family had reached voting age.

Ahern was reared in mid-century Ireland when the all-persuasive influence of the Fianna Fáil founder, Eamon de Valera, was waning and a new Fianna Fáil and a new economic order in the Republic was being formulated by his successor, Sean Lemass. The frugalities of the de Valera years, of Fianna Fáil, with its unquestioned allegiance to the Catholic Church and its haemorrhaging emigration, had produced an Irish economy with a conspicuous chip on its shoulder and a profound inferiority complex. Indeed, the Irish economy of Ahern's early childhood in the '50s and of de Valera's declining dog years in power depended as much on weekly registered letters bearing remittances from loved ones forced to leave Ireland for Britain or the United States to find work to support their families, as much as on any great economic initiatives from Government buildings. Fortunately, this era was giving way to Sean Lemass's dream of an economically independent Ireland.

As a wartime Minister for Industry, Lemass pioneered the electrification of rural Ireland which in turn underpinned his development of the Shannon Free Enterprise zone – the precursor for Ireland becoming a premier location for multi-national employment, particularly from the United States. He gave his economic guru, Ken Whittaker, the political space to develop his Programmes for Economic Expansions which would further open the economy and begin the process of repatriating the Irish emmigrant population in the '60s. Lemass even toyed with the idea of developing a reproachment and a new relationship with the Unionist oligarchy which ran Northern Ireland as their fiefdom, and crossed the border to Belfast to hold talks with their leader, Captain James O'Neill.

When Ahern became politically active during the mid-'60s, Fianna Fáil politics was at the crossroads between the old and new and there was no contest about which Fianna Fáil Ahern favoured. To this day, Ahern sees none of his predecessors holding a candle to Lemass in terms of using power to change the lot of the electorate. For Ahern, Lemass is a political hero. The 'slightly constitutional' predecessor, famed for his enduring political maxim of 'rising economic tides lifting all boats' is the only Irish Taoiseach worthy of any extensive and diligent study. When he was first elected to the Dáil in 1977 and was just another political greenhorn in a herd of greenhorns who made up the record-breaking majority for the Jack Lynch-led government, Ahern spent his obscure backbench days in the Dáil library swotting up on Lemass's speeches and legislation.

There is an inevitability that Ahern's time as Taoiseach will mirror the Lemass standard because, so far, the past 20 years of Ahern's political activity is textbook Lemass in terms of political and economic pragmatism. Already Ahern has begun to emulate his 'slightly constitutional' hero by ensuring that the territorial claims on the north of Ireland, so sacrosanct to de Valera's Fianna Fáil, have been abandoned in the Republic and this without internal party dissent while the Ahern economic dogma of creating the labour and market conditions for growth and investment belongs to the Fianna Fáil of the mid-'60s. The fact that Ahern as Taoiseach talks of crushing those violently opposed to the Good Friday Agreement and speaks of being on the same team as Unionist leader, David Trimble, in developing the non-territorial island of Ireland, is a mere extension of what Lemass was contemplating with Captain O'Neill.

Aside from politics, an equal influence on Ahern as he was growing up in the '50s and '60s was his home-life.

The Aherns were a relatively fortunate lower-middle-class family in that they did not have to endure the curse of family emigration like most similar Dublin families of their status. The family ethos prized education which was neither free nor easily accessed at the time, but which would have been routine for the Aherns considering their associations with the All Hallows seminary.

The home environment was also unique from the perspective of today's heavily urbanised Dublin lifestyle – here was a family living and working on a 30-acre farm a mere mile and a half from the Liffey. Nearby villages like Finglas, Whitehall and Santry, now sprawling, densely-populated suburbs, were open countryside then. The public houses in these villages were classed as 'bona fides' and could serve 'travellers'' drink after the normal licensing hours. People living in these areas would travel into Dublin during the '60s to shop in department stores like Clery's and Arnotts or buy food and wine in city centre outlets like Findlaters, Liptons and the Monument Creamery on Parnell Street. The Dublin Riviera of the time was Skerries, a mere eighteen miles from O'Connell Street but a good and slow two-hour journey from a capital not yet reduced in size by roads, cars and urban sprawl.

In this countrified Dublin, Ahern spent a unique childhood on a big farm on the edge of a capital city and to all intents and purposes, he might as well have been reared back on his cousins' land in Cork.

'All Hallows was a big farm. They had all the land between Gracepark Road and Griffith Avenue and a big farm at the back of the airport,' Ahern recalls. 'The Da, as farm manager, had to look after both and move between the two of them. We spent all our time helping him. I did everything – milked the cows, fed the pigs, brought the swill down from the college. I never mastered ploughing but my father ploughed with two horses – he didn't drive. Even near the end of his time at the college in the '70s he still didn't drive a tractor. He kept on ploughing with the horses. We were really growing up on the land in the middle of a city. The college was effectively self-sufficient and all my summer jobs were on the farm there. I spent all my time market gardening. I did cabbages, cauliflowers and celeries. Guys like Joe Reynolds who worked with us taught me everything there was to know about plants. I was even a member of Dublin 5 Horticultural Society. I still have a huge interest in plants and I still do my own hanging baskets to this day.'

And the rural idyll in the heart of the Dublin was reinforced every year when the Aherns decamped Drumcondra for the 'free holliers' on the cousins' farm in Cork.

Living as he did within the shadow of the GAA's headquarters in Croke Park and just a stone's throw from Tolka Park where Drumcondra and Shelbourne kept Division One League of Ireland soccer alive on the city's northside and just down the road from

Dalymount Park where the Irish soccer internationals were once played, where he also followed the fortunes of Bohemians FC, it was pretty certain that the young Ahern would take a serious interest in both football codes as a schoolboy. The 'Dubs' and 'Drums' were his teams but his interest in football was not a mere sideline. In his early '20s he set up All Hamptons with his friend (now Fianna Fáil senator, Tony Kett) and this side still thrives in the amateur soccer leagues.

Ahern's sporting interests remain, much to the relief of sporting administrators, particularly the GAA bosses, who find Ireland's ninth Taoiseach always willing to listen to development proposals. In the first budget introduced by his administration last December, the Government chipped in £20 million towards the multi-million redesign of Croke Park. When he was Minister for Finance in the early '90s, Ahern gave the GAA £5 million to get the modernisation project up and running and privately he is on record as saying his Government would be open to giving soccer the same financial breaks, 'whenever they get their act together' and come up with a viable plan for a national soccer stadium.

Back in the '60s, however, things were less crowded.

'The agenda in the Ahern household was very simple depending on the day it was – GAA, politics and religion, in whatever order you liked. And each of them was hotly argued,' Ahern explains.

Chapter 2

The King of the Poster Boys

A hern's introduction to grassroots politics came at the tender age of 14 when he was roped into the Fianna Fáil by-election campaign in Dublin Central as a 'poster boy'. Ahern had just started his secondary school education at St Aidan's, a run-of-the-mill Christian Brothers school in Whitehall, about a mile from his home in Drumcondra. It was a new school taking the oversupply of students from nearby O'Connells on the North Circular Road and St. Vincent's in Glasnevin, and its only conspicuous accolade in the early '60s was its decision to expel Irish and Arsenal soccer hero, Liam Brady, because he refused to play Gaelic football for the school and instead opted to play soccer for an external club. The Christian brothers were like that in those days.

Once Ahern's teacher, Stan O'Brien, was forwarded as the Fianna Fáil candidate in a Dublin Central by-election in 1965, he press-ganged every available body into the campaign. Young Ahern's job was to shimmy up lamp posts throughout the constituency and get the best vantage point for O'Brien's election material. More importantly, he had to make sure the election material was not torn down by O'Brien's opponents. In turn, Ahern dragooned his classmates to work the lamp posts and the blitz on the constituency earned the precocious teenager the soubriquet of 'King of the Poster Boys'. Fianna Fáil may not have won the by-election but the Dublin Central constituency won Ahern.

The O'Brien campaign would be his first insight into the social and unsocial geography of a constituency which would return him to Dáil Eireann as TD some 12 years later. The hopping and trotting for O'Brien was remarkable in one other sense: during the campaign he was introduced for the first time to Charles J Haughey who was to become his mentor and subsequently, many would say, his tormentor.

'I was introduced to him at a polling booth during the election. I was 14 or 15 at the time. I was very impressed by him, really. I remember Charlie giving a bit of his time to talk to me though I don't remember what we talked about,' Ahern recalls.

Haughey's arch-rival, George Colley, was the local TD at the time and was a regular visitor to the Ahern's home in Drumcondra. Although he was only counting and mounting Fianna Fáil posters, the then Inter-Certificate student had a passing acquaintance with the two Fianna Fáil heavyweights that would slog it out for the leadership of Fianna Fáil in the late '70s when Jack Lynch retired. Ahern had been marked down as a 'potential' by the two Fianna Fáil ward bosses, Noel Booth and Tom Houlihan who ran the local Fianna Fáil O'Donovan Rossa cumann – then and now the biggest of Fianna Fáil's nationwide network of branches. Both men were neighbours and friends of the Aherns and were fixtures in the Ahern house, talking Fianna Fáil politics late into the nights with Con and Julia. Young Ahern ran the poster detail again in 1969 when Haughey and Colley jointly sought and won office there.

When the teenager was not working out the Fianna Fáil transfer percentages or good sites for election posters, he was applying himself to his education at St Aidan's CBS Secondary school (he attended primary school at St Patrick's in Drumcondra) and percentage, too, was the operative word. His only remarkable aptitudes involved figures and one of his teachers, Cyril Coughlan, who taught business studies, would focus the mind of his pupil on accountancy.

'He really made me concentrate on accountancy. You go from a stage of liking a subject to loving the subject. He got me to the stage that I was doing trial balances and balance sheets for fun on the bus to school. I don't know what it was about him but he even got me to read the *Financial Times* at school every day. Instinctively to this day I will read the *Financial Times* first unless it is a heavy news day when I will read the other papers,' Ahern says. 'I had many teachers but Cyril Coughlan gave me the love of accountancy.

Fair credit to him – he was just a great, great teacher.'

His sporting interests revolved only around football but it would have taken ten Cyril Coughlans to get him past parklife in either soccer or gaelic. He played for Home Farm, the nursery soccer club in Whitehall which has produced a sufficiency of Irish players for the English Divisions, but the bankrollers from Manchester and Liverpool were never going to break into a sweat over the abilities of one Bartholemew Ahern. He also played around the corner from his home with Drumcondra, a League of Ireland first division outfit that played at Tolka Park. Their most famous player in the early '60s was a red-haired goalkeeper called 'Sheila' Darcy, whose claim to fame was his parallel gymnastics on the cross bar at the start of every game and after he let in yet another goal.

The lack of money wrecked Drumcondra's dreams, causing the owners, the Proole family, to sell out and force the side to drop out of semi-professional football. Ahern, along with his 'lieutenant' Tony Kett, were deeply involved with the club but before long they hatched the idea of setting up their own team which they called All Hampton United. Some colleagues might argue that it had the virtue of guaranteeing the two teenagers a first-team place, but more importantly for Ahern, the bonus in the venture came when he met his wife, Miriam, who was a fan of local northside soccer.

They were in their late teens at the time and just finishing their secondary school education. The romance blossomed in nearby tennis clubs like the Charleville on Cross Guns Bridge, at 'the Nevin' up in Glasnevin and in Carty's Ivy House and the Cat and Cage pubs in Drumcondra where the All Hampton footballers adjourned for post-match post-mortems. As we shall see, the relationship would survive everything except politics. All Hamptons still strive as a junior side in the Amateur League, where Drums are still playing out their days. Ahern, meanwhile, maintains his association with both sides and is honorary chairman of Drumcondra.

His interest in Gaelic football was as natural as his interest in Fianna Fáil. It was compulsory in the Ahern household and anyway, GAA could hardly be ignored as the Aherns lived virtually under the shadow of Croke Park. As with soccer, he played heroically and valiantly but was never going to leave his day job due to his precocious footballing skills. He played with nearby Whitehall Colmcilles Gaels but the only county football jerseys he got were bought in O'Neills. He remains proud of the fact that be stood alongside Dublin GAA hero, Tommy Drum, in the battleground that is Dublin County club GAA. He refrained from setting up his own GAA operation on the northside and contented himself with becoming the 'Dubs' most high profile fan and the GAA's most generous benefactor when he later came to power.

Ahern flew through his Leaving Certificate and immediately went to the College of Commerce in Rathmines to study accountancy. It was a second-line college which produced accountants primarily, but also had a useful line in journalists and commercial secretaries: it was just one of the various southside colleges which northsiders depended on to get qualifications. The students would have joined the usual students' strikes or, more precisely, the 'away days' that the national student body had called, but by no stretch of the imagination would the college have been called a hotbed of political activity. It was a heads-down-and-get-your-exams sort of place.

He led a frugal student life. 'It was a great help not having any money – I just couldn't do anything that needed cash. After paying for the books, extra tutorials and so on, there was next to nothing left. I lived on nixers – doing the books for shops and pubs. I was part of the black economy, then,' he says.

Within three years, Ahern was out of Rathmines with his primary accountancy qualification and later completed further diploma courses through the London School of Economics in taxation, business administration and computer studies. He briefly worked with the State company, An Bord Bainne, one of the minority there that could actually milk a cow, and then, with his now established pattern of keeping things 'local', he got a job as an assistant accountant with the Mater hospital less than a mile from his home in the opposite direction of his old school.

'I was about 22 and I answered a job advertised by the Mater hospital and got it – slaving away with the nuns in the Mater and working 100 hours a week.' Apart from sorting the books out for the nuns, Ahern was rapidly sorting out his own political career in Dublin Central.

By 1972, he had met his wife-to-be Miriam Kelly, sorted out his accountancy examinations and set up a career. For good measure, his passionate interests in GAA and soccer were catered for in nearby 'Tolka', 'Dalyier' and 'Croker'.

The whole structure of his life was concentrated in the narrow corridor of Dublin, between the Liffey and the Tolka rivers through the middle-class suburbs of Drumcondra and Glasnevin and the derelict northside inner city of the capital. Little has altered in the intervening years, though in personal terms his political career would cost him his marriage.

Chapter 3

'Never Met a Socialist in my Life'

With his personal and work affairs on a secure footing, it was time for Ahern to start moving in his political career. He became secretary of the influential O'Donovan Rossa cumann with the help of Noel Booth and, within a year, was on the cumann's organising committee increasing his status within the party locally and at headquarters. When he joined the constituency's organising committee, he became something of a 'noise' at local level, though not yet a ward boss which would be a political imperative if he were to progress into national politics.

Pro temps, Ahern and his faction – all still in their early '20s – bided their time and backed Celia Lynch, a long serving Fianna Fáil backbencher who was nearing retirement. They used the time to put together the election machine which would turn Ahern into one of the biggest vote-getters in the country. Their machine would take on and destroy allcomers at every election in Dublin Central over the following 20 years as any candidates there over that period will testify.

Ahern's populist political fiefdom was created and developed for him in the constituency by an initially small inner circle which would later expand with Ahern's relentless rise through the ranks in Fianna Fáil. Around the table when the plot was being hatched in 1975 were Tony Kett, his long-time friend and footballing buddy, and now an elected Senator; Daithi O' Broinn, a school teacher from Ard Scoil Ris in the nearby suburb of Marino who has since dropped out of ward politics; Brian Curran, who married and moved to Galway; and Paul

Kiely who has effectively run Dublin Central since Ahern's election to the Dáil in 1977. It was this small group which decided that Bertie Ahern would contest the 1977 general election and set about putting together the necessary votes for the selection convention.

Significantly, in 1969, Ahern decided to become involved with trade unionism and joined the Federated Workers Union of Ireland. He used to do part-time work for the unions as a scrutineer and became friends with many of the activists that he would later spar off when, as Minister for Labour, he negotiated successive National Economic Plans with the Irish Congress of Trade and the employers. He was thought to be the right stuff for the unions at the time and was even encouraged by a trade union friend, Jan Easken, to go forward as a union branch secretary but was deemed too young for the job by the union's national executive. But the interest meant he came into contact with leading members of the union movement like young Jim Larkin, Paddy Cardiff and John Foster and for the first time, got his head around the intricacies of proportional representation and how to use it profitably. His tutor was Roddy Coughlan, a Labour party TD who was a wizard tallyman. He remained active in the trade union movement well into the '70s and was seconded onto various FWUI conference delegations.

'It was great working with the unions. They'd bring me down to the Labour club on the Quays for a few pints. I used to love drinking with those guys and it was the only job I had where you got two steak dinners a day,' he recalls. 'They would go to the Anchor hotel on Cavendish Row for their lunches and dinners. And steak was always on the menu. It was on the basis that nothing was good enough for the working man and I can tell you I never got two steak dinners a day out of Fianna Fáil.'

His work with the FWUI though would never inspire him to take a socialist route in politics. 'They knew I was Fianna Fáil and Republican and that I didn't believe in that socialist stuff. I've never met a socialist in my life and if I do I'll tell you,' he continues.

His FWUI days gave him an insight into trade union politics and their social priorities and negotiating imperatives. It also produced an enviable network of contacts within the greater trade union movement which would pay a handsome dividend when he joined the Cabinet in 1987 as Minister for Labour. According to former SIPTU union boss, Bill Attley, Ahern's shop floor and construction site contacts were extensive.

'We discovered when he was Minister for Labour that he had better contacts with the ordinary trade union activists than trade union officials themselves. There was an electricians' dispute when the Financial centre was being built down on the Docks and Ahern just arrived at the site one day, spoke to his local trade union contacts and solved the problem without any reference to the trade union officials,' Attley explains.

That type of hands-on approach to solving industrial disputes would make Ahern's reputation but would also alienate the middle ranks of the union plutocracy who quietly wished the busy-body Labour Minister would fall on his face in one of these interventions which at the rate he was going, could see him winning with a single figure swing. He was convinced that not more than a 5 per cent swing was needed in Dublin to clinch victory for Fianna Fáil. 'It was a mathematical thing,' he says today.

'There was a gang of us. We wrote this document which showed that Fianna Fáil could win an overall majority if there was a 5 per cent swing in Dublin. We presented it to Seamus Brennan [then party general secretary and now Ahern's Government chief whip] and the boys. Brennan thought it was interesting and he asked myself and Colette Meleady [a party activist from the Sycamore area of Finglas East from where a Fine Gael TD, Mary Flaterty, would subsequently emerge] to present the theory to an Ogra Fianna Fáil meeting.

'Brennan had just set up the youth wing of the party at the time. I was as nervous as hell but made a reasonable twist of the presentation,' he reveals.

As luck would have it, RTE television's political pundit, Brian Farrell was in the audience and approached Ahern afterwards about his figures. He asked Ahern and Meleady onto the television station's lead political programme of the day – *Seven Days* – to run through his figures with a national audience.

Fianna Fáil had been out of power for the previous four years as a consequence of the Arms Trial Crisis which saw four senior Fianna Fáil Ministers, including Finance Minister Charles J. Haughey, relieved of Ministerial Office, on the grounds of an alleged conspiracy (never proven) to import arms to Northern Ireland. The political wisdom of the mid-'70s suggested that they would be out of power for another five years. To make sure of this eventuality, the Fine Gael–Labour Coalition of the day redrew the constituencies to maximise their support as was their prerogative at the time. Critically, they decided to turn the vital Dublin constituencies into three-seaters. The redrawn constituencies were referred to at the time as the 'Tullymander' after the Local Government Minister, the late Jimmy Tully of the Labour party who had written the political insurance policy for the Coalition Government.

The unpopularity of Fianna Fáil combined with the electoral bias which these eleven three-seater constituencies would give to the Coalition would copperfasten their vote. It seemed to be a watertight plan, but it depended on a 'no swing' to Fianna Fáil. Nevertheless, the main political commentators could not see how Fianna Fáil could wrest power back while there was no immediate evidence of any swing coming through the various media and party political polls that were being commissioned in the lead up to the general election. The only positive news for Fianna Fáil in the election lead-in period seemed to be the pushy 5 per cent swing theory from the Ahern greenhorns. Ahern and Meleady braved the *Seven Days* programme, pouring forth about the mathematics of pending elections and, providentially for Ahern, Fianna Fáil party leader, Jack Lynch, appeared on the same programme. The would-be politician had got his five minutes of fame and left his calling card at party headquarters.

The 'Tullymander' had truncated most of the Dublin constituencies and the traditional boundaries of Dublin North Central were scattered into neighbouring constituencies leaving even-sitting TDs with a problem as to where they would stand. Again providentially, most of Ahern's base in Drumcondra and Glasnevin was pushed into Dublin Finglas leaving a substantial amount of potential votes outside the traditional bailiwick of local Fianna Fáil TD, Jim Tunney, who was a Finglas-based politician. Tunney had a view that some 'local' should stand to cover the potential votes in Drumcondra and this encouragement was sufficient for the Ahern faction to pounce.

They failed. Ahern missed out on a nomination by three votes to Danny Bell, a Finglas city councillor who joined Tunney on the ticket. Fortuitously, this left two politicians vying for the same Fianna Fáil vote in the Finglas end of the constituency and left the party completely exposed without a candidate at the Drumcondra end where some 40 per cent of the electorate resided. The Fianna Fáil National Executive took immediate action to close the electoral gap and imposed Bertie Ahern on the ticket. The time had come to see if the Ahern swing theory was moonshine or sunshine.

Chapter 4

Hoovering up the Vote
in Drumcondra

The Fianna Fáil organisation left Bertie Ahern and his coterie in splendid isolation in the southern part of the Dublin Finglas constituency to hoover up the votes of the party faithful there and to wait for the much-hoped-for swing to the party. Tunney had no problem with the carve-up of the constituency because he knew his quota would be produced in Finglas in any case and he was confident that he could handle any challenge from his running mate, Danny Bell. The deal with Tunney was simplicity itself. 'He'd take a slip in his support to bolster my first preferences and he would stay out of my areas. He came down in votes and I went up,' is how the incumbent Taoiseach describes the sideline pact with Tunney today.

In a three-seater constituency, vote management is the only political tactic that shows any dividends but even the most rigorous management of votes would not have been enough in 1977. A swing to Fianna Fáil was still needed. And the quickest way known to politicians anywhere to finesse a swing is to bribe the electorate. When Fianna Fáil published its 1977 election manifesto they brought good, old-fashioned political bribery of the electorate to new heights. Few in Fianna Fáil would deny as much today. Domestic household rates and car taxes were to be abolished and social welfare rates across all sectors were to rise. That was just for starters. It was said of the manifesto that if the electorate wanted the moon, Fianna Fáil would have written a

24

promise to buy Cape Canaveral, so desperate was their need to return to Government. The manifesto was the brainchild of Trinity College Economics Professor, Martin O'Donoghue, and seemed solely predicated on the notion that if the Government put money into the economy, the economy, of itself, would grow.

The electorate were slow to bite on the Fianna Fáil giveaway with the polls showing no immediate shift of allegiance. The policies themselves were being brutally rubbished by independent economic commentators as 'spending our way out of a boom' – indeed, political commentary in the media was generally hostile to the party. Gradually, however, the middle classes, who were set to benefit most, began looking at their personal bank balances and started moving their votes to Fianna Fáil. The Fine Gael–Labour coalition fought the election on their record but on the economic front this was not their leading suit and, on the political front, it was to be their downfall.

One of the Ministers, Conor Cruise O'Brien, emphasised his views on Northern Ireland and the 'impending civil war' there and frightened the electorate with other fear and loathing security issues. When the penny dropped that Fianna Fáil's manifesto was making an impact, the Coalition lightened up on the economic front but they gave too little too late – a fact which seemed to underline that there was indeed scope to reduce taxes as O'Donoghue had preached.

This shift by the electorate, however, did not reveal itself, at least publicly, through polling information commissioned by the newspapers. It was rumoured that polling information commissioned by one leading national newspaper identified the swing to Fianna Fáil, but the information was so out of kilter with what had been published throughout the campaign and with the prevailing wisdom of political commentators, that the newspaper spiked the poll.

Whatever the truth about that story, the actual poll on election day saw over 50 per cent of the electorate backing Fianna Fáil as voters voted with their wallets and destroyed the outgoing Government. It was a political bloodbath of Alamo proportions: Ministers like Conor Cruise O'Brien and Justin Keating faced total humiliation by their constituents who switched to Fianna Fáil and gave the Republican party its biggest ever majority for a single party Government. The three-seat 'Tullymander' blew up in the Coalition's faces and had handed Fianna Fáil a twenty-seat majority. It was indicative of the political cack-handedness of the Tullymander that one of the first measures announced by the incoming Jack Lynch administration was its intention to cede the redrawing of constituencies from the political élite to an Independent Judicial Constituency Commission. The election was a triumph for Fianna Fáil in general, and for Bertie Ahern in particular. On his first electoral outing for the Dáil he notched up over 4,000 first preferences and won the second seat for Dublin Finglas on transfers.

The Fianna Fáil election pledges would have accounted for much of this encouraging tally but looking at Ahern's transfers, it emerged that many of his second and third preferences were marked down for the Labour party's candidate, Brendan Halligan and Fine Gael's Luke Belton. It became apparent that Ahern had the makings of a substantial personal vote in the constituency as he was getting the 'first scratch' in the polling booths from people who would otherwise have voted for different parties. This ability to attract votes or later preferences from other parties would build up Ahern's electoral base in subsequent elections and would be critical to Ahern becoming Taoiseach 20 years later, as it would be preferences – even from sworn political foes like Fine Gael – that would clinch power for him.

Another feature of the campaign mounted in Dublin Central by the Ahern team was the introduction of 'focused canvassing' which required plenty of shoe leather and brass neck. The Ahern campaign canvassed every vote in the constituency up to three times and introduced 'breakfast' canvassing in which every household in the constituency was blitzed with early morning literature drops. In Ahern's textbook, 90 per cent of a politician's job lies in close interaction with his constituents while a mere 10 per cent depends on election manifestos. The only vital information flow as far as he is concerned, is what is coming from the households in each constituency – it is the kernal of politics, and after the 1977 election he set about making sure that his constituency headquarters became the centre of the political information flow on the northside of Dublin.

In retrospect, Ahern believes that the 1977 Manifesto was economic make-believe. Other economic commentators are not as kind in their analysis, claiming the manifesto led to a huge national debt that dominated economic and political life for the following decade and took a further decade to get under control.

'The car tax thing was a nonsense and abolishing rates was totally wrong. All we needed was a waiver scheme. I remember at the time there were a lot of old people – Garda widows and retired teachers –

who had huge houses but no money and they were being screwed for rates. All we needed to do was bring in a good waiver scheme for the people who hadn't got the bread. Instead, we abolished rates and here we are, 20 years on, and Dublin Corporation have to do everything on a shoe-string because they can't have a local charge.

'I agreed with local charges but you'll not get rates back again. The game is over on that one. It has to be indirect taxation now,' he says.

Chapter 5

A Raucous Backbencher

A hern passed his first two years in Dáil Eireann anonymously, just another backbencher in a parliament full of Fianna Fáil voting fodder. It was hard to get noticed and harder still to get inside Lynch's tight circle which was dominated by George Colley and Dessie O'Malley. His time at Leinster House was mainly spent reading up Lemass speeches and legislation in the Dáil Library and streamlining his constituency operation with Kett, Kiely, Curran and O'Broinn. Meanwhile, the only political manoeuvrings going on in the background concerned the succession stakes to Jack Lynch.

Haughey had been returned to Cabinet as Health Minister while Colley, the favourite to succeed and the candidate backed by the party's establishment, had the far more important Finance portfolio.

The huge majority was always going to be problematical when it came to the succession fight as there were swathes of backbenchers left outside the loop of power. They were loose canons, in fact, that could not be constrained by an aloof Lynch Cabinet when a secret vote on a new party leader would take place. The Ahern vote was not particularly canvassed by George Colley who may have believed that the vote was his because the influential O'Donovan Rossa cumann would have mandated their TD to back George Colley if required to do so. Nevertheless, Ahern would have known Haughey better. Ahern was on an internal party committee in the

28

mid-'70s set up to advise the then shadow spokesman on Health, Charlie Haughey, who at that stage was on the comeback after the setback of the Arms Trial – he got onto that committee because of his associations with the Mater hospital. In the run-up to the leadership vote some 18 months after Lynch's record-breaking general election victory, Colley faced Haughey with an obvious favourite's chance.

'I had met George but I didn't really know him. A lot of cumann people in the constituency would have been Colley people but Tunney and myself were given a free hand in who we voted for,' explains Ahern.

But Colley was part of an aloof élite which ran the Cabinet and was typified by Ahern's revelation that he never stepped inside Jack Lynch's Taoiseach office. He was not alone: neither did the other backbenchers.

'I knew Charlie well because of my involvement in the health committee when he got back onto the front-bench. He was very positive about the party and kept in touch with the new raft of TDs that came with the election victory.'

When the leadership vote was sprung on the Fianna Fáil parliamentary party in 1979, the two TDs from Dublin Finglas cancelled each other out with Ahern backing Haughey and Tunney publicly backing Colley which he memorably justified in his much-repeated phrase – 'I don't buy my colours coming out of the stadium.' Tunney, who was junior Minister at the Department of Education with specific responsibility for sport, fully expected that his political career would be curtailed on the evening that Haughey won but was pleasantly surprised when he was retained by Haughey and subsequently made chairman of the Fianna Fáil parliamentary party, and later Leas Ceann Comhairle of the Dáil. Ahern, on the other hand, was too 'politically downtable' to expect any real preferment in the new Haughey Government set-up. He was, however, appointed Assistant Government Whip by Haughey – a vacuous title which meant nothing beyond the fact that it was better than *not* being Assistant Government Whip. Lady luck would again intervene, though in unfortunate circumstances.

Sean Moore, the actual Chief Whip who also had the rank of Minister for State, was ill throughout 1980 and Ahern was effectively doing the job but without the perks of an extra salary and a State car. The job meant that Ahern was in direct contact with all the Fianna Fáil parliamentary members and their nationwide political networks as well as being the conduit between the Cabinet and voting fodder in the Dáil – it also gave him the opportunity to negotiate Dáil business with the opposition parties for the first time.

The job got Ahern to the doors of power but it would take another seven years before he was actually shown through them.

Chapter 6

'All Politics are Local'

With a cushion of 20 seats in the Dáil there was little or no need for a Government Whip and less for an Assistant Whip, though Ahern's dry run at the job, due to Sean Moore's illness, would be invaluable later, when the heaves against Haughey got underway. His constituency colleague, Jim Tunney, remained as a Junior Minister in the first Haughey administration and in accordance with usual political practice, he ceded his seat on Dublin Corporation to his junior constituency colleague. Ahern could not have been happier and considering his penchant for local politics, he thought all his birthdays had arrived at once. City Hall was and remains the passport to publicity and popularity in Dublin politics and all Ahern had to do was make sure he was more popular and more publicly known than the rest of the Fianna Fáil's backbenchers in the city.

The Ahern machine took three years to put in place and by the early '80s it had become unstoppable. The '77 election tally of nearly 4,000 votes rose to 5,000, 7,000 and then 11,000 votes in the three snap elections called during 1981 and 1982. In the final election of 1982, he polled over double the first preference tally of his running mate George Colley, who only three years previously had expected to be leader of Fianna Fáil and Taoiseach in succession to Jack Lynch.

It was an achievement noted and remarked upon by party leader, Charlie Haughey, who saw the ruthlessness and ambitions of the Ahern organisation as the only way that his party would ever again win a majority of seats in Dublin and thereby achieve his cherished aim of single-party, Fianna Fáil government. The machine's electoral methodology was simple. The constituency was divided into 25 ward areas, each of which was run by 'ward bosses' who were known and respected in their localities. In Ahern's view, any Dublin city constituency can be split into 'distinct villages' with problems and issues quite separate from each other. It harks back to his upbringing on the 'farm in the city' when areas like Drumcondra, Glasnevin, Whitehall and Finglas were independent of each other and quite different, so that Ahern still sees the geographic framework of separate and different villages in what is now a vast north Dublin conurbation. These ward bosses, in turn, had up to seven workers who could be relied upon to canvass and recanvass the constituency properly. Canvassers who annoyed people on their doorsteps and argued the toss with potential voters were ruthlessly dropped and given envelope-filling jobs.

The reliability of canvassers and the dependability of the information they were bringing back to constituency headquarters were paramount, and the same is true in Dublin Central today. Crucially, this hardcore committed element canvassed for Ahern first and Fianna Fáil second. Their primary job was to pinpoint exactly where the Fianna Fáil voters resided and to know precisely the individual and collective problems of the local electorate.

By the second 1982 election, the Ahern machine could judge from its extensive profile of the constituency the amount of Ahern votes coming from each single house and whether intensive canvassing and glad handing of wavering voters had been successful.

'When the election machine went into action it was purely for Ahern. We have some leeway now but in the early days we were ruthless. Other Fianna Fáil candidates would complain about the way we ran things. We just ignored them,' Senator Tony Kett explains.

'We were determined to run Dublin Central and we were determined that nobody, not even our own people in our own party, would get in our way. Even in our first election we ignored warnings not to go into Jim Tunney's area and we made forays there all the time,' he adds. 'We succeeded, and we still run the constituency in the same way today. Anyone who says otherwise doesn't know what they are talking about.'

Today the machine can give you better information on the 'hatches, matches and despatches' (births, marriages and deaths) in Dublin Central than the various City registries. It is one of their boasts. The second critical part of the Ahern operation dealt with fund raising.

From the very beginning it was accepted that Ahern would run a full time professional office and constituency service for Dublin Central. He was one of the first of the new generation to drop the haphazard clientelism that was favoured by constituency politicians for a straightforward, professional service for his electorate, run from a central location and staffed by professionals. Today the office is staffed by Cyprian Brady (the son of one of the original Ahern workers), who is seconded from the Department of Social Welfare and two secretaries, Grainne Carruth and Sandra Cullagh, who have been with him for years. This service is in addition to his political office in Leinster House which is run by Ahern's partner, Celia Larkin.

In the early days, the operation depended on race nights and limited draws to raise the necessary cash to pay staff, but when Fianna Fáil's National Treasurer and financial guru, Des Richardson, joined the Ahern inner circle in the early '80s, the financing was restructured. Richardson did away with 'bitty' fund-raisers and decided to pitch for funding in one single hit – an American-styled, £120-a-plate dinner at the Royal hospital in Kilmainham. The dinner was an immediate success and attracted up to 500 guests, mainly from building, business and political circles. As Ahern grew in political stature over the years so did the Royal Hospital beano which now attracts a good deal of Corporate interest. The dinner raises sufficient funds to payroll the constituency office and defray the substantial mortgage on St Luke's, the Dublin Central constituency headquarters located in Drumcondra. It has been the main source of income for the day-to-day running expenses of the Ahern operation for the past 15 years.

The third and most important part of the constituency jigsaw was Ahern himself, and right from the word go this depended on Ahern not being backward about coming forward once he entered the Dáil. With no Government profile to fall back on, Ahern had to fend for himself and that meant getting raucous. An example of this occurred in his early years in the Dáil when his constituency, like most other Dublin inner city communities, was devastated by a heroin epidemic among its young population. The whole horror of drug abuse was clearly visible to anyone who walked down Dublin's main thoroughfare, O'Connell Street, and was more tragically obvious to the people who lived in the flat complexes in Dublin Central. Through his soccer activities, which included organising street leagues in these flat complexes, Ahern saw the drug epidemic unfold before his very eyes and also knew at first hand the *modus operandi* of the main city pushers like Larry Dunne and Tony Felloni who were then serious players in the drug trade. Both are now behind bars but have been replaced by other, equally lethal, drug barons and gangs.

'You could see it starting off from 1978 onwards. It was ferocious. The Dunnes were around then and the Italian guy, Felloni, was involved big time,' Ahern recalls.

By the early '80s these drug families were flaunting their wealth and their trade, and literally thumbing their noses at the authorities. The Gardaí didn't seem to be getting anywhere in their battle – even to contain the drugs problem – so eventually the direct action neighbourhood groups, like Concerned Parents Against Drugs, emerged to fight the drugs barons. This group, backed mainly by Sinn Féin, with the implicit suggestion of IRA assistance, marched out to the homes of drug pushers, and in the Cabra West area of the northside they actually knee-capped two well-known heroin dealers.

Ahern said publicly that he could understand why communities had been driven to take such action. He explained on RTE's *Day to Day* programme that the vigilantes' action against known criminals had been 'quite effective' although he stressed that he condemned their extra legal move.

'Groups of residents often came to me,' he told interviewer John Bowman, 'to say they were setting up vigilante groups and are seeking my advice. I tell them it is dangerous and then they come back months later and say that crime has been cut in their areas through the vigilantes. It's hard to keep saying, well, "it's not a good idea".

'In my own area they've taken various actions, some of which I'm totally opposed to. But unfortunately, John, I must say they are quite effective. In one particular part of the constituency [Cabra West], very severe action was taken against known criminals and the area has almost cleaned itself up since.'

His remarks were taken by Garda chiefs as support for vigilantism and by opposition leaders like Proinsias de Rossa of the then Workers Party, as implicit support for direct community action. A spokesman for the Association of Garda Sergeants and Inspectors condemned Ahern's remarks. 'Even such hinted or tacit support or recognition of vigilante groups is too much,' he said. 'Seemingly, according to Bertie Ahern, these people who were knee-capped were criminals. You are not a criminal until you have been convicted by the courts.' Political foe Proinsias de Rossa, described Ahern's remarks as 'outrageous'.

'Not only is it outrageous for a member of the Oireachtas to imply support in this way for such activities, but it is equally outrageous because it is completely untrue that vigilantes do anything other than threaten the protection which the law should afford to all citizens and simply replace one terror with another.'

Ahern remained unfazed during the controversy and the incident did little harm to the 'ordinary guy', grassroot image he was trying to portray at the time.

Another aspect of the drugs epidemic in his constituency was the rivalry it created between Ahern and Tony Gregory – an independent TD who was elected as an anti-drugs campaigner and champion of the working-class in the constituency. Gregory came to national prominence when the formation of a Charlie Haughey government in 1981 depended on his vote. He extracted what seemed a high price for his moniker in terms of housing and facilities for his patch in a negotiation which Haughey opened with the immortal words – 'You know what I want – so what do you want?'.

The problem for Ahern was that the deal was being done for his constituency and there was no political kudos for him in the divvy-up between Haughey and Gregory. Haughey would explain later, with some justification, that he was merely rescheduling what was going to take place in the inner city area anyway. The publicity secured Gregory's Dáil seat alongside Ahern but the idea of Gregory masquerading as the saviour of the inner city got up Ahern's nose. That was a soubriquet he wanted reserved for himself. During the 1985 local elections to City Hall, Ahern decided to settle the issue of who ran Dublin Central, once and for all. His view of that 1985 election and of Gregory's performance is scathing.

'Tony Gregory was small fry. When I went head to head with him in the 1985 local elections people soon stopped talking about how great he was. I got 5,000 votes and he got 1,800. The argument was about who ran the inner city. I did. It was as simple as that,' Ahern says today.

A footnote to the mutual enmity between both politicians came in a Rachel Borrill interview with Gregory in *Ireland on Sunday* earlier this year in which he claimed that Ahern's lieutenants offered him a Junior Minister's job to support the new minority Ahern administration. 'In his dreams,' retorts Ahern.

As for the drug-pushing in the constituency today, Ahern says the remedies are only now beginning to work.

'I was down recently in Champions Avenue [inner city], where the local school was burned down. There were eight Guards around the park off Cathal Brugha Street. Eight Guards in uniform down there, and all of the residents were saying – "Fair play to you Bertie, fair play to you."

'These people are absolutely delighted. We're having some problems with drugs being back on the streets again, because there are some new operators, but the Guards are moving them.'

To consolidate the various strands of the Ahern *modus operandi*, he then love-bombed the entire constituency each year and canvassed each household between May and September. Even now, as Taoiseach, he is as likely to do spot canvasses in the constituency to keep in touch with his electorate. And though most of his clinics in the various clubs and pubs in Dublin Central are carried out by subordinate councillors or his own professional staff, he still makes it his business to drop in to these gatherings whenever time permits at weekends. The net effect of the thoroughness of the operation is seen on the eve of each election when all the various foot soldiers of the Ahern machine gather in the Gresham hotel. Up to 400 can attend those meetings, and they are all primarily Ahern people as distinct from Fianna Fáil people.

Chapter 7

The House

One of the hardy, annual stories peddled by Dublin's tabloid press in general and the Fine Gael press office in particular, concerns the purchase and ownership of St Luke's – Ahern's constituency office in the heart of Drumcondra. It's a typical 'nudge, nudge' story flogged every now and then in Dublin pubs which suggests that there is something irregular about the purchase. The redbricked, two-storey building is situated on the busy airport road about half a mile from Ahern's family home on Church Avenue in Drumcondra. It is conveniently opposite 'Kennedy's' – Ahern's local pub where he has been drinking pints of Bass for the past 20 years.

When Ahern was first elected to the Dáil, the constituency political work was run from an inner city property on Amiens Street which was owned by party headquarters in Mount Street. It was not the most salubrious of addresses at the time and to Ahern's cost, his car was burgled or vandalised as often as not. 'You would go to do a clinic there or go to a meeting and the car would be robbed,' he remembers.

With the machine getting into full swing, the Kett and Kiely faction decided it was time to move from Amiens Street into a more law-abiding area. The backroom boys knew that St Luke's, which was owned by a local doctor called Daly, was about to be put on the market and they decided to put in a bid. To finance the purchase, they brought together 25 local well-to-do supporters who pledged £1,000 each, with further contributions over a five year period. This was sufficient to put together a mortgage for the house with the repayments paid through the constituency organisation's own bank. The purchase price in the mid-'80s was £57,000. The house was assigned to a group of five trustees – again, not party activists – who for legal purposes vested the property in the Dublin Central Fianna Fáil organisation. The senior TD was Bertie Ahern and St Luke's effectively became his headquarters.

The trustee arrangement states that Ahern's rights to the use of the property corresponds to the longevity of his political career in the constituency and if Ahern were to die suddenly, St Luke's would be passed on to the next senior Fianna Fáil politician in the constituency. If a bomb dropped on Drumcondra and all the elected Fianna Fáil politicians went to the parliament in the sky, the property would revert back to the party's headquarters for disposal or retention.

When the purchase of St Luke's was closed it became obvious to all and sundry that the house needed serious refurbishment as there was a foundation crack in the structure. This was costed at a further £50,000 and, when approved by the trustees, the work took over a year and a half to complete. Some of the original contributors dropped out over the following few years or simply made occasional donations to the mortgage on St Luke's. This shortfall on the purchase and redevelopment of St Luke's combined with the salaries of the full-time constituency workers there together with sundry expenses, were causing serious headaches and making huge inroads into Ahern's private time, until Des Richardson arrived and restructured the fund-raising requirements of Dublin Central through his annual Royal Hospital dinner.

St Luke's itself is far from being a Taj Mahal. Situated on one of the city's busiest traffic arteries and sandwiched between a petrol station and a row of small businesses, it doesn't even boast a garage. Local passers-by can gauge whether something important is afoot there by the amount of large cars parked on the public pathway outside. The bottom floor of the house comprises Ahern's constituency office, a personal office, a small bar, a kitchen and a large meeting room to the rear. The meeting room is used for meetings and clinics by Ahern and all the Fianna Fáil public representatives in the constituency who include Ahern's running mate, the 'Doc' Fitzpatrick, TDs Pat Carey and his brother Noel, and City Hall politicians, Senator Kett, Paddy Farry and recent Dublin Lord Mayor, John Stafford. It is occasionally used by local community groups.

The walls of the lower floor are festooned with photographs of Ahern taken during the various phases of his political climb – from Fianna Fáil backbencher, to Labour and Finance Minister, Fianna Fáil leader and Taoiseach – as well as staged hand-shaking photos of Ahern with all manner of world leaders from FW de Klerk to Bill Clinton. The most prominent exhibit as one enters the meeting room shows Ahern and his partner Celia Larkin, with President Clinton and Hillary Rodham Clinton.

Interspersed with the photographic gallery are various political mementos from presentations of encased Mountmellick lace from John Maloney, a new Laois–Offaly TD, to a large inscribed mirror presented to him by Fianna Fáil activists after the signing of the Good Friday Agreement. You wouldn't lose track of time for the amount of timepieces in St Luke's, all of a presentational nature and all over the place. The amount of nick nacks from pewter tankards to cast iron horses would be heaven for fans of these collectibles. Some would describe the bottom floor of St Luke's as cluttered.

The upper floor was converted shortly after the time of the purchase into a private apartment which includes a bedroom, kitchen and living areas, all of them of a modern design.

Ahern, as senior constituency TD and Minister in the late '80s initially used the apartment as a glorified changing-room between political gigs in the constituency or as a late-night stop-over *en route* to an early flight from Dublin Airport up the road. It was also used as a venue for strategy meetings – local or national – for the Dublin Central 'mafia'. Ahern's stays at St Luke's became more regular when his marriage to Miriam got into difficulties in the late '80s. When, under the legal separation of the couple, the family home was signed over to Miriam, St Lukes became Ahern's home.

It was from St Luke's that he made his journey to the Dáil to deliver his first budget as Minister for Finance in 1991; it was where he considered challenging Albert Reynolds for the leadership of Fianna Fáil after Haughey's demise; and where he thought he had concluded an Agreement for Government in 1994 with the then leader of the Labour party, Dick Spring, only to be told later that all deals were off.

He rarely stays at St Luke's these days. He moved out to his new home two years ago and in keeping with the habits of a lifetime, he didn't bother to move very far. It's about half a mile up the road in an exclusive estate off Griffith Avenue called Beresford. Again, keeping with the patterns of his life, the house is built on grounds once owned by the parish. It cost him £139,000 to buy and is today valued at over £200,000 in the highly inflated current property market in the capital – friends say it's the only time he has come out on the right side of a balance sheet. His personal mortgage on the property is over £100,000.

Chapter 8

Bigger House on Dawson Street

Populist politics is not for the faint-hearted or the lazy: it requires a boundless capacity to be polite to people – especially drunks and bores – and a clear realisation that your personal time is no longer your own. A typical day for Ahern in his early years in politics would see him into his constituency office by 8 a.m., spending the rest of the morning at City Hall and most of the evening at Dáil Eireann. Night times would be taken up with political meetings with his inner circle, constituency meetings with local communities or social events which had to be attended, so a 16-hour day would not be exceptional.

When he was Haughey's Whip, week nights became part of working days both due to Haughey's endless capacity for driving his minions and partly because of the ongoing revolts within the party against his leadership. The week would also require travelling down the country to attend Fianna Fáil party functions in his capacity as a Fianna Fáil executive officer while the weekends were a nightmare with up to a dozen functions to attend in his constituency.

He would possibly have a drink at the first port of call and then remain on mineral water for the rest of the evening.

'I would have hit anything between seven and eleven locations, like the local prison officers' club or the CYMS in Fairview, and then some parish and sporting clubs at the start of the weekend,' he recalls.

Saturdays were kept strictly for clinics which always began at 10.30 a.m. at the Tolka House public house in Glasnevin and moved on to other locations in the inner city.

His life with Miriam was rostered around his Fianna Fáil and constituency obligations and the best he could offer her was a Saturday night watching the television, a visit to relations or dinner in a quiet restaurant. The couple travelled very little distance in their marriage; there was no glamour in the whole business for Miriam and all she was getting was a Saturday night.

'Saturday night was the only night we'd get a chance to meet any of my relations or Miriam's family. We tended not to go out on Saturday nights. I don't like pubs on Saturday night, anyway – they're too bloody packed and if you were sitting at a meal you'd gather a captive audience which would pull up a seat and stay there.'

Sundays were usually reserved for football which was, at least, a mutual pastime for the couple, but in the Haughey years – especially when he was Minister for Labour – even the Sabbath could mean Cabinet meetings. For Miriam who was always underwhelmed with the politician's life in any case, being rostered between national and constituency dramas while rearing a young family was not her idea of fun.

The only time Ahern would have on his own from one end of the week to the other would be on Sunday evenings with his 'own guys' drinking pints in Kennedy's, the Beaumont House or the Brian Boru in Glasnevin. Apart from the pure drudgery of the lifestyle, Ahern had to constantly invent ways of keeping his name before the public and for the most part during the '80s he used the City Hall route for publicity. He accused Dubliners of 'moaning, bitching and growling' incessantly about their city shortly before he made his grab to be Lord Mayor in 1987.

'When was the last time you said to someone – "Great city this – I'm glad I live in Dublin"? Or indeed, have you ever said that to a client, to your children, to a friend?', he said at the time.

Four weeks later, with an essential grasp of how to get raucous publicity, he led a table-thumping Corporation delegation to the Minister for the Environment to press for more money and power to develop the capital's city centre. The delegation built up the head of steam that would lead to the development of Temple Bar and later to the urban renewal projects which transformed the dereliction within the inner city.

When he snatched the Lord Mayor's chain he expanded his brief to include Irish emigrants to Britain which at the time were running at record levels of 25,000 a year because of the near-collapsed state of the Irish economy. It was good, headline-grabbing stuff when he visited Irish centres in Camden and Hammersmith in London to highlight the problems of employment and accommodation for Irish emigrants. Ahern said at least 10 per cent needed help of some kind and quickly launched an information service for emigrants: the aim, he said, not to encourage emigration but 'to discourage thoughtless, ill-prepared emigration.' It was pure, Irish Diaspora stuff which Mary Robinson would patent as her own some years later and clinch the Irish presidency to boot.

Keeping to tried and tested means of maximising publicity for public profile purposes, he once again played the crime card in 1988 with the same controversial results as before. The only issue of the day, he claimed, was bringing 'law and order to the streets'. Conservation, traffic and development were secondary to making the streets of the capital safe to live, work and visit, he raged. Gardaí were too ready to adopt a softly, softly policy with petty thieves, joyriders and vandals, and the community itself was willing to tolerate 'an unacceptable level of violence' in central Dublin, he added. He claimed that the then Garda Commissioner, Eamonn Doherty, was perhaps concentrating too much on organised crime while houses in Stoneybatter could not be sold because of crime and vandalism. Business people and householders could not get insurance cover in the inner city and a red light district on the north quays had been holding up development for years, he continued. He rejected suggestions that social deprivation was fuelling lawlessness. The same social problems existed in the 1950s but the level of crime was not the same. He added, 'They do not turn on their own and beat up old people; that is a new problem. Many of the criminals live in expensive Dublin Corporation houses and avail themselves of some of the best community facilities.

'What is wrong is that we accept a level of violence as long as it is in central Dublin,' he pointed out. 'If one window is broken in the suburbs, an urgent meeting of Neighbourhood Watch is summoned. But if it happens in the inner city, we are glad it is only one window or one stolen car in a single night.'

His outburst brought an immediate rebuttal from Garda groups and his old chum, Tony Gregory.

'It's a statement he makes on a regular basis, a calculated attempt to grab headlines on a popular issue which gets votes for him and achieves absolutely nothing apart from stigmatising the area and perhaps making the problems worse,' stormed Gregory.

The Workers Party's Pat McCartan, now a judge, poured scorn on the Ahern analysis as 'totally superficial'. George Maybury, secretary of the Association of Garda Sergeants and Inspectors, dismissed Ahern's diagnosis as 'rather shallow and simplistic'. He protested that at any rate, the Gardaí needed reinforcements. Ahern had the last word, and on national radio as per usual, stated: 'I believe there are plenty of Guards, and if you had another 5,000, that still wouldn't stop people robbing cars.'

He had established his populist credentials by the time he became Minister for Labour and had also established his political tactic of 'burying' the opposition, especially if the opposition was Tony Gregory or the Workers Party.

Chapter 9

The Women

Urban myths, rumours and lies tend to plague many people in the public eye and none more so than Bertie Ahern. He too has had to put up with his fair share of scurrilous accusations, often whispered in the back lounges of bars by jealous enemies or prurient gossips.

Ahern is one of the few politicians in Ireland who has gone through a public separation and, having got over the trauma of that, found happiness with a new woman in his life. It appears that the only mud his decryers can throw at him are unfounded allegations regarding his life with both his separated wife, Miriam, and present partner, Celia Larkin. Despite a plethora of journalists avidly pursuing what they supposedly heard from the friend of a Garda or an aunt of a nurse in a hospital, not a shred of wrongdoing on his part has been shown to exist. Yet the lies and vicious mudslinging continue. Ahern is reluctant to even acknowledge the rumour-mongers – he would not even wish to give them that satisfaction – but for the sake of his loved ones and friends, he is hoping that the declarations he makes here will finally put an end to the vicious circle of untruths about his personal life.

The Irish electorate expect their representatives to be a combination of the Pope, publican and a fixer. But if these representatives over-recite the rosaries or become conspicuous attendees at funerals, they soon become known as craw-thumping hypocrites; if they are not hail-fellow-well-met enough to hold their own in pint-drinking contests, financed from their own wallets, they are stingy losers; and if they cannot organise a quick planning permission on the 'q.t.', they are practically useless.

If they manage to scrape through those rule of thumb tests at constituency level, they are best advised to wear armour-plates when dealing with their fellow TDs in the Dáil, especially those from their own party, and if they safely negotiate the Leinster House chamber of horrors, they still have the Irish media to contend with. Most of the Irish media is strictly of the small town variety. Its values are small town and most of its leading practitioners, with less than a handful of exceptions, rarely rise above the level of nosy Sunday school teachers. The exceptions would include the revelations by journalist Sam Smyth which led to the Payments to Politicians judicial enquiry, soon to be convened, concerning Charles J. Haughey and former Fine Gael Minister Michael Lowry, and their experiences of the Dallas-style generosity of supermarket supremo Ben Dunne, and to a lesser extent, the still unsubstantiated third party planning allegations against former Fianna Fáil Foreign Minister, Ray Burke. Such exceptions, of course, elevate thin gruel rumours of every description into stories of Watergate proportions and turn many of Dublin's news executives into headless Carl Bernsteins. The financing of Ahern's constituency office and the roguish possibilities it offered to the more off-the-wall news executives in Dublin is an example of this type of journalistic frenzy. The second media frenzy about Ahern concerns rumours about his personal life, peddled bar-room style by his fellow politicians in the main and sometimes by his own Cabinet colleagues.

Ahern got married on his 24th birthday on 12 September 1975 to Miriam Kelly at the Catholic Church on St. Alphonsus Road near Croke Park. The couple had been going out together since their late teens. They met when Ahern was running the Hamptons junior soccer club in Drumcondra and their social life centred around the soccer club and game post-mortems in the local pubs. Miriam was one of a large family (11 children, no less) that lived down the road from Ahern on Clonliffe Road. She was a bank official who continued working in the early years of their marriage but eschewed political life when Ahern gave himself entirely to a political career. In 1981, they set up home in the seaside suburb of Malahide, in a detached modern house at Muldowney Court, and Miriam departed the bank when their children Georgina and Cecilia came along.

By that stage Ahern was a backbench TD and was making no bones about his political ambitions. The nature of his constituency operation and his ambitions required full-time attention – to the level of a workaholic, according to friends. This personal drive imposed huge strains on the marriage which was only compounded when he became Haughey's Chief Whip in the '80s. The strains became unbearable when Ahern was elected Lord Mayor in the summer of 1986 and this period of populist activity, while immensely profitable for Ahern in political terms, was disastrously unprofitable for him personally. When Lord Mayor Ahern and his wife Miriam waved from that gaudy relic of British colonialism called the mayoral coach, their marriage was in the intensive care unit. Close friends like Ahern's best man, Daithi O'Broinn, and his right hand man Tony Kett, could see the strains developing on the marriage.

'The plain reality was that Bertie was never home and when he got home Miriam's family were *in situ*, keeping her company. It was no way to keep a marriage going. Like many marriages in politics and other walks of life, one partner got careless and that led to the collapse of the relationship. At that stage Celia was not involved,' Tony Kett remarks.

The marriage was in deep crisis when Ahern became Minister for Labour in 1987 and his habit of conducting all-night negotiations on national pay deals with the employers and unions, or mounting fire brigade interventions into every industrial relations flare-up in the land, was not helping matters.

Celia Larkin, a civil servant and Fianna Fáil activist from nearby Finglas East came on the scene around this time. She had been engaged to a promising civil servant at the Department of Enterprise and Employment, John X, who tragically died from a brain haemorrhage in his 30s. Both were part of the extended Ahern network in the constituency. Both would be in the same company drinking after late-evening constituency work and from there the relationship developed. Miriam became aware of the developing relationship and gave Ahern an ultimatum which was not met. Ahern's inner circle also tried to intervene to save the marriage but to no avail.

And so the Ahern marriage formally ended in the Family Law Courts at Dolphin House in Dublin in 1992. The hearing ran intermittently over four days where a judge disposed of the assets of the marriage in the propriatorial fashion which ends every failed marriage. The arguments were over routine matters like Ahern's future earnings, pension entitlements and access to his daughters,

Georgina and Cecilia, the latter amounting to an annual holiday, usually taken in Co. Kerry, and every Sunday. When all the papers were signed, the couple agreed that retaining lawyers to argue over such details was one expense that could have been avoided.

District court reporters from various Dublin newspapers who were working elsewhere in the Dolphin House complex were aware of what was going on over these four days and had spoken with Ahern during adjournments in the case. They reported the news to their newsdesk, but as family law matters conducted in private hearings are subject to reporting bans, the details of the settlement remain private between the two parties concerned. What did not remain private, however, was the fact that they had been separated for a number of years and that Ahern's fellow politicians in the Dáil, not least those in Fianna Fáil, would capitalise on the tragedy of the broken marriage in a tawdry fashion.

When the succession race to Haughey had begun, everyone knew there were only two alternatives – Albert Reynolds and Bertie Ahern. The Reynolds faction, which included Padraig Flynn and Maire Geoghegan-Quinn, were already outside the power loop, having been fired by Haughey, and were gagging to get back into power.

One of their number, the then Environment Minister, Michael Smith, was quoted in the *Tipperary Star* newspaper as suggesting that there were question marks over Ahern's suitability for the job because of his indefinite marriage situation. Today, Smith denies indulging in smear tactics and claims that simple comments about the wholesomeness of the Reynolds family were 'twisted' by supporters of Tipperary Fianna Fáil politician, Senator Des Hanafin, to reflect on Ahern's marriage situation. Smith is now a member of Ahern's Cabinet and whatever twisting went on at the time has now been resolved to the satisfaction of both men.

But in the heat of the race to succeed Haughey, the implication of the newspaper report in Tipperary was simple – Ahern's marital status was fair game if he intended to stand. When this was taken in tandem with another rumour swirling around Leinster House at the time about Celia Larkin being pregnant, the potential depth of human baseness became obvious to Ahern.

There is no reason to suggest that Albert Reynolds and his immediate circles of campaigners had anything to do with this vicious whispering campaign but, fortunately for them, the intimidation of rumour, although not causing Ahern's withdrawal from the leadership race, certainly influenced the decision.

Ahern appeared on Pat Kenny's widely-viewed Saturday night television show to do an interview in connection with the leadership issue. He also publicly confirmed then that his marriage had broken down and revealed that he was in another relationship with Celia Larkin. He says today:

'I have no big houses or mansions or yachts or studs. All I've got is a mortgage. The only thing they have on me is the fact that my marriage has broken down and I'm with Celia.'

The rumour about Celia Larkin being pregnant had become an urban myth of Irish politics. It used to pop up every two or three months in the early '90s. The Dáil rumour-mill had her depicted as a one-woman population explosion, as Ahern's aides are wont to remark. When Ahern took over Fianna Fáil after the political implosion of Albert Reynolds in 1994, the rumours became more fraught with suggestions of public house pint-throwing incidents between the couple and other physical contretemps. Celia, it appeared, was out of the birth business and in and out of hospitals for 'walking into doors'. Compounding these rumours were allegations that a barring order had been issued against Ahern by his wife Miriam.

The story was doing the rounds that some journalists had discovered the existence of the barring order and were about to publish the same. Independent newspapers fanned the rumour but nothing was ever produced.

Ahern has heard all the rumours and knows of alleged offers of money from a certain reporter to a civil servant for anything embarrassing and incriminating. In one instance, he explains, a four-figure sum was allegedly offered to a junior civil servant who one particular reporter thought might have useful information. The offer, in Ahern's view, was all the more disgusting as the civil servant concerned was in need of money, having just come out of a particularly harrowing separation agreement.

The rumours have even escalated so much that not only is Miriam supposed to have a barring order against him, but Celia too. And he is also candid in his criticism of *Sunday Independent* gossip columnist, Terry Keane, for stoking up an artificial flame that he and Miriam may be getting back together again. Today he is more forthright in telling the Irish public that there are black rumours circulating about him which are nothing more than lies – damned lies.

'I know all the rumours and so do Celia and Miriam,' he reveals. 'I can do sweet nothing about these things.

'You can sound me out 'til the cows come home: you'll find no Garda reports, no barring orders, nothing. I'll tell you, there's not a whole many things in my life that I can 110 per cent swear on, because I'm no more an angel than anyone else in this life, but of the barring orders, there is zilch.'

He re-emphasises: 'There were no Guards ever involved. To Celia's house, to Malahide, when I was in Pinebrook before I was in Malahide. Ever. There was no barring order of any kind; there were no threatened barring orders.'

And as for the allegations that he and Celia ever came to blows, this is another unfounded allegation he categorically denies. He does admit, however, that Celia did hurt herself once when she accidentally slipped at a party.

'There was never a hospital incident. Celia fell at a party and that was it. And the following day she went out and joked about it with Mary Harney.'

Celia is alleged to have visited the Mater so many times for sustaining so many wounds now that she could almost be canonised for having stigmata.

'It is rubbish,' Ahern stresses. 'You can march into the Mater yourself and you will find nothing.

He and Miriam remain good friends to this day and often have a meal or a drink together. As for a possible divorce, he maintains that it is a private matter, a belief reinforced by a recent *Sunday Independent* opinion poll which found that over two-thirds of the Irish population believe his private life is his own business.

Miriam herself is leading a happy life and for somebody who was allegedly getting a hellish time from Bertie she was remarkably favourable towards him when she gave a rare interview in January 1992 during the height of the heaves against Haughey and the possibility that Ahern and Reynolds might be vying for leadership of Fianna Fáil. Indeed, she said she saw 'no difficulties' in their marital situation that should stand in the way of any leadership ambitions he may have.

'I don't see why they should. I don't think they would,' she said. She added: 'I am cautious of talking to the Press because of the way anything I say may be twisted.'

Ahern and his current partner Celia spent several days on a State visit to China recently which was again the subject of intense media speculation. Ahern is aware of a regular number of right-wingers who 'have been on my back for years' and have cooked up a storm over Celia accompanying him on that trip. The Irish edition of one British tabloid, the *Mirror*, even ran a headline 'DEAR TAXPAYER – GREETINGS FROM CHINA, WISH YOU WERE HERE' with a picture of Ahern and Celia on the front page. It also 'revealed' that the taxpayer was forking out some £120,000 for the trip. It neglected to highlight that the couple accompanied 26 business people on the trip to reap valuable investment opportunities for Ireland and that this was the total cost. One Sunday newspaper ran an opinion poll shortly afterwards which showed that over 70 per cent of the Irish public were of the fair-minded view that Ahern had every right to take Celia on such a trip.

To Ahern, his family, friends and party, the whole nasty innuendo over his private life has in itself been one long Chinese puzzle. Hopefully, the Irish public can now solve it for themselves.

Chapter 10

The Status Quo Is Not an Option

By 1987, the Irish economy was almost bankrupt and Dr Garret FitzGerald's coalition Government were getting nowhere fast: the national debt had spiralled to tens of billions and was absorbing over a quarter of annual Exchequer revenues to service. The country's international credit rating was of a third world ranking; inflation was soaring, as were interest rates. Income tax and levies took over 60 per cent of workers' taxable income and unemployment was languishing in double figures. The economic valve of emigration was fully thrown with tens of thousands of young people leaving for Britain, Europe and the United States. The only difference between the emigrants of the '80s and their parents in the '50s was the fact that the second wave of emigrants were, in the main, educated to third-level standard. Recruitment embargoes in the public sector were imposed and pay freezes, and even pay reductions, were the norm in the private sector. Industrial relations between employers and trade unions were in shreds such that the then Teachers' Union leader and now chief executive of the Labour Relations Commission, Kieran Mulvey, characterised the economic situation in 1987 as 'disastrous'.

'It is hard to remind people what it was like in the '80s. Inflation was rampant, interest rates were rampant and factories were closing by the half dozen every Friday.

'There was huge unemployment and huge problems with the balance of payments,' he explains.

'If there are any problems in negotiating future national pay deals, they will involve how to share the national wealth and how to tackle the complacency of the modern workforce who don't seem to know how bad things were just ten years ago.'

By 1986, communications between the Coalition government and the trade union movement had been virtually discontinued. Every curbing action the Government put on pay was met by an equal and equivalent industrial reaction from the trade unions. The economy was withering and the only lifelines the electorate and the trade unions were getting from the Fine Gael–Labour administration were lectures on 'fiscal rectitude' and various unappreciated economic plans. Government had become a mere classroom and the electorate, inattentive or truanting pupils.

Opposition leader, Charles Haughey, delighted in the political discomfort of the FitzGerald administration and rubbed salt into their wounds at every turn. However, in parallel to the cheap but politically necessary posturing for headlines in Dáil Eireann, Haughey decided to open up the lines of communications with the trade unions and employers and formulate some consensus-driven plan to get the Irish economy out of its stagnant mire. These overtures were listened to by the trade unions who at the time were deaf to anything the Government were saying. The status quo of the '80s was simply not an option for either the unions, the employers or any new government likely to take over the economic stagnation from FitzGerald.

'Whatever was going to happen, Haughey knew he had to get a new deal of some kind if the national economy was to be salvaged and public expenditure brought under control,' Mulvey says.

Haughey delegated Ahern to mark the trade unions and to sound them out about a possible national deal which would achieve peace on the industrial relations side and control on the public expenditure side.

As Ahern recalls, 'The relationship between the FitzGerald Government and the trade unions had broken down. John Boland was the Fine Gael Minister in charge then. We decided to go to the Irish Congress of Trade Union in the autumn of 1986 to sound them on a possible national deal.

'We had never been in Raglan Road [the headquarters of the ICTU] before, though in Lemass's time there were connections between the party and the trade unions so I decided to reinstate them by setting up a Fianna Fáil trade union group.

'Haughey gave me a free hand in setting up our contacts with the

ICTU and in fairness to him he never put an obstacle in my way,'
Ahern stresses.

The trade unions had no problems in liaising with Fianna Fáil
because at that point in time they were talking to nobody else. It was
a mutually profitable relationship as the trade unions were getting
their side of any given industrial argument put free gratis and for
nothing in the Dáil while the Fianna Fáil spokesmen in general, and
Ahern in particular, were getting inside information on strikes and
broken pay promises that in turn could do real damage to the
FitzGerald administration.

'Within months we produced a document called the "Jobs Crisis"
and another called "Social Consensus". They were researched by and
large by myself and a small group of trade union guys and former shop
stewards. We used to meet in an office over Fagans every Wednesday
night.

'We did two things – a paper on FÁS where we brought together all
the micro agencies like ANCO, Cert, the environmental schemes for
young people and the Youth Employment Agency and then we made
proposals to streamline them.

'The second document, "Social Consensus" was based on a 1950s
programme carried out in Austria.

'In 1951, the year I was born, the Austrians felt that Russia was
going to invade. The Russians had already created a national strike in
Austria from the outside so something had to be done. Eventually the
Austrians copped themselves on and by 1954 they started working on
the idea of social consensus where the unions and employers worked
together in their own mutual interests. We also researched other
examples of partnership from Scandinavia but the Austrian method
seemed the best example of what we were looking for,' Ahern says.

The trade union side needed to stabilise the economy as much as
the Government. The standard of living of their members was
dropping by 7 per cent a year in real terms and the unions were
suffering from strike fatigue with their own financial resources being
drained by the level of industrial action that was being undertaken.

Across the Irish Sea they were watching the unnerving war of
attrition that the Thatcher government was waging and winning with
their colleagues in the British trade union movement and in the Dáil
they were listening to the Thatcher cheerleaders here. Dessie
O'Malley's new Progressive Democrat party had no misgivings about
echoing the Thatcher mantras on industrial relations and were

prominent in backing new enterprises like Ryanair with their stated policy of not recognising trade unions. Within the Government itself there was more than a sufficiency of anti-trade union members including heavyweights like Fine Gael's John Bruton and John Boland who at the time, thought the idea of centralised bargaining was all but a communist plot. In many ways the developing relationship between the trade unions and Fianna Fáil carried the fingerprints of mutual preservation although the common interest of both parties was to get the economy going once again.

By the start of the election year of 1987, Fianna Fáil and the Irish Congress of Trade Unions were effectively a Coalition in opposition.

'I was dealing with all the unions who were feeding me with all the stuff that we needed. Irish Shipping was going down the tubes then and the teachers were in open revolt. All the trade unions were working with us. I won't say I turned them into Fianna Fáil, but I managed to get them to co-operate with us,' Ahern remembers.

As Bill Attley, boss of the country's largest trade union, SIPTU, recalls: 'The principle of a national agreement was agreed with Fianna Fáil in advance. There were discussions between Haughey, Ahern and the Irish Congress of Trade Unions to get a deal up and running once Haughey returned to Government. It was Ahern's job to make sure that the trade unions could deliver on any deal that was gong to be struck.'

Uniquely, what was going on was, in effect, a negotiation for a new economic consensus with an opposition party with no powers of implementation. What made these talks even more different and would cause considerable problems for individual Government Ministers later was the fact that the ideas being bandied about went beyond crude percentage pay increases and productivity concessions, as had been the norm in other national deals in the '70s.

What was being conceded by Haughey and Ahern – Finance spokesman, Ray MacSharry, was always lukewarm about this project – was an input into the Government budgetary, taxation and social planning policies which up until then was underheard of. The Austrian model discussed between Ahern and his committee of trade unionists and former shop stewards over pints in Kennedy's pub in Drumcondra was going to be given a twirl.

In the run-up to the 1987 general election, the main opposition party had the basis for a new national pay deal in its back pocket. It would be the first Programme for National Recovery (PNR): it would begin the transformation of the Irish economy from being the economic basket case of Europe into the the fastest-growing economy in the EU over the following ten years. The deal would be a 'bitch to negotiate', according to Bill Attley, and it would make Ahern's reputation on the national political scene.

Chapter 11

Spit or Swallow Time

When Haughey returned to power in 1987 with a minority administration, he decided that Ireland was going to have an enterprise economy come hell or high water and if this meant ceding some additional negotiating powers and rights to the trade unions, employers and farmers, then so be it. The Government's job, in his view, was to turn the economy over to the entrepreneurs to generate the wealth that would create the jobs: no Government policy could hinder the idea of the enterprise economy. It was a case of straightforward economic dominoes – enterprise leads to jobs which cut welfare queues which lead to tax reductions which lead to low inflation which lead to low interest rates which eventually lead to a prosperous enterprise economy. The previous five years of what appeared to be State intervention in everything from clearing streets of snow to penny community raffles had been a spectacular failure so anything, however fanciful, was worth a try in 1987. The state of the economy was so scary that Alan Dukes, who succeeded Dr Garret FitzGerald as Fine Gael and opposition leader, suspended normal political opportunism in the Dáil to give the new administration a free reign at regenerating the economy. In his groundbreaking Tallaght speech, Dukes said he would not bring the minority Government down if it pursued policies that tackled the underlying causes of the malaise – excessive borrowing and an exploding public service pay bill. It has since been known as the 'Tallaght strategy' and it was the only blank cheque ever written for a minority government by an opposition leader. It was Dukes himself who paid for it with his own Fine Gael leadership career later.

Ahern received his first Cabinet posting as Minister for Labour in Haughey's minority Government. Ahern was 35 years of age. The Labour portfolio was not regarded then as a critical 'economic' Ministry but by the time he left Mespil Road some four years later, its importance had moved from downtable Cabinet to centre stage. Ahern immediately opened detailed negotiations on the agreement in principle he had with the trade unions chiefs on a national deal.

As Kieran Mulvey, one of the negotiators on the union side remembers it:

'Haughey and Ahern were the main players on the Government side and it was clear that their relationship was very close. MacSharry (then Minister for Finance and dubbed 'Mac the Knife' for his ruthlessness in carving up public sector expenditure) was initially very lukewarm on the idea of the notion of a centralised national deal and recoiled from the idea of his budgetary policy not being totally independent and seen to be so. He was not enamoured with IBEC, the employers organisation, nor with the Irish Congress of Trade Unions coming on board as designing partners for public policy. MacSharry changed his attitude when the second programme was being negotiated.

Mulvey continues: 'Without Haughey, there wouldn't have been a deal. Ahern played the right-hand man in the first negotiations and was the cement in the deal because of his extensive union contacts and the amount of ground work that he had done. He seemed to grow with the negotiations. He was a natural negotiator. He was prepared to put in the hours and, most importantly, it was, and still is, very hard to have a row with Bertie Ahern.

'You've got to remember that in national negotiations you are dealing with people who have the biggest egos in the country. Every one on each side actually thinks they run the country,' Mulvey quips.

Ahern's style allowed the super egos on the union and employer side to erupt for as long as they had breath and, when they subsided, he would remark that no problem was insoluble and start reworking the argument. It is a style that requires patience throughout the entire process and the ability to wait and listen for the 'important statement' or the words from either side that change the direction of the negotiations from rhetoric to reality.

'Ahern's biggest asset in these negotiations was his patience. These deals took infinite patience and in the context of the Good Friday

Agreement it was his grounding in industrial relations here that brought him through that. The dynamics in conflict situations are not necessarily different from national and economic talks. The only differences are scale and personalities,' Mulvey adds.

For Bill Attley, the negotiations were a nightmare. The economy was on the floor and the employers were used to kicking the trade unions around and were not being discouraged in doing so by some of the leading opposition politicians. The employers were dragging their feet in the negotiations and were hauled into Haughey's offices in Government buildings where he ranted and raved about his administration putting their policies into operation. He read them the Riot Act and told them to 'piss or get off the pot'. The Haughey tirades were not exclusively reserved for the employers.

On another occasion he called in the Irish Congress of Trade Union bosses during one late-night, negotiating session and bluntly asked them if they were going to 'do a fucking deal'. When they were having problems with some of the statistics being forwarded from the Department of Finance he reputedly raged: 'If you're not going to do a fucking deal then get out of the fucking building – you're frightening the staff.'

Haughey's main man at the first negotiations was Seán O hUiginn, the predominant civil servant of the Haughey era and someone who was involved in every important Government policy departure both in relation to the economy, the European Union, Anglo–Irish relations and the North. Lightweight he was not. Attley and his colleagues were negotiating to stabilise the incomes of trade union members which made up the majority of the workforce in the private and public sectors. The game plan was to achieve improvement in living standards through a combination of tax cuts and modest income increases.

'At one stage O hUiginn arrives and offers us a ½ per cent pay rise a year over the period of the agreement and he was not joking. We were utterly speechless,' Attley recalls.

Ahern and his senior civil servant, Kevin Murphy, now the Ombudsman, were assigned to keeping the trade unions 'onside' which, considering the stinginess of the offer, took a considerable amount of arm twisting.

'What would happen was simple,' Attley recalls. 'We would conclude some part of the deal with Ahern and Murphy and they would go to Haughey to get the imprimatur. Usually they would have only one shot at it and most times they would come back with what was required after Haughey and MacSharry did their usual ranting and raving.'

The first national deal in 1987 was worse, then bad, for the Irish workforce. It was penitential. But the trade unions decided to swallow it and wait for the upturn in the economy. 'At least,' says Attley, 'we got an hour off the working week which was a help.' For Ahern it was a personal triumph. It was sufficient for Haughey to cut him loose to develop and husband the national consensus approach to economic planning.

Ahern was quickly running an independent operation at Labour, which many of his Cabinet colleagues resented, while a minority – seeing the huge credibility he was getting from successive interventions in major industrial disputes – began to secretly hope he would fall smack, bang on his face.

Chapter 12

Payback Time for the Unions

The good times in politics take no managing at all. The talent is to manage the bad times, and the bad times in Irish politics were from 1987 to 1992. Haughey had decided to throw caution to the wind and deliberately turned the economy over to the most talented entrepreneurs available in the country and, in the process, brought the stock exchange ethics of men with red braces too close to the levers of power. The gamble would create thousands of jobs at the International Financial Services Centre in Dublin, secure countless others in the still under-utilised Irish Bloodstock industry, would re-invent tourism through commercial oddities like Temple Bar in Dublin and would jack-up the construction industry through various urban renewal incentives. His enterprise culture would also throw up some real turkeys like TEAM Aer Lingus, which was going to be a 'jewel' in the economic crown by creating an aircraft maintenance industry at Dublin airport, but which calamitously crash-landed not long after take-off.

The quick, fast and loose economic push by Haughey also created monopoly players in various strategic industries like the beef industry, which in turn led to the unedifying Beef Tribunal – a multi-million pound legal extravaganza which unearthed a glut of petty tax-dodging in the sector, some deft writing of export insurance and a lot of much-travelled beef carcasses.

Finance Minister Ray MacSharry, on the other hand, was given the task of sorting out the accounts which he carried out with the enthusiasm of a born-again Scrooge. The MacSharry tenure at the Department of Finance saw the worst round of slash-and-burn cutbacks ever seen in Government buildings.

Ahern was the third man of the triumvirate whose job was to keep the trade unions in the loop and stabilise industrial relations. This turned out to be a 24-hour-a-day job. Circumstances were in his favour when negotiating the first Programme for National Recovery (PNR), but by the time the second deal – the Programme for Economic and Social Progress (PESP) – came to be negotiated, the trade unions were looking for some payback.

The economy had improved slightly by this stage and in percentage terms, the salary increases were nearing double figures over the course of the second agreement. But now the trade unions called in their card to have their own input into the taxation, employment and social agendas of the Government. Simple and crudely applied, pay rises were no longer enough – the partnership idea had to be developed and direct influence on the levers of power had to be secured by the unions if they were to deliver the workforce to the Government. The implications of the demand were obvious. For industrial peace and employment growth the social partners, the unions and the employers, wanted direct influence on the Government's fiscal policies.

MacSharry, who was initially against any parlay with the social partners, came round after the PNR and decided to do business through Ahern. The effect of the new approach shocked traditional politicians like Fine Gael's John Bruton who was horrified that employer and unions leaders could troop into Government buildings at the drop of a hat and start making demands on taxation and welfare and, as often as not, get their way. He remarked at one junction that there was another 'parliament somewhere else' outside Dáil Eireann making the real decisions on the economy. He was right.

The partnership approach quickly had a knock-on effect throughout the Government. Ministers who were not inside the Cabinet loop on the social consensus soon realised that their individual ministerial priorities accounted for nothing unless they were within the perimeters of the national programme. Finance Ministers hoping to make their mark also quickly discovered that their style was cramped with up to 90 per cent of their annual budgets written up through measures agreed in the partnership process.

'There was residual resentment from individual Ministers who would find out that the deal cobbled together committed their departments to certain programmes and costs to which they had no input as legislators or Ministers of Dáil Eireann. The social partnership was expanding quickly and the pay element to the negotiations became only one part of a negotiation that would cover investment in education, welfare, health and local government. The agenda just kept getting wider,' Kieran Mulvey outlines.

'When you systematically set out on a course like that it takes a cataclysm to break it up but you'll get times when there is a lot of shadow boxing from one or more of the super egos who have to jolly their troops back into the trenches on some employment or welfare policy which might be important to the individual union,' he adds.

There were some near catastrophes in the early days of the partnership, not least when Ray MacSharry decided to shave a mere half a billion pounds – just like that – from the public finances. Everyone, in the colourful words of Attley, went off their trolleys – firemen, teachers, nurses, prison officers the lot. 'It was a credit to Ahern that he managed to calm everyone down, including MacSharry, and keep everyone in line,' Attley adds.

Chapter 13

Once More with Feeling –
1989 General Election

A hern was preparing for the second economic social partnership agreement (PESP) when Haughey decided once again to throw the electoral dice in his quest for the Holy Grail – an overall Fianna Fáil majority. It was a case of 'once more with feeling' for Haughey but when the results came through, the predominant feeling was one of numbness: Haughey went out with 81 seats, a mere 3 away from a majority and came back with 77 seats, putting the idea of a single-party Government run by Fianna Fáil on hold for the immediate future. Worse than that, the percentage vote which Fianna Fáil got in the 1989 election was exactly the same as in 1987 – 44 per cent. As a political manoeuvre, the '89 election was a totally futile and useless exercise with no benefits whatsoever for Fianna Fáil. Although the percentage poll for Fianna Fáil remained static, the party lost some 50,000 first preferences in the 1989 election and the idea that they could achieve single-party government was, and still remains, suspended indefinitely.

The scandals which would later engulf the Haughey administration were only bubbling under the surface at the time of the election but posed no real threat to the minority administration. A routine weekend report in the *Sunday Press* about a run-of-the-mill raid on the Eirfreeze meat plant in Dublin by Department of Agriculture officials investigating the beef trade which would be a prep raid for worse to come, was one of the few oddities on the horizon. Fine Gael leader, Alan Dukes, had been as good as his word and was persevering with his constructive opposition policy while Labour leader, Dick Spring, had yet to clear the phlegm from his throat for what was later to become the most sustained, effective and excruciating verbal laceration of Haughey's public reputation.

To this day Ahern is still perplexed by the decision to call that snap election.

'There was no reason for that election. We could have held on for another year and gone into the election better prepared. Haughey completely mistimed his move and we were left seeing the joke,' he remarked.

The only question being asked about Ahern's Dublin Central constituency in the run-up was whether the Ahern machine could retain their record number of three TDs for the constituency. There were opposition hopes that the huge personal vote built up by Ahern was on the wane and that his organisation in Drumcondra was not the force it once was.

One of his running mates had to go, political commentators believed, and it was only a question of whom.

The *modus operandi*, by now familiar, went into full swing. Around 380 of Ahern's election workers gathered in the Gresham hotel and were rostered for saturated canvassing with at least 120 of them working the door steps at any given time during the campaign. Each house in Dublin Central was covered not once, not twice, but three times by the Fianna Fáilers with a final swing through the constituency by Ahern himself on the eve of poll.

In the previous '87 election, a vote management pact managed to win a record 60 per cent of the seats with 42 per cent of the vote or management saturation. A repeat of that record performance was essential if Haughey's ambitions were to be achieved. From a voting electorate of just over 41,000, Ahern cornered 13,589 votes or virtually 2 quotas. His two running mates, the Doc Fitzpatrick and John Stafford, shared just over 5,000 between them which, when they divided the Ahern surplus, kept them comfortably ahead of their rivals with their seats in the bag. It was a master class on how to clinically maximise every available vote which was only repeated by Haughey himself in the nearby Dublin North Central constituency. The only consolation for Ahern and his organisation when the final tally of 77 Fianna Fáil seats was confirmed was the fact that the 1989 election was good practice.

The figures immediately suggested a Fianna Fáil–Progressive Democrat coalition (even though the PDs were in a pact with Fine Gael in the '89 general election). The six Progressive Democrats members with Fianna Fáil could scrape together the numbers to form the Government. The Labour party had ruled themselves out of Government, leaving Fine Gael out of the loop in the process. The idea of Fianna Fáil and the PDs going into government before the election would have been regarded as surreal material for a stuttering stand-up comic but after the election all that was left was electoral numbers.

The first to break ranks was Mary Harney, the former Fianna Fáil TD, who conceived the PDs as the new, cleaner-than-clean, virginal political party. Speaking at her Euro election count, she said the electoral mathematics from the poll suggested as much. Haughey was going nowhere with his 77 seats anyway, and a hung Dáil would mean another election where, as likely as not, another batch of Fianna Fáil seats would be reallocated.

By the beginning of July, Ahern was told by Haughey to announce the imprimatur on a possible FF–PD deal, saying the most likely solution to the impasse caused by the election was a government between Fianna Fáil and the PDs. Still acting Minister for Labour, he suggested that any further general election, if necessary should be contested in the autumn, rather than July and August, as many people would be on holiday and in which case agreement between the Dáil parties on the estimates would be needed to avert a constitutional and financial crisis.

'I raised the issue first and Haughey thought I was mad but he changed his mind quickly,' Ahern says.

'We have 77 seats and we're prepared to share power and responsibility, as we did with the mechanism in the Programme for National Recovery, when we shared it with the farmers, with the trade unions and business people. We believe we can do likewise with the parties in opposition,' Ahern said at the time. He said Fianna Fáil was prepared to discuss coalition with the PDs and even putting aside the issue of coalition for the meantime and talk about policy matters and new structures and see how close Fianna Fáil and the PDs were: 'I don't think we should be arguing about perks; we should be arguing about policies.'

Haughey was still out in Kinsealy trying to work out the

conundrum regarding the same percentage coming up four seats light and extemporising publicly about forms of power-sharing and alliances with the PDs while having great difficulty confronting the word coalition publicly. His Cabinet, which was still in office pending the Dáil ratification of a new government, was also opposed to the idea – some vitriolicly. Padraig Flynn and Albert Reynolds saw it as betrayal most foul. But everyone was missing the signals being sent out by the Haughey camp. The idea of coalition was conceded – all that had to be devised was the form of words that would be used in the public announcement of the fact. The Cabinet in Haughey's own words didn't really matter anyway because they were only a 'crowd of gobshites'.

For Ahern, still smarting at the lunacy of calling a snap election for no reason at all and getting a perverse result of less seats with the same percentage vote, it was negotiation time again. On coalition generally, he said then: 'I can see that perhaps in the future, with the PR system, turning out results that it does, it would be difficult not to be looking at parties in coalition.'

He admitted that Fianna Fáil had objected to coalitions in the past but whether in a majority or minority position, they had always been able to provide stable government on its own.

'What we're not going to do is throw away what we believe in just to make people who are traditionally against us happy,' he added. 'We're not going to do that. We are making decisions for the future of our party based on philosophies and ideologies that we've had for 60 years.'

It was a luxurious position Ahern might have been able to afford if his party had not lost four seats in the general election.

The negotiations between Fianna Fáil and the PDs concerning the formation of the new government focused on policy issues and on a joint legislative programme. Early on in the negotiations, Fianna Fáil conceded that the PDs should have one senior Minister, with portfolio, at the Cabinet table, and perhaps a further two junior ministers. Some Fianna Fáil acting Ministers were still gloomy and embarrassed since even as late as 4 July they were being encouraged by Haughey to issue public statements ruling out any coalition arrangements. When Haughey and O'Malley gave the go-ahead for the parlay, Ahern was sent in with Albert Reynolds to bat for Fianna Fáil and faced Pat Cox and Bobby Molloy for the PDs. The negotiations were fractious with Molloy insisting on two Cabinet seats for the PDs, which was proportionately out of line with their relative strength. It was a move Ahern believed to be breathtakingly acquisitive.

The talks dragged on and wavered on core PD issues like sharing Dáil committees and giving these committees the power to subpoena witnesses. These points of difference were blown up into federal cases, especially for media consumption, until a joint programme for government was hammered out. Since there were no great differences between the two parties on the economy, the talks then mainly on specifying the priorities for the government.

Seven days later, the Fianna Fáil and the PDs announced the formation of the Government. Haughey was returned as Taoiseach, the PDs were given two Senior Ministers at Cabinet level – Bobby Molloy at the Department of Energy and Des O'Malley at the Department of Industry and Commerce, and Ahern returned to his position as Minister for Labour. Normal service had resumed.

Chapter 14

The Holy Ghost

Ahern became omnipresent in the industrial relations sector during his tenure as Labour Minister, leading one wag to remark – 'He's like the Holy Ghost. He's everywhere.'

By his second term as Labour Minister, he had intervened in what seemed intractable disputes at Waterford Glass, Barlo engineering in Clonmel, ESB on two occasions, Dublin Fire brigade and the Irish Press newspaper group. His interventions always followed a set *modus operandi*. Before any announcement was made, he would get ICTU bosses, particularly the Congress deputy, Kevin Duffy, to find out the bottom line for the workers involved in the dispute. The same approach would be made to the employers side and only when a general outline of a solution to the problem was on the horizon would a Ministerial intervention be announced. Ahern would go to great personal lengths to make sure he was fully briefed on any given intervention.

He remarked of his Waterford Glass intervention: 'You cannot be of any use to the sides in a dispute if you do not fully understand what they're talking about. At the end of the the Waterford Glass dispute, I almost knew how to bloody make glass!'.

The word would then go out to the Federated Union of Employers (now called IBEC) and the ICTU to get the perimeters of what was likely to settle the dispute. Then, and only then, would the disputing parties arrive at Ahern's office at the Department of Labour where facilitators would run from room to room with proposals and counter proposals until settlement terms were reached. Two other traditional industrial relations tactics would be employed – exhausting the parties by running the talks well into the early hours of the morning and ensuring that representatives of FUE and the ICTU were available to exert the maximum amount of pressure on the warring factions to settle. The media could be relied upon to hype up the dispute and run regular bulletins on progress, thereby further increasing the pressure on those assigned to do the negotiating.

Usually, after about four days and nights of 'dramatic, eleventh-hour crisis talks', Ahern would come out with a piece of paper and announce to the print and electronic media the recommended settlement. The saner shop stewards involved in these set pieces would thank the Minister, go home to bed and forswear any involvement in dispute mediation for the rest of their lives.

The disputes mentioned above, it should be stressed, were extremely serious negotiations and not cosmetic pieces of theatricals created to benefit the public image of Ahern. To the certain knowledge of the authors, the *Irish Press* newspaper group would have permanently ceased publishing during the 1990 dispute there but for Ahern's intervention. The intervention kept the *Irish Press* newspapers alive for another five years until the titles collapsed for want of marketing and investment and the weight of a long-running boardroom litigation between the partners who owned the Press Group. At the time of their demise, 25 per cent of the Press titles were owned by Independent Newspapers, the rival newspaper group it out-circulated on aggregated sales a mere ten years previously.

The interventions made Ahern a local hero, the guy who could talk straight and get things done. They also insulated the social partnership programmes against its many critics in the establishment. But the hands-on approach from the Minister's office to every fire storm in the industrial arena could not last forever.

Although the Labour Court was there to arbitrate on industrial disputes, it had become too legalistic for the pragmatics of modern industrial mediation as was proved by the fact that the Minister himself had to intervene where the Labour Court failed. Ahern decided to give the whole area a make-over and in 1990 set up the Labour Relations Commission (LRC) to take care of the fire brigade actions required in the sector. The LRC is the first port of call, and usually the last, for disputing employers and trade unions alike these days, though the Labour Court remains as the final arbitration court on industrial disputes. Since Ahern left the Labour department there have only been a couple of Ministerial interventions in trade disputes. As a rule, the high-wire, eleventh-hour dramas are nowadays left to the mediators on Haddington Road.

By 1990, Ahern had established the LRC and put a new Industrial Relations Act, which among other things, banned secondary picketing and made trade unions financially responsible for profits lost in such wildcat actions. The streamlining of the labour support services for trainees, as promised to the unions during their Wednesday night soirees in Kennedy's pub, had been implemented. The social partnership agreements were ticking over with the PESP, by far the best deal achieved by the workers, were now down for renewal and days lost through industrial action were at record low levels.

There was little left for Ahern to do at Labour and he made it known that he wanted out. He reputedly tried to get out on three occasions but Haughey would not let him go.

'By Christmas in 1990 I was finishing the PESP agreement and the night before we were due to sign the agreement, my father died. The same thing happened with the Good Friday Agreement, when my mother died just before it was completed,' Ahern explains today. 'I came back from my father's funeral and went straight back to the PESP negotiations.

'After the PESP there was no more for me to do in the Department of Labour. I had brought in the new Industrial Relations Bill, which had been around for years. Paddy Hillary even had it back in the 1960s. I had brought in the 'Part-time Workers Act', which protected casual workers, set up the Labour Relations Commission and established the Health and Safety Authority. Strikes were at their lowest in history. There was just no more for me to do in the place.

'I had gone to the trade union conferences; I had met every trade unionist in Ireland and it was just getting boring. There was talk of a change in the Cabinet by Easter and I was being tipped in the papers for Environment or Health. At that stage I just wanted to get out of Labour,' Ahern adds.

Bill Attley has a clearer view of Ahern's Ministerial becalming: 'He was too good at the job; Haughey was never going to let him out,' he remarks.

The reshuffle never materialised that Easter and it took another leadership challenge and a scorched earth response from Haughey to the challenging 'Country and Western Alliance' (a tag given by Haughey mainly because of Reynolds's past as a dance hall owner and showband empressario) before sufficient gaps were created at Cabinet to allow Ahern to kick over the traces at the Department of Labour.

Chapter 15

Is There a Bomb under this Bus?

If the cultural trauma of having to go into coalition with the Progressive Democrats was harrowing for Fianna Fáil, the presidential election campaign of the party's favourite senior statesman, Brian Lenihan, was a scarifying experience.

The election should have been a shoo-in for the party but for the first time in its history, Fianna Fáil systematically dismantled their campaign through a combination of downright ignorance, political dissembling and hamfistedness. Ahern had the misfortune of being the Lenihan Director of Elections and as he arrived to hear the official announcement of the defeat, an ashen-faced Minister for Labour remarked that it was the worst experience of his life.

'It got to the stage that I was looking under the campaign bus every morning to see if there was a bomb on it,' he remarked to these authors at the count.

That 1990 election was set-up for Lenihan, a hugely popular politician with an easy-going, no problem style. The opposition looked pretty weak, with radical lawyer, Mary Robinson, representing the left and Fine Gael backbencher Austin Currie. Neither looked like a political handful initially.

The fact that Fianna Fáil had never lost a presidential election and on polling evidence would only require a moderate transfer of preferences from either Robinson's or Currie's votes, gave the campaign a sunny disposition at the start. The optimistic form was reinforced by polls which showed that Fianna Fáil were holding their

40 per cent share of the vote while Robinson kicked off with a modest 13 per cent.

In the first few weeks of the campaign, Fianna Fáil were pinching themselves for their good fortune. It was like shooting fish in a barrel – just a question of making sure there was no complacency with the organisation. Then, quite suddenly, all the wheels fell off the Fianna Fáil campaign: the curse of the early '80s was to return in spades.

A young political science student called Jim Duffy interviewed Lenihan in the course of work on his thesis and brought up allegations about Lenihan and Haughey contacting the then Fianna Fáil President, Patrick Hillary, urging him not to dissolve the Dáil following the failure of the FitzGerald coalition to bring in its Budget. *The Irish Times* carried the general information of the academic conversation in an article penned by Duffy and the opposition went blazing for Fianna Fáil. As far as Ahern was concerned, everything was hunky dory. Previously Lenihan had told him that no such call was made and Fianna Fáil had issued a public statement to that effect at the time of the supposed phone calls. The party had simply outlined the options available to President Hillary in that particular budgetary crisis.

'Brian Lenihan had made it quite clear to me, as his director of elections; I've spoken to him about this in the last few days, he recalls what's been said before, what's been written before, and he says he did not make any phone calls,' Ahern told the media when the story broke out.

Fianna Fáil went in to classic denial-mode with Lenihan continuing his disclaimers on RTE's *Questions and Answers*. With nowhere to go with their story but full disclosure, *The Irish Times* stage managed a press conference where the Duffy tape was played to a Dublin press corps. The political torpedo had hit its target.

Lenihan put his hands up and with a now famous phrase, admitted that 'on mature recollection', he had indeed made telephone calls to the Aras. The PDs were left with no option but to move in on Haughey, who in turn threw his best political ally to the wolves and requested his resignation. Lenihan refused and forced Haughey to fire him. And if that was not enough, Padraig Flynn threw his twopenny worth into the argument by going on national radio with an unsolicited, vituperative harangue regarding Mary Robinson's new, reconstructed image as 'a mother'. Fianna Fáil were proving they could shoot themselves in the foot and then try to head the ricochet away for good measure. For the most professional election machine in Ireland, the Lenihan campaign showed how incredibly inept they were at managing a crisis – it was a headless chicken party trait that would return to haunt them again some four years later when Albert Reynolds was in power.

The campaign had become a total shambles but the public humiliation of Brian Lenihan at the hands of his political master, Haughey, generated a sympathy for the popular politician. The view held by former Labour leader, Dick Spring, that *Haughey* was the politician that should have resigned was a general view held by the electorate. The whole debacle also rejuvenated the Fianna Fáil core vote which in the end came out in droves to support their wounded hero.

Remarkably, Lenihan polled over 44 per cent of the vote, which in other circumstances would have been sufficient to win the prize on transfers. It certainly buoyed up Ahern on result day in the RDS, who read the result positively by stressing that the Lenihan tally was remarkable considering the campaign that had taken place. He admitted that the 'Duffy incidents' had caused almost irrevocable damage to Lenihan's chances.

'That issue forced us into a fair bit of mud slinging,' he admitted.

He said that before the controversy, Fianna Fáil had estimated they had around 46 per cent with 8 per cent of Austin Currie's transfers. But after the Duffy revelations, the Currie transfers had dropped to just 2 per cent with the election closing in early November. At a remove of eight years, Ahern looks with personal regret on the fortunes of his political friend.

'We started off with Brian at 46 or 47 per cent of the vote (Robinson around 13 per cent) and then he drifted back to about 43, but the share of the transfers going to him was huge,' Ahern recalls. 'We had worked out that even if he could stay at 41 or 42, he was very safe on the transfers. There was no doubt about it. Then the Duffy tape was published in which Lenihan admitted ringing the Presidents in the early '80s in a bid to halt a general election. He just forgot the bloody interview and the campaign was in serious crisis.

'We had gone down to 29 per cent. I made the decision to continue the campaign, not to change anything – just keep going. And we gradually got the percentage to come up and come up. We were doing the polls and it looked as if we were back on a good 45 per cent that last weekend and we needed just another push to get another few points.

'But two things happened in the last period. The transfers died. The people who liked Brian Lenihan unfortunately went back and voted political. They stayed with Fine Gael and Labour. And those remarks by Flynn, claiming Robinson was a reconstructed mother, just drove a whole lot of women mad. It stopped our rise, which had been brilliant because we had gone from 29 per cent to 45 per cent,' Ahern says.

Ahern believes Lenihan would have made an exceptional president despite the fact that his health was weakening.

'He was a great character and a great statesman. He was highly thought of at Foreign Affairs. He was highly respected in Europe for the work he did on the Bahrain Agreement. Lenihan was extremely able. Once he got a brief he was brilliant at it.

'There is no doubt Mary Robinson was a very good President. I mean, Brian Lenihan himself said that if wasn't him, he would have voted for her. Mary Robinson turned out to be a superb President and esteemed by all of us. I think it surprised a lot of people that as soon as she was elected, the first time Fianna Fáil hadn't got the Presidency, I think people thought we might have some sort of begrudgery and we didn't. Across the country, the party said "this is our President" and from the very first day we worked with her.'

The fact that Brian Lenihan was sacked by Haughey was a terrible turn of events, in Ahern's view, for the relationship between the two men. 'Two great friends, who worked together through thick and thin for 40 years. Here you are in 1990, these guys had been in the Dáil since '57, and the gun was put effectively to Charlie's head and Brian was fired. Charlie Haughey would never have done that to Brian Lenihan were it not for PD pressure,' Ahern claims today.

'Brian was Brian – he was a gracious fellow, but he didn't like being fired. But I can tell you he continued on and that night and the following day we were back on the trail and in spite of everything, we literally pulled the campaign together in 12 hours and kept going. It was extraordinary.'

The suggestion that Lenihan's sister, Mary O'Rourke, told the FF election team, including Ahern, to 'fuck off back across the Shannon' when she met them in Moate, County Westmeath, is denied by Ahern.

'That was always overstated. I was there. Mary was a bit hyper. She never said that. I was Director of Elections, so I just told everyone to calm it down. They were tense days – not stuff for the faint-hearted. Just tough raw politics. I'm not saying it didn't have the potential to get very nasty; there was real tension, but Mary didn't say that.'

According to Mary O'Rourke, now deputy leader of Fianna Fail and Minister for Public Enterprise: 'I would never use bad language, anybody who knows me knows that. But I did say to Padraig Flynn, "Get back across the Shannon from whence you came." This was said in Moate. I was in the campaign bus with Brian and Padraig Flynn came along in his car with Bertie. Padraig Flynn wound down his window while Brian was addressing people from the steps of the bus in Moate.

'I knew that he had been sent on an errand (by Haughey to ask for Lenihan's resignation) and yes, obviously I was very determined that Brian was not going to resign. I said, "You come not in friendship but in guile." I don't think Bertie came on that errand, I think Padraig Flynn came on that errand. Bertie was the Director of Elections and he had his own task to do, which was to mind his candidate. We hold no rancour for Padraig Flynn, none of us do because time goes on and people's emotions assuage themselves eventually and we're in another era now.'

Chapter 16

'Just Aimless Haggling and Arguing'

At the start of the '90s there was only one consistent thread through every aspect of Ahern's personal and political life – haggling. The Social Partnership deals were fought tooth and nail by employers and trade unions and whenever a breach was detected by either side they would camp in his offices until they got satisfaction. The crisis in his marriage was coming to a head and was being negotiated to a settlement by lawyers who would soon sign, seal and deliver a separation agreement in their clinical fashion in Dublin's Family Law courts. In Fianna Fáil, meanwhile, nothing short of civil war was breaking out between the predominant Haughey faction and the ambitious 'County and Western Alliance' which was led by the remarkable Albert Reynolds but whose ranks, with the possible exceptions of Padraig Flynn, Maire Geoghegan-Quinn and Michael Smith, were not bursting with political talent.

'When I came into the Dáil in 1977 things were grand for about 18 months. From 1979 on it was just aimless haggling and arguing and it went on for over 20 years,' Ahern says today.

His attempts to get out of Labour were pointless because Haughey was not going to hand over what had become a sensitive department, in terms of the economy, to any of his other senior Ministers. It would have been a recipe for disaster and, as we have seen, his view of many of Haughey's colleagues was biased. They were a 'crowd of gobshites'. Ahern, whether he liked it or not, would have to grin and bear it.

His public pronouncements from 1990, however, were overlapping with those of the Minister for Finance (MacSherry) and he left nobody in any doubt where his next port of call was going to be. He continued hassling the employers on his pet hobby-horse of poor pay rates for working women, noting that the average female hourly rate at the turn of the decade was a mere 68 per cent of the male rate with many women working in 'female-only jobs' and not advancing into middle management, much less top management. He called on the Social partners to adopt positive action to redress the equality imbalance: positive action was the key to building on the legal entitlement to equality at work, he preached. This means taking vital steps to ensure that disadvantages are eliminated. Merely sticking to the letter of the law was not enough – the principles behind it must form part of the way of thinking of management, colleagues, trade unions and women themselves.

The Labour Relations Commission, which was legally formalised under the 1990 Industrial Relations Act, came into being the following January under the chairmanship of Dan McAuley, the former respected chairman of the Federated Union of Employers (now IBEC) with Kieran Mulvey, the former teachers union leader, as chief executive. The Commission took over responsibility for conciliation, advisory and equality issues in the sector and, as Ahern explained at the time, restored responsibility to the industrial relations sector and allowed the Labour Court to resume its original role as the court of last appeal in industrial matters. The establishment of the Commission spelt the close of Ahern's career as a hot-footing interventionist Minister for Labour. In a flattering editorial, *The Irish Times* said Ahern had distinguished himself as a mediator since he became Minister and had now correctly put in place machinery to deal with industrial relations which would replace high profile, but not necessarily desirable, Ministerial interventions in disputes.

The Special Partnership model was also beginning to pay dividends. The worst year in the '80s had been 1984 when 191 strikes, of which 75 were unofficial, were reported. The downward trend in strike action and particularly unofficial strike action was kicking in and by the end of the '80s, the lost working days' total had fallen to 132,000, while strikes relating directly to pay issues had dropped to a mere six.

A climate of realism had been created within the workforce. Ahern was also demanding that voluntary action be taken to deal with the problem of absenteeism in Irish industry which was losing industry an estimated £1 billion a year. The main cause of the losses was alcohol abuse though covering up industrial accidents was an additional factor.

Progress was also been reported on Ahern's other pet project – the rationalisation of the trade unions. Small trade unions had proliferated since the foundation of the State and such was the propensity to organise that it would not raise an eyebrow if the painters union poached members from a scaffolding union. The sheer amount of unions was delaying the process of solving industrial disputes and causing closures – because bigger unions would not pass pickets placed by minnow unions.

To rationalise matters, the Government decided to grant aid any proposals in which the unions had to amalgamate. During his tenure as Minister, ongoing discussions on merger proposals among about 20 unions were in the pipeline, the most major being the amalgamation of the Irish Transport and General Workers Union (ITGWU) and the Federated Workers Union of Ireland (FWUI) into a new super trade union – Services, Industrial, Professional, Technical Union – SIPTU. As he prepared to wind down his days at the department of Labour, Ahern had successfully established FÁS, the employment and training agency, which merged AnCO, the Youth Employment Agency, and the National Manpower Service.

An act to enable employees to elect worker directors to major State companies like ESB and Telecom Eireann had been passed while other bills had been introduced on Unfair Dismissals, Employment Equality and methods of paying salaries. The Safety, Health and Welfare at Work Act was revised and extended from the 20 per cent of the industrial workers which had previously benefited from the provisions to all categories of worker. A National Authority for Occupational Safety and Health was also put in place and laws had been designed to end the exploitation of part-time workers. Ahern's earlier prediction that the social partnership approach to the economy would introduce a period of industrial harmony not seen in the country since the late '50s was looking good. All that remained for Ahern to do at the Department of Labour, it appeared, was to clean the ashtrays and think about a new strategy to convince Haughey that he should be in another and more senior economic ministry before bidding adieu to his ever-efficient Ministerial secretary, Freda Nolan.

On the marriage front, the weather was becoming stormy on the hurricane end of the scale. The persistent calls on his time from the moment he was elected to Dáil Eireann back in 1977 and his workaholic approach to setting up an unrivalled constituency organisation in Dublin Central was proving to be too much of a strain on the marriage. As one of his close friends observes today – 'There is a time when arriving home after midnight with the excuse that there has been another political drama to deal with is no longer an excuse. A pattern was emerging with Bertie arriving home late to be greeted frostily by Miriam who might be there with her parents or sisters. This would lead to the inevitable argument and when that goes on over a long period of time, a carelessness sets in around the relationship.'

His own inner circle in Drumcondra were witnessing the lack of communication on a regular basis as were the Ahern and Kelly families, but falling for Celia Larkin was a wholly unpredictable outcome according to his friends.

'Everyone knew Bertie and Miriam would get married. They were made for each other. But if you were to tell me that Bertie would end up with two women ten years later I would have told you you were mad' an insider points out.

'He wasn't that type of guy. When we went out to dances looking for women Bertie used to come along just for the fun of it. He would be in hysterics at our efforts to chat up women. He just never bothered with the women. Of all the gang back in the '70s he would be the last one you would think would have these problems.'

It is generally conceded by those close to Ahern that carelessness was the cause of the drift between the couple while local happenchance led to the relationship with Celia Larkin. The contact was purely political initially as Larkin had developed a reputation for being a particularly astute grassroots organiser at election time. Initially it was a casual and unthreatening relationship as Larkin herself was engaged anyway. But by the local elections in 1985, something more personally significant was going on between the pair.

In those elections, Ahern had decided to go for a clean sweep in his political bailiwick. His constituency covers the urban sprawl between the Liffey and Tolka rivers and in local government terms took in three smaller wards – the inner city, Drumcondra, Glasnevin and Finglas. The Ahern machine was all powerful and effectively decided who stood where after the democratic fashion of ward bosses who knew what was best for the electorate. The line-up for the sweep on

City Hall had Bertie Ahern running in the north inner city, his brother Noel taking the slot in Drumcondra and the fledgling politician, Celia Larkin, running for the Finglas ward. All were duly nominated and confirmed and those who were not nominated and confirmed were ready to tell anyone that Ahern was turning Fianna Fáil in Dublin Central into a dynasty. They were also quick off the mark with the obvious favouritism shown to Celia Larkin in the shake out of nominations.

Ahern, as we have seen, wanted to politically pulverise Tony Gregory who was advertising himself as a self-proclaimed hero of the working-classes. He duly despatched Gregory with ease, polling some 5,000 votes to his 2,000 minus, in what is best described as a wholly over-the-top piece of populist bragging. Noel Ahern duly swept up the family vote in Drumcondra but the third leg of the political bet – Celia Larkin in Finglas – came spectacularly unstuck. Despite what observers describe as a dawn to dusk campaign, Larkin make no impact whatsoever despite plenty of door to door combat. Her uninspired performance in terms of votes had as much to do with the Finglas Fianna Fáilers stepping aside from the Larkin campaign and switching their allegiance to other party candidates. The experience of the 1985 local elections was enough to put Larkin off seeking elective office for life.

From that point, the relationship between Ahern and Larkin developed and she was working within the Ahern machine. She was seconded from the civil service to take over Ahern's constituency office in the Dáil, a job she has consistently carried out with impressive professionalism to this day. She runs his office on a same-day reply system and on the basis of an empty 'in tray' by 5 o'clock.

After the '85 City Hall elections, the relationship developed initially in an unseen fashion. 'She would be with Bertie in Kennedy's for a late-evening drink and would be seen around much more often,' insiders remark.

Like any other relationship, things seemed to take their own course, they added. What was going on, of course, was no different from what was going on in 70,000 other similar relationships in Ireland at the time, the only difference being there were not 70,000 Ministers for Labour.

Divorce had been resoundingly thrown out by the electorate in a 1986 Referendum, much to the shock of the proposing FitzGerald government, so Ahern, like everyone else in a disrupted relationship, was effectively left in limbo waiting for another Referendum to politically confront the reality of what was happening to so many marriages. Emotionally and politically it was an unpleasant time for Ahern to say nothing of Miriam, their daughters, the Ahern and Kelly families as well as Celia Larkin and her family.

These private and personal matters remain private and personal. What is publicly known about the separation is that Ahern has and always uses his access to his daughters Georgina and Cecilia. Sunday is reserved by Ahern for both of them. They regularly attended the Dáil with him on set political occasions like Budget Day and the day he was elected Taoiseach last year, and they holiday with him in Kerry during August of every year. They share his interest in sport, particularly the fortunes of Dublin's GAA team and the greater fortunes of the Manchester United soccer team – a team they see regularly with their father at Old Trafford. Indeed, Manchester United is supported by the Aherns with such interest that Ahern felt obliged recently to state that he was opposed to the sale of the club to media tycoon, Rupert Murdoch. The statement had the same effect as every other protest about the sale – zip.

After the separation, Ahern lived at St Luke's and only relatively recently bought his own four-bedroomed home at the Beresford estate off Griffith Avenue about a mile away from St Luke's, where he has moved all his personal effects. Celia bought her own home, a modest middle-class residence in the Ashington estate off Navan Road just beyond the northside suburb of Cabra around the time of the Ahern separation. She resides there today.

On the political front, 1990 marked the final run in for Charlie Haughey who from the time of the Lenihan election debacle was losing friends at a rate of knots and influence over his Fianna Fáil party even faster. By the end of the year, a beleaguered Haughey would be saved by Ahern's negotiating adroitness and he bestowed on his protégé the soubriquet of 'the most clever, the most cunning and the best of the lot'. It was a sobriquet that Ahern needed like a hole in the head, as we shall see.

Chapter 17

'The Most Cunning of them All'

The Programme for Government between Fianna Fáil and the Progressive Democrats was down for renegotiation in the Autumn of 1991, but according to Ahern, what should have been a routine task began to unravel as soon as the negotiating teams met.

The Lenihan election effort had cut straight into the heart of the Government with O'Malley demanding, and getting, Lenihan's resignation from the Cabinet as Tánaiste and Minister for Defence, but they could not be assured of the cohesion of the coalition which was, in the famous words of Albert Reynolds a 'temporary little arrangement'. The idea of sharing power was a culture shock to the 'Country and Western Alliance' and all they could do was persevere with it. They were also convinced that Haughey would yield on every core principle of Fianna Fáil if it meant that he would remain in power. Allegations that a golden circle of businessmen associated with Haughey's Fianna Fáil were getting the best deals that were available in the economy, rumbled on.

A valuable Telecom Eireann site in Ballsbridge which was sold by the company for £3 million to a second company which and then sold on for £9 million, threatened the stability of the Government when it was discovered that Telecom director, Michael Smurfit, had a beneficial interest in the second company, along with known Haughey associates. When Haughey asked Smurfit and Séamus Páircéir to 'step aside' from their jobs at Telecom Eireann while investigators probed how the sale of the Ballsbridge site was embarked upon, both men left, but they also left a huge question mark over the governance of Ireland from Leinster House.

The privatisation of the Irish Sugar company also hit the headlines when it was revealed that off-shore companies benefiting from the State disinvestment had associations with the State company personnel.

Questions were raised about the forced purchase and resale by University College Dublin of another lucrative educational site at Carysfort on the southside of Dublin while the Irish beef industry was by then getting the FBI treatment with the machinations of who approved State insurance for beef exports and why Larry Goodman, the beef baron vested with reviving the beef industry by Haughey, had become the most important player in the home market. About the only suspicious-looking act which was not left at the door of the Haughey administration was the kidnapping of Shergar.

For the Progressive Democrats, whose political *raison d'etre* was to clean up Irish politics, the whole farrago of Fianna Fáil politics and business was becoming hard to bear, more particularly since the Labour party leader, Dick Spring, had launched a sustained attack in the Dáil about standards in Government and a scarifying assault on the Haughey method of governance, which he shockingly likened to a cancer in the body politic. For all their political sanctity, the Progressive Democrats were left looking like latter-day political Canutes shooing away what looked to the public like tides of business-type sewage.

The same teams were assigned to the renegotiations as in 1989 – Albert Reynolds and Bertie Ahern for Fianna Fáil and Pat Cox and Bobby Molloy for the PDs, with both teams reporting progress back to their respective leaders.

'They were ferociously tricky talks,' Ahern remembers. 'Everyone was losing their heads, which can be routine for these kind of talks. Cox wouldn't agree with Molloy, Molloy wouldn't agree with O'Malley and Reynolds wouldn't agree with Haughey. The talks were all over the place and it looked as though the Government would collapse,' Ahern reveals. 'The headless chicken brigade had taken over. I just sat back and tried to piece together what we actually agreed upon. Nothing special – just seeing where the common ground was. I got all the agreed bits and pieces in the Programme for Government together and pointed out to them that there was little point in arguing, as much of the package was already agreed. By telling them that they were arguing about things that were not in the Programme, we managed to put the whole thing together literally overnight.'

In the end, the simple task of collating what could be agreed was sufficient to keep the show on the road. However, the sequel to this piece of routine negotiating nous was not appreciated by Ahern.

A delighted Haughey, now back in the driving seat, happened upon the political correspondents of the national media in Leinster House. He was fulsome in his praise of his protégé when he put his head around the door of the political correspondent's room and pointed at Ahern.

'He's the most clever, the most cunning, the best of the lot,' he enthused. It was a piece of overdone PR for his protégé which was hardly going to delight a would-be Taoiseach just making his way in politics.

'When it was said that day I didn't like it. I didn't like the way it was said and I haven't liked it ever since,' Ahern says today. 'It was all about what had happened over the previous 48 hours of those talks with the PDs but now it has come to mean this, that and the other, usually libellous, depending on who you are talking to,' he adds.

For a politician who was able to keep his head and keep a Government in place, he was still showing a singular inability to negotiate his way out of the Department of Labour. Asked today where he actually wanted to be if Haughey let him out of Labour he replies: 'I wanted Environment to be honest. There was clearly a perception in Dublin that the capital was getting nothing, especially in the area of housing. All the flats were falling down, even the windows were falling out. The Dublin TDs wanted me there. I had been Lord Mayor a few years previously and my constituency was Ballymun, Finglas and the inner city, so I knew what had to be done in Dublin,' he points out.

Politically, the Environmental Department is a plum. It's a high-spending Ministry and impacts directly on the social fabric of every constituency in terms of housing and infrastructure. It is also important from an internal Fianna Fáil party viewpoint as the Environment Minister has the captive attention of the party's local authority members nationwide and with this Department comes significant internal party approval. Unfortunately for Ahern, the man in possession was Padraig Flynn, the Reynolds loyalist, who put the final nail in Brian Lenihan's presidential coffin. It would take a political JCB to shift Flynn from the Custom House which Ahern hadn't got.

With Haughey back at the helm, the manner of the renegotiation and the wafting smell of scandal around Leinster House would ensure his grasp of power was temporary.

Reynolds and the 'Country and Western Alliance' (that which Haughey called the rump led by Albert Reynolds) had decided Haughey had to go and the only question on their agenda was when. During the Smurfit and Páircéir resignations, Haughey went one joke too far at the expense of the 'Country and Western Alliance' when he suggested in a radio interview that he might pant on into his '80s as leader of Fianna Fáil after the fashion of 'those Chinese guys'. That was sufficient to induce shades of purple around the gills of the 'Country and Western Alliance' cabal who were exhausted at that stage by what they saw as Haughey's Pavlovian responses to every Progressive Democrat demand. They hatched their attempted putch for that November of 1991. Reynolds wanted Ahern in on the ousting because it was essential that the Dublin TDs backed the usurpers for political and public perceptions. Ahern refused to come on board and vainly tried to defer the challenge by claiming that Haughey was on the verge of going anyway.

Everyone knew of Haughey's promise to retire as leader when he adjudged the time was right, but as far as Reynolds and Co. were concerned, that time had long since passed. Ahern publicly said he was happy that Haughey would stay on as Taoiseach.

'I do want him to stay,' Ahern said at the time. 'I think he is a tremendous leader. He has given 35 years of service to the public and if he wishes to continue on working, then I'm quite happy with it.'

He would not, Ahern then said, be in favour of any group of people going along to the Taoiseach to discuss the leadership issue. The alleged business scandals were causing the political unrest which was turning into the proposed motions of no-confidence in the leadership of the Government, he emphasised. There was an unwillingness at the time among Fianna Fáil TDs to openly support a no-confidence motion after Haughey appealed to be allowed to pick his own retirement date.

The Reynolds camp were believed to have had 42 out of the 77 deputies behind them, but less than a dozen would have been prepared to address a no-confidence meeting. Environment Minister, Padraig Flynn, was believed to have been the only senior cabinet minister willing to speak in favour of the no-confidence motion.

Reynolds initially marked time by saying: 'The leader of the party set out a time frame to complete an agenda. I'm flattered by the amount of support offered to me, not having campaigned at all in the situation. There was a strong request that honorable time be given for the completion of an agenda and we responded to that.'

However, by early November, the issue was finally pushed to a formal leadership vote. Ahern nailed his colours to the mast and proclaimed he would be supporting Haughey and expressed confidence that he would prevail. Asked why he was supporting Haughey, he replied: 'I believe in supporting the leader. If I am leader in 25 years time, I would like to think that people would support me. I am going to support the man in power. I am going to support the Taoiseach.' He asked reporters at the time to 'underline 25 years' when it came to his own prospects for leadership.

On reflection now, Ahern feels all the political drama generated by the Reynolds side of the party only hastened Haughey's retirement by a fortnight.

'My view from the autumn of that year was that Haughey was going. I knew him well enough to know he was going,' he says today. 'The first time Albert, Flynn and the boys had a go in November, I led the campaign openly to keep Haughey in power and we succeeded. The second time they came after him with the Doherty interview about the telephone buggings, Haughey was gone. But all their efforts only shaved two weeks off Haughey's time. Haughey would have been gone during the following fortnight anyway.'

He adds: 'I met Haughey over that Christmas period and it was emphatically clear that he was going. I know people will still say, 'Ah, he would have hung on,' but I knew Haughey relatively well – at least I thought I knew him well and I knew he was going.

'I get all the credit now for knowing Haughey so well and all the blame from people for not knowing this or that about his personal life. And I get none of the credit for knowing when Haughey would step down,' Ahern reflects.

Reynolds, Flynn, Maire Geoghegan-Quinn and Michael Smith were ejected from Government after losing the challenge to Haughey quite miserably from a numbers viewpoint. They only managed 22 votes against 55 votes for the status quo. Their temporary disappearance from the top table at Cabinet left the way clear for Ahern to get out of the Department of Labour at last and transfer to the Department of Finance. He had just turned 40 and was some five years ahead of schedule in the personal Ahern political plan.

'Who would have thought that an ordinary guy from Drumcondra could get this far,' he told these writers at the time.

Finance was scheduled as a stop-off at 45 years of age for Ahern en route to becoming Taoiseach before his 50s. The exit of the Reynolds group speeded up the process nicely.

By the turn of 1991, Ahern was finalising his first budget – his predecessor Albert Reynolds having done most of the ground work on the document – when the Exocet missile which sank Haughey was fired off by Senator Sean Doherty, the born again Christian but one time Minister for Justice who a decade previously was responsible for the illegal bugging of the telephones of political journalists, Geraldine Kennedy and Bruce Arnold. Doherty revealed in a television interview (with Shay Healy on the late night coffee bar style *Nighthawks* chat show on RTE) that Haughey was personally aware of the telephone tappings and their contents. The Haughey era in power was over. Haughey made no apologies. He just set a date for his departure and left. The Reynolds 'Country and Western Alliance' have always denied that the Doherty interview was a set-up, preferring to think of it as a kind of political miracle given Doherty's rediscovered Christian fervour. Even today, Ahern firmly believes otherwise.

'I don't know who set it up. But Albert, Flynn and the boys obviously knew about it, because Flynn had gone on the radio the previous Sunday about the same thing,' he stresses.

The manner in which the Reynolds loyalists went about doing down Haughey infuriated Ahern because it was, in his view, unnecessary and only publicly reopened divisions within Fianna Fáil. It was a pointless exercise since the gain for Reynolds was a mere 14 days out of power.

However, the manner in which Reynolds's loyalists made sure that Ahern was neutralised in the succession stakes, which included a whispering campaign about his personal life, led to a cautious distance developing between Ahern and many of Reynolds's lieutenants.

Chapter 18

'I Hope Haughey's not Proved of any Wrongdoing'

Bertie Ahern makes no bones about the fact that he admired Charles Haughey's political and public style and was thoroughly unhappy about the way his hero was 'shafted' by the 'Country and Western Alliance'. He first met the controversial politician when he was a teenager at an election count in Dublin Central, and later come to the attention of Haughey through the spectacular results the party were achieving in the constituency when Ahern took over. The Ahern election machine was held up to Fianna Fáilers as the model of how to run a constituency effectively, and ruthlessly if necessary. Ahern was only 18 months in the Dáil when he was given observer status in the corridors of power through the 'makey up' job of Assistant Whip of Fianna Fáil.

The first 1981 election for Fianna Fáil was a disaster. 'We were buried mainly because of the H Blocks,' he recalls today. 'They were on that bridge [over the Tolka river at St Luke's] every day of the campaign that summer and they took thousands of votes off us and got TDs elected in the border constituencies. It was a nightmare. We started off with a 20-seat majority and ended up in opposition.'

The first election results of 1982 caused by the failure of Garret FitzGerald's Finance Minister, John Bruton, to bring in a Budget, produced a minority Fianna Fáil administration supported by the so-called 'Gregory Deal' and a handful of Workers Party TDs. The ensuing six months were calamitous for Fianna Fáil, as Ahern recalls. He found himself working day and night to keep the Dáil numbers up for the Government. The Gregory deal, which annoyed Ahern, kept the minority administration on the road but the three votes of the Workers Party had to be shepherded constantly on an issue-by-issue basis.

'I was an Assistant Whip when Fianna Fáil had a 20-seat majority and it was easy, but then I was Whip when we were in a minority and trying to get the Workers Party to vote for the party on every issue,' he explains today. 'I had to deliver the three guys from the Workers Party – Joe Sherlock from Cork, Pat Gallagher from Waterford and Proinsias de Rossa. Then of all a sudden everyone started dying. John Callanan down in Galway, Loughnane in Clare and Jim Gibbons [an old adversary of Haughey's within Fianna Fáil who was incapacitated by a heart attack]. 'Your man, the murderer, [Malcolm MacArthur who bludgeoned a nurse, Bridie Gargan to death in broad daylight in October 1982 – in Phoenix Park], was arrested in Paddy Connolly's, the Attorney General's flat. Everything happened during that period.

'It got to the stage that your time was not your own. I once drove and drove for six-and-a-half hours, with Georgina as a baby, to Ballyferriter, when I got the call to come back immediately because of some drama in Dublin. I had to leave the kids in Ballyferriter, turn around with an escort and drive back again. That was some year – '82,' he sighs.

'It's a terrible pity that the Fianna Fáil minority Government didn't survive. The numbers were impossible, and you couldn't control events, but MacSharry had decided how to tackle the public expenditure problems. MacSharry was already dictating the task in front of us on public expenditure, but unfortunately the Government was dropping votes every day and had no alternative but to take things easy.

'People say that it took a period in opposition for Fianna Fáil to realise the urgency of getting the public finances in order. That's entirely wrong. Haughey and MacSharry published the document "The Way Forward" in 1982 – also called the blue document – which showed the way to sort things out. But by the end of that year we were out of office and the new Coalition was elected. By the time we got back to power five years later, the national debt had doubled.'

The Haughey–Ahern relationship strengthened during this period of crisis Government and Ahern would have been a regular visitor to

Haughey's mansion in Kinsealy as part of the crisis management team.

'My job was to bring him the bad news,' he reveals today. 'I'd give the news to him straight – he would start arguing and railing and we would fall out. The next day everything would be back to normal. He respected you for telling it straight. A falling-out with Haughey would last a day, unlike others in Fianna Fáil,' he adds, pointedly.

Back in opposition, the political falling-out with Dessie O'Malley became permanent as the fledgling party of O'Malley, Mary Harney and Bobby Molloy, had left Fianna Fáil to form the Progressive Democrats. The PDs were formed from a rump within Fianna Fáil who were totally disillusioned by Haughey and saw themselves as cleaner-than-clean in political terms.

Ahern shared an office with Molloy up until the split and was aware firsthand how the divisions exacerbated. The PD faction made its royal progress through the constituencies, attracting huge audiences and remarkable support which would shore up future problems for Fianna Fáil. Back in the Dáil, Haughey appointed Ahern shadow leader of the House, which he found 'interesting but boring'.

'I learned a lot then because the Dáil was starting to reform itself. I got on very well and worked well with John Bruton, who was the Minister in charge (of Dáil reform), and between that job and being Haughey's Whip, there isn't a thing that I don't know about Dáil precedents and procedures and points of order.'

From there, as we have seen, Ahern went to Labour where he would make his name nationally and this period in opposition would also give him ample opportunity to build up his image as a senior Dublin TD and the time to become the city's Lord Mayor ('86–'87) and chairman of the city's Millennium committee. Ahern's cruise through the ranks of Fianna Fáil was largely down to Haughey spotting him early and the politician grabbing the opportunity with both hands. Politically, he was as close as you could get to Haughey without being intrusive, but personally, he would never have been called his best buddy in the party.

'I was often in Kinsealy and enjoyed myself there – we enjoyed ourselves as a family there. Recently I was bringing the girls home and we passed the place and they remarked how they loved going there. I enjoyed his hospitality and, yes, I was often given a brace of duck from the estate to bring home for the pot,' he chuckles.

'But I didn't know anything about what was going on in the background and I didn't suspect anything and had no grounds to suspect anything. I believed he had made his money from shrewd business deals and was keeping the place going on his investments. Everyone believed that down the years. He was Taoiseach but he was also a shrewd businessman so there were no grounds to ask him about his money,' Ahern points out today.

'Now it turns out that he got money [from former supermarket magnate, Ben Dunne: a £1.3 million gift when the word went out that Haughey was in financial trouble after leaving office]. He was wrong to take the big bucks. I don't know what got into him. Whatever got into him that he needed those big bucks to live a lifestyle he couldn't afford is beyond me. I think the Haughey lifestyle was too much. Who wants to have islands, helicopters and boats? I'm just happy going to Croker and Daylier.

'Politically, he served the old party well, if controversially at times, and I still believe that he should have been left to resign the leadership in his own time.

'I hope he's not proved of any wrongdoing. If he is, he'll have to pay the penalty. The laws of the land are there for everyone whether you're Charlie Haughey, Bertie Ahern or anybody else.'

Chapter 19

Let Not Ambition o'er Leap Itself

As Charles Haughey was fine-tuning his resignation speech, which would be laboured with Shakespearian quotes from *Othello* about being of 'some service to the State', Ahern, his protégé, was sticking the verbs between the numerals of his first Budget speech as Minister for Finance. Albert Reynolds, meanwhile, was in his counting house counting all his votes and fashioning his first Cabinet. The rest of the Fianna Fáil Cabinet were in the 'sweats' wondering where the axe would fall when the 'Country and Western' leader took over as Taoiseach. People like Gerry Collins, who in a near tearful plea to Reynolds on the television news during the attempted putch of the previous November, begged him not to 'burst the party', only to become a comedy turn overnight, had every cause to look in the Motor Mart sections of the newspapers. Ray Burke, Haughey's storm trooper of every previous administration, also had good reason to believe his days of curling up in the back seat of a State Mercedes were over. Their only realistic hope of hanging on to Cabinet rank was to line up behind the only candidate with a chance to halt Reynolds' roll – Bertie Ahern.

When the flag went up the Reynolds campaign started issuing public bulletins on the hour, every hour. Their head count was accumulating.

'We believed we had between 45 and 55 votes by Day Two of the campaign and this would have been sufficient if the contest went to an election,' Michael Smith, one of Reynolds's campaign managers, explains today. 'If there was going to be a real contest, there was no question but that it had to be between Reynolds and Ahern, but we designed our campaign so that TDs and Senators would declare for our man at different times and that's how we built up the pressure. We had sufficient votes for our man by Day Two of the campaign, I believe. When John Wilson [Haughey's deputy leader] declared for Reynolds, that clinched the matter,' Smith adds.

Among the Haughey loyalists, things were becoming just frantic. They knew the political reaper was barging in the door and they needed a champion. They all but squatted in Ahern's constituency headquarters at St Luke's in one of the biggest collective acts of implorement seen this side of Lourdes for decades. 'Save us from the Country and Western hoards who are intent on bursting us', might have been their prayer if Gerry Collins was in charge of the script.

Ahern refused to emphatically rule himself out of the leadership race but switched the tenure of his public statements to his upcoming Budget, which was pressing almost contemporaneously with the leadership election.

'I'm honestly not going to think about anything like the leadership until after the Budget. I really don't want people saying that Bertie was not concentrating on the Budget. Budget day next Wednesday will be the biggest day in my life since I came into politics,' he told reporters.

He recalls today that the level of pressure on him to run was intense. 'The boys were saying you've got to go, you've got to go. All the senior guys – Lenihan, Ray Burke, Rory O'Hanlon, Gerry Collins. I had them all with the exception of John Wilson. I had good rural support, especially down the Western seaboard. I had all the senior people outside the parliamentary party as well. In the Dublin vote at that time, [Ben] Briscoe and David Andrews, Seamus Brennan, Tom Kitt, Eoin Ryan were all for Albert. In my view, if you were going to have a base, you needed your own county. When it came around a few years later, if there had been a vote I would have had every single vote in Dublin,' he says today.

Ahern had an unpromising choice: concentrate on his Budget – his was, after all, only a wet week in the job as Finance Minister – or chance a run for the leadership with the backing of Cabinet members running scared about their status. He took soundings but made no emphatic statement about his intentions (although twice the previous November he had ruled himself out of the succession stakes) which only encouraged the implorers to believe they had a candidate. His old senior colleague, Deputy Jim Tunney (Haughey's party chairman and former mentor) was called in by Ahern to run the rule over the field.

Tunney's headmasterish and often aloof manner disguises a cold grasp of the political machinations within the Fianna Fáil party and an even more calculated grasp of how the figures fall when the parliamentary party met to elect a new leader.

'I told him not to run because he just wouldn't win,' he says today, matter of factly. 'He hadn't got the numbers. If he had run and lost, it would have affected him in a future leadership election. Better to let Albert Reynolds win now and take over the leadership later without any opposition. Anyway, he was young and he needed more senior Cabinet experience.'

In keeping with the tendency of the day to quote Shakespeare during times of great Fianna Fáil drama, Jim Tunney emphasised his parting advice to Ahern with the words – 'Let not ambition o'er leap itself'. The quote from *Macbeth* couldn't have been more appropriate given the Cabinet bloodbath that would follow Reynolds's assumption of power.

The real politic of the situation therefore indicated that there should be a re-opening of the accommodation which existed between Ahern and Reynolds. They were not political enemies: on the contrary, they were seldom out of each other's company in the preceding years in Cabinet. If you saw one at a sports event like a race meeting, the other would be just around the corner.

A personal mutual respect had been the cornerstone of the relationship which Fianna Fáilers, in happier times, had regarded as the 'dream ticket for the future', with Reynolds bringing the rural and business vote to the party and Ahern providing the urban and worker constituencies. It was not a huge secret that both men worked in each other's interests while in Cabinet and the only thing to upset what was a happy relationship was what Ahern perceived to be the unnecessary, divisive and cackhanded manner in which the Reynolds wing got rid of Haughey. The fact that some elements within the 'Country and Western Alliance' liberally laced their calling cards with vulgar abuse did not improve Ahern's mood at the time. While Ahern's inner circle believed that Reynolds could not be held responsible for that tendency, they thought the least he could do was control it.

The Lenihan campaign debacle two years previously still touched FF nerves and was laid at the door of Padraig Flynn's outrageous criticism of Mary Robinson as a 'reconstructed mother', in terms of pure electoral mathematics. While during the interregnum, between Haughey deciding to step down and the actual election of a new leader, Ahern himself came under attack from a whispering smear campaign about his collapsed marriage. The cruder version of this smear heard politicians wondering aloud where the potential leader of Fianna Fáil and the country slept at night – a crude reference to his relationship with Celia Larkin. The latter version horrified Reynolds and his campaign manager, Michael Smith, who immediately took steps to halt the vulgar abuse.

The nature of political rumour in Dáil Eireann and its short-term efficacy for political rivals, the bar flies propping up the Kildare Street waterholes and the media in general, are best illustrated by the rumour mill that turned during this leadership campaign.

An exasperated Ahern remembers today: 'Michael Smith came out and gave an interview to the *Tipperary Star* and Albert Reynolds apparently said, "we should know where the Taoiseach lives." I was annoyed with them, but I was more annoyed, I have to say, with the way they shafted Charlie Haughey.'

As Michael Smith recalls today, the newspaper interview merely said that he was greatly taken by the Reynolds family and this was inverted to cast Ahern in a bad light.

'I made a comment about the Reynolds family and how united they were,' he explains. 'That's all I said. But for the week preceding the leadership contest it was peddled around the Dáil by people on our own side that I made some remark about Bertie's family life. My remarks were twisted to make out that I was saying something disparaging about Bertie.'

The rumour mill for Ahern had begun to turn during that leadership struggle and it would be cranked up on several occasions subsequently, usually by Fianna Fáilers whose nose fell out of joint, sometimes by the opposition and sometimes by the media as the rumours travelled around for the second time. It was sufficient for Ahern to make a public statement about his domestic situation. He lashed out at 'outrageous rumours' about his domestic life being pandered during this Budget–Leadership period.

'I spoke about my domestic problems on the television because I wanted to be honest about the situation. I'd hoped people would accept that I had been straight about the matter and leave it at that, but there have been so many rumours and newspaper stories since that it makes you wonder if it's a good idea to be honest,' he said at the time.

Those rumours, on the back of his budget and on the back of a putative run for the Fianna Fáil leadership, informed the conversation when Reynolds decided to parlay with Ahern about who was to succeed Haughey.

Before 'the summit', Ahern told *The Irish Times*, 'I suppose more tactically than anything else I haven't officially declared my support. But my supporters are canvassing as if I was in the race in a normal way. I have a long-standing commitment that I will talk to Albert Reynolds and we have to set that up.'

But he admitted that he was canvassing his party colleagues on the basis that he was in the leadership race and Brian Lenihan's understanding (he told Dublin radio station 98FM that Ahern would run) that Ahern was in the race 'would hold'. He also predicted that the majority of the Cabinet would back him in any race.

The 'summit' was held in a suite in the Berkeley Court hotel in Dublin which Reynolds had a key to.

'Albert and myself met on the Saturday morning,' Ahern recalls today, 'and I told Albert – "listen, I'm not really interested in any of this. I'm just interested in the Budget". Reynolds said, "Well, you know, I'll win it," Reynolds said, to which I replied, "Well that wouldn't be hard for you because I'm not canvassing."

'We had a very general chat about the Cabinet, which was subsequently leaked and was very unfair to the individuals concerned because we were only bantering – there was nothing serious about the conversation.

'Albert made it very clear to me that he wouldn't stay around very long. He wouldn't be a Haughey, trying to hang on forever. He would do his stint. I told him that he wouldn't have a more loyal friend and he didn't,' Ahern says today.

An informal deal on the future of Fianna Fáil's leadership was completed at that meeting by the only two men that were likely to lead the party through the new Millennium. It was an understanding which Ahern himself alluded to in a Sky News interview when the details of the Berkeley court meeting also later leaked out.

Reynolds's campaign manager, Michael Smith, says such a deal was never actually thrashed out in detail: 'Nothing was ever talked about but I think it would be quite fair to think that such a deal was agreed. It would be an easier way to explain why Bertie was not standing against Reynolds and it's the type of deal Reynolds would have done,' Smith says. 'I did not expect Reynolds to stay on for a long time as leader. I expected him to fight another election and then retire midway through his term. Once he was out of the equation there was no real challenge to Ahern.'

The whole episode left Ahern open to sustained public criticism for the first time for what appeared to be dithering. It also left the Haughey wing of the party and his own personal support sore and anguished after putting their money on a horse that never even entered the stalls.

Ahern's defence is simple. He was not interested in the job of Taoiseach at that time:

'I was on my feet giving the Budget,' he stresses today. 'My first budget, my big day, my chance of a lifetime. And as soon as I sit down all the guys [TDs] are out on to the road canvassing.

'I remember Emily O'Reilly wrote an article claiming "Bertie is dithering". I was so annoyed with that.'

O'Reilly described Ahern as a 'ditherer' for his reluctance to lay his cards on the table over the leadership issue. 'His behaviour at the time smacked of indecisiveness, political immaturity and an inability to extract himself from the poorman Machiavellian clutches of his constituency mates,' she wrote.

'Here I was, doing my first Budget, going over to do Pat Kenny for two hours, going over to do Farrell and *Primetime*, doing *Saturday View*, doing the Sunday programmes, doing everything to sell my Budget. I couldn't have cared two damns if there had been 55 Taoiseach positions on offer. I went into Finance in the middle of November. I'm nine weeks in the job and I wanted to sell my Budget. That's all that was on Ahern's mind,' he points out today.

The Berkeley Court hotel meeting between Reynolds and Ahern meant the leadership contest to follow the Budget was a foregone conclusion, though Mary O'Rourke and Dr Michael Woods went ahead with candidacies. Dr Woods made an issue of the apparent 'divvy-up' of power, between Reynolds and Ahern, saying that the future of the party was not for bartering in hotel suites. But the resistance to Reynolds was only token in nature and was brushed aside.

The bloodbath that followed, however, was not token and even surprised many of Reynolds's most ardent admirers in both Fianna Fáil and the media. It was scorched earth time again. Eight Ministers were chopped, including Gerry Collins, Rory O'Hanlon and Ray Burke, and in what many observers saw as an act of conspicuous pettiness, Mary O'Rourke was relegated to junior Ministerial status. The only senior Cabinet Ministers to survive were Dr Michael Woods and Bertie Ahern.

Chapter 20

On His Tod

Bertie Ahern was on his tod for his first Budget. He confirmed to reporters that he would not be with his wife, Miriam, for the traditional Budget Day photographs.

'I'll be on my tod. The marital situation does not allow it,' he told reporters, adding that it was 'quite possible' that this fact would be used against him by his rivals in the upcoming Fianna Fáil leadership battle. 'However, I would like to think that nobody would do that; it shouldn't be an issue.' Another divorce referendum was 'absolutely inevitable', he added. Miriam, who had foresworn politics long since as a bad job, however, did not influence the couple's daughters, twelve-year-old Georgina and ten-year-old Cecilia who were in the Dáil with their father, as was Ahern's mother Julia and other family members for the 'Big Day'.

Ahern's first Budget began the process of cutting income tax rates which was implicitly agreed with the employers and trade unions in the Social Partnership process, now into its second term with the signing of the Programme for Economic and Social Progress (PESP). It introduced a wide range of reforming measures aimed at curtailing the abuse of tax reliefs, extended the provisions for corporation taxation, while simultaneously broadening income tax bands. The biggest winners were higher paid employees without 'perks', like company cars, who gained substantially from the cut in the top rate to 48 per cent who were also relieved by the fact that mortgage and health insurance reliefs were left untouched. The chase against tax evaders was intensified. Extra cash was found for the health requirements of the mentally handicapped and the elderly while all the 'old reliables' were, to use a favourite Ahern word – hammered. Cigarettes went up by 16p a pack, largely, it was said, at the insistence of the soon to be demoted, Health Minister, Mary O'Rourke. Opposition parties and investors reacted with Ahern's decision to dispose of a 15 per cent stake in Greencore, the former State sugar company, for £33.1 million.

The sale was necessary to meet budgetary pressures resulting from the renegotiated parts of the PESP, Ahern said, despite a two-year moratorium of the sale for 'unforeseen circumstances'.

The Ahern budget was criticised in the time-honoured fashion of the previous 70 Budgets since the foundation of the State as a 'missed opportunity'. Fine Gael's Michael Noonan raged in his flinty way that the move was 'little short of insider trading', a charge rejected by Ahern. It was described as the 'Liberation of Pay as You Earn Worker' by Progressive Democrat leader, Dessie O'Malley, in one of the few rushes of political hyperbole he was to experience in his life, while the Minister himself confined himself to describing it as a 'socially caring Budget'.

The *Sunday Business Post* dismissed his efforts as being the work of a 'civil servant who was splashed by a Mercedes on his way to work' while *The Irish Times* pondered in an editorial: 'The hand of the Progressive Democrats is very much in evidence in this, Mr Ahern's first Budget. But more so than other budgets in this administration, it deserves the appellation tax reforming.' The only person who was missing the opportunity that day was Albert Reynolds who sat in the back row of the Dáil observing the delivery and listening to the sustained applause his successor was receiving from the Fianna Fáil backbenchers.

As soon as the Budget was delivered, Ahern went on the TV and radio selling circuit while everyone else in Fianna Fáil went on the election trail as we have seen.

He pulled out of the leadership race the following weekend remarking that his domestic situation had no bearing on his decision. But he admitted he firmly believed there had been a deliberate campaign by some elements in the party to exploit his marital difficulties. However, these smears would not have affected any vote amongst the members of the parliamentary party on the outcome of the leadership race, he maintained.

'I have to say, at the end of the day, that it wasn't a factor. The most conservative people in the party were with me in this, bar one or two, and the rural areas were very supportive of my running.'

Even the anti-Divorce candidate, Des Hannafin, was behind him. Ahern confessed this was all the more surprising given that there had been some opposition to his running in Dublin, particularly in some south and west constituencies.

Ahern retained the Finance portfolio under Reynolds's new administration and the much feared bloodbath took place with a savageness seldom seen at the top of Fianna Fáil politics. Ahern prepared himself for a slightly detached sojourn at the Department of Finance as Fianna Fáil's Country and Western Alliance took over Government buildings.

Chapter 21

Beef and German Burghers

In 1992, Ahern began regrouping on the political front and putting together a tight inner circle at the Department of Finance for what was going to be a rollercoaster year which would make the Chinese torture of negotiating the vulgar fractions of Social Partnerships seem like child's play. The year would start off with the first part of a double whammy for Ahern arising from the privatisation of the Irish Sugar company – the most controversial of the sell-offs of State companies. It would be followed by gloomy predictions about the national dole queues rising to over 300,000, and by autumn the beginnings of a ferociously fought currency crisis which would lead to the devaluation of the punt within the European Monetary System. The proverbial icing on the cake would be the collapse of the Government followed by a disastrous election in which Fianna Fáil would lose seats as though they were going out of date.

Ahern embarked upon his *annus horribilis* with a team many of whom are now at the centre of power in his current administration. Gerry Hickey, a senior departmental civil servant with a particular expertise in the agricultural sector, headed the team: his experience at the fiscal end of agriculture would be critical in cleaning up the Greencore mess and he was made Ahern's departmental programme manager. The Department of Finance press operation was led by Paddy Duffy, a personal friend who was seconded to Merrion Street from his job as a headteacher in Ashbourne in Co. Meath. He was backed up by civil servant Nick Reddy. Their press operation was tighter than a bodhran and even tighter throughout the currency crisis that raged later in the year: they elevated the concept of being sparing within information to an art form.

Brendan Ward was the Minister's private secretary – a role he now carries out at the department of the Taoiseach. Additionally, there were people like civil servants Sean Cromien, secretary of the department, Maurice Doyle, Governor of the Central Bank and Michael Somers, Head of the National Treasury who would all become pivotal players in the various unfolding crises. Externally, Ahern relied on a coterie of financial market experts and confidantes to keep him abreast of what was going on in the financial services sector. These included the late Brendan Hayes, of the now privatised State Assurance company, Irish Life; Brendan Menton from the Whittaker days; and Peter Bacon, an economist who would reappear to price the Government's report on stabilising the Irish property market.

In a surprise move that year, the Government announced its intention to sell 15 per cent of the Greencore–Irish Sugar company to finance budgetary targets. The company was subject to a High court investigation into how it purchased a subsidiary, Sugar Distributors, at an inflated price and how a financial trail through off-shore companies could be traced back to the State company. It was unfinished business which Ahern inherited with the job but it just blew up in his face. The investigation, costing over a million in taxpayer's money, blamed the company's chief executive and other executives for the scandal but exonerated the Board. Ahern described the wheeling and dealing which went on at the company as 'deplorable' while his PD colleague, Dessie O'Malley, said the High court report provided enough material to justify it being sent to the Director of Public Prosecutions.

New money speculation against the punt within the ERM began to develop and the activity was sufficient for the Government to sanction a temporary support scheme for industry and agriculture at a cost of between £20 and £30 million. By October, Ahern was giving public lessons on the cost of devaluation, especially to mortgage holders.

By November the gathering economic storm was full blown with allegations that even the Irish financial institutions were joining in on the speculative spree with claims of some £400 million punts being sold in advance of an emergency EU monetary committee meeting. The weakened position of the punt, Ahern then maintained, was being exacerbated by the speculative activities of the Irish financial institutions, whom he had warned to put national interests before their treasury interests.

At this stage the main banks had decided that a 10 per cent devaluation of the punt was inevitable and were warning their treasury managers to act accordingly. At the same time the banks emphatically denied speculating against their own currency. Ahern himself did not 'name names' as was demanded by the trade unions. The Spanish and Portuguese currencies had devalued by now but Ahern steadfastly held out saying the punt would only realign with the French franc and the Danish kroner. The economy was now all but halted with interest rates up to 35 per cent and building society mortgages set to soar. Some respite came by 1 December when the punt began to rally. But by the time Ahern called in the opposition leaders to brief them on the crisis, the national consensus was beginning to crumble.

The Irish Congress of Trade Unions remained steadfast behind Ahern saying a unilateral devaluation of the Irish punt would be a 'potentially greater disaster' for Irish workers but the banks were acting in their own self interests and the farmers were demanding an immediate devaluation, preferring it to crippling interest rates, while the Confederation of Irish Industry were emphatic that a realignment had to take place.

The National Treasury Management Agency arranged a top-up borrowing facility of 4 billion DM to call upon if further speculation materialised against the punt. More would be required before the currency crisis ran its full course.

Running in parallel to the currency crisis was the political crisis caused by the Beef Tribunal. The Tribunal had been running with intermittent public interest throughout the year under Mr Justice Liam Hamilton at Dublin Castle and involved a voyage around the country's beef industry, particularly the commercial activities of beef baron Larry Goodman, an alleged friend of Charles Haughey. In the public mind, the legal fees charged were remarkable. They were running into millions for a grim entertainment about the quality of meat on a cow's shin, the level of income tax-dodging by the literal cowboys in the industry and the preference or otherwise given to a cabal of beef barons on state-funded export insurance for meat in all its forms to Middle Eastern markets. The political entertainment was provided by PD leader, Dessie O'Malley who raged against what he believed was the preferential treatment given to Goodman by the

Department of Industry and Commerce – Albert Reynolds's baby during the minority Fianna Fáil government of '87 and Reynolds's contrary view. Both opinions were bounced around the Tribunal by that autumn and both accused each other of being economical or previously, with the truth. Reynolds's final night saw a fleet of Ministerial Mercedes screech in to the gravelled courtyard of Dublin Castle followed by a rush of Ministers into the Tribunal chamber to witness whether Reynolds would withdraw his accusation against O'Malley. Ahern was not among their number. They stood at the back of the Tribunal chamber in a collective act of solidarity with their 'man'. When Reynolds refused to withdraw, a fleet of Ministerial Mercedes screeched out of the castle yard again with Ministers preparing for a general election.

From the word go, it became obvious that Fianna Fáil were going to pay for the antics of its leader at the Beef Tribunal. The electorate were thoroughly bored by the Tribunal itself and horrified by the actual legal costs of the charade. The idea that personal political interpretations of arcane points about export insurance made at an unpopular Tribunal would animate the electorate seemed a few sandwiches short of an electoral picnic. If the taxpayers were paying for an expensive Tribunal, the least they could expect was some suggestion of the Tribunal reaching a verdict.

In electoral terms, it was like asking the voters to buy a Tribunal dog and then doing the barking themselves.

In a lack-lustre campaign, more remarkable for the phenomenon of Fianna Fáil TDs battening down the hatches in their own constituencies to save their own skins, the party was buried, especially in the greater Dublin area. The party lost nine seats in its worst percentage tally since the late '20s and its worst attrition in lost seats since the Second World War. It was, in a word used by Reynolds during the campaign, a 'crap' performance. The only silver lining for the party was that John Burton's Fine Gael lost 10 seats which effectively debarred them from forming an administration. The power brokers were the Labour party who gained the entirety of the floating vote and pushed its Dáil tally up to 33 seats or just under a record-breaking first preference tally of 20 per cent. They had replicated the 1990 performance of the President Robinson election campaign. Dessie O'Malley's Progressive Democrats were the only centrist party to gain in the election, going up from six seats to ten seats and proving, at least, that his performance at the unpopular Beef Tribunal did not cause his party any collateral damage. Five votes in Dublin South Central kept Albert Reynolds and Fianna Fáil in the political game despite the trouncing the Fianna Fáil leader had received at the hands of the electorate. It took a marathon election recount in that constituency which finally confirmed the election of Fianna Fáil veteran, Ben Briscoe, over Democratic Left's Eric Byrne, to keep FF's faint hope of holding on to power alive.

The mathematics of that result left Fine Gael, Labour and Democratic Left just one short of the slimmest of Dáil majorities, but Fine Gael had ruled out an alliance with Democratic Left, preferring a link-up with the Progressive Democrats: Bruton's argy-bargy over Democratic Left opened the door to a possible deal with Fianna Fáil.

Most commentators initially thought the idea of a coalition between the parties that won and lost most seats was hardly the Government configuration which the electorate had in mind. Brian Lenihan, Bertie Ahern's right hand man, however, wasn't backward about coming forward regarding the possibility. He, like Ahern, believed a Fianna Fáil–Labour coalition was a natural alignment within Irish politics and Lenihan took to giving impromptu history lessons to all and sundry about the left wing history of the party going back to Lemass and the creation of the semi-state companies – it was an infectious belief that had stalwart Fianna Fáilers scratching their heads about their political history. Lenihan was also in contact with Labour's deputy leader, Ruairi Quinn, about the options available. In the background, Ahern and Fianna Fáil's one-man think-tank, Martin Mansergh, were mixing and matching Labour and Fianna Fáil policies in advance of any possible negotiations. It was an inspired team.

Mansergh, though, only associated in the public's mind with the long, drawn-out and sensitive negotiations with the Northern paramilitaries which led to the Peace Process, is one of Fianna Fáil's great liberals. Writing up a Government programme to match the needs of the Labour party was second nature to him. Ahern's long time association with the trade unions and with union leaders like Bill Attley would also be critical in putting together the deal. Pro temps, Fianna Fáil marked time until the inevitable stage-managed approach came for Reynolds's parlay with Spring in the Berkeley Court hotel. The usual negotiating routine was observed: with Ahern, Brian Cowen, Noel Dempsey and Seamus Brennan for Fianna Fáil and Ruairi Quinn, Brendan Howlin, Mervyn Taylor and Pat Magner for Labour – with the contentious items referred upstairs to the party leaders for resolution. It was a Labour gig as far as Fianna Fáil were concerned because they were in the driving seat for power. The talks turned over slowly but surely and by early January, the momentum was unstoppable.

To Labour's surprise, the basis of a Government agreement had been prepared for them in advance and most of their demands in terms of the social agenda, Cabinet seats and the creation of a cumbersome system of programme managers and advisers for each Minister were conceded without much ado. Against impossible odds, Brian Lenihan began his revisionism of Fianna Fáil political history maintaining that when a Government with 101 seats and an audacious Dáil majority could, in typical optimistic Lenihan banter, last for ten years at least – no problem. The deal was carried through without any great fuss at the Labour party's special conference at the National Concert Hall, with the most pointed remarks coming from the party's trade unionists, particularly Bill Attley, who typically and curtly remarked that he was glad that the burden of fighting the workers' case at Government level had passed from the trade unionists to the politicians in the Labour Party.

Back at the ranch the currency crisis continued unabated and the delay in creating some kind of Government was causing more than public disquiet. Interest rates were going through the roof as Ahern and his team held out for a realignment of the Irish punt alongside other European currencies within its fiscal basket. The Germans who had been drip feeding the Irish government's defence of the currency with lines of DM credit were now ready to fly the white flag. The defence of the punt was now looking like a Pyrrhic endeavour with the national reserves all but exhausted and the lines of credit drying up. Ahern's monetary team demanded an emergency meeting in Brussels and asked for a 10 per cent devaluation. The Germans wanted to give far less. There was a moral victory in defeat, and it was the Germans what done it. Victory in defeat was the spin coming out of Ahern's office. The cost was substantial. In February 1993, Ahern told the Dáil that while he believed the worst of the EMS crisis was over and the system would quickly restore its equilibrium, he admitted that the devaluation had become inevitable. He rejected the view that an earlier devaluation would have avoided difficulty. Devaluation had imposed significant costs on the State, adding about £50 million to the cost of servicing the national debt in 1993. The debt of state-sponsored bodies would be increased by £160 million and servicing would go up by £15 million. He noted that on the positive side there would be a stronger level of economic activity in 1993 than if Ireland had not devalued and on the budgetary front the effects would be 'only slightly negative'. The extra costs in debt servicing would be balanced by gains in other areas, he added. But because Ireland's foreign debt had increased, there would be a premium in the longer term on the country's interest rate and that premium had to be reduced, he warned.

Ahern's second budget came on an early Ash Wednesday and, in keeping with tradition, Ahern attended Mass in the Pro cathedral and came out suitably blackened with Ashes and looking more like a coal miner than a Minister for Finance. The penitential appearance of the minister reflected the advance publicity for the 1993 Budget which was being touted as the toughest ever. He was jeered by the opposition as he rose to his feet as the 'Ghandi of the Northside' and the Budget itself turned out to be an anticlimax with the Fianna Fáil–Labour administration opting for minor fiscal surgery and a package of measures designed to slow down, rather than halt, the level of unemployment. Ahern increased levies on people with incomes in excess of £9,000, released new spending for the construction sector with a view to maximising the crane count in Irish cities and introduced a complex package of mortgage–interest reliefs and benefits for the least well-off sectors of society. He adhered to the strict disciplines of the Maastricht Treaty on government borrowing and opted for a financial holding operation in the expectation that the international economic situation would improve.

The only bad news for a surprised public was a 1 per cent income levy with tax biting harder on the higher paid. The projected unemployment figure of 315,000 for the year could be revised downwards, he predicted.

Ahern says today that the Government could have devalued the currency at any time but if the punt had fallen out of the EMS because of the Sterling withdrawal in September of that year, it would only have gone the way of the Spanish peseta, Portuguese escudo and Italian lire.

The group advising him included Maurice Doyle, then governor of the Central Bank, Maurice O'Connell, who was head of the Monetary Division and who is now the governor of the Central Bank and Seán ÓCróinín, a senior monetary civil service who had previous experience working with the International Monetary Fund in Washington. 'A sizeable amount of IBEC [the employer's federation] sided with the defence, as did most of the banks. Allied Irish Bank stuck with the policy all the way through though the Bank of Ireland were a bit more jittery,' Ahern recalls. 'We agreed from the outset, and passionately so, that if we folded easily and just went out of the system with Britain, then for all time we would be linked with sterling in the public's mind, and as things went on, we would never be able to make decisions on our own.

'And I remember Padraic O'Connor – I think he's now Number One at NCB stockbrokers – saying to me, "How will we ever be able to go into the Euro if we are linked to sterling; we would be left with no decision on whether to go in – Minister, it doesn't matter to me as a person but it does as an Irishman. We have to fight for as long as we can, even if ultimately we have to move."

'But the view was, which has now turned out to be absolutely true, that he was right. I wouldn't have thought of it – I wouldn't have seen six or seven years ahead – but what was more important was what the group, who were all experienced financial people, said: that if we devalued in September when the British were out of the system, we would have to have gone and devalued again in October when the horrendous pressure came. Spain and Portugal did; Greece, Britain and Italy were gone out of the system by then.'

Ahern's monetary committee advised that Ireland would hold out until the New Year despite the waves of speculation on the punt. 'We didn't devalue in September, we didn't devalue in November and we held out until the last day of January,' Ahern continues. 'Events were happening in the North; there was a beef crisis and there was an election on top of the currency crisis. Christ, it was hard. It was tough and there was pressure and hassle.'

When the devaluation of 10 per cent came in the last week of January, it was the only devaluation. 'We went once and within six months, interest rates fell 16 times and the Irish economy has never looked back,' he adds. 'We didn't let ourselves be kicked and bumped around and gave ourselves a chance of creating a thriving economy afterwards and that has happened. I don't claim it was my decision. I claim it was very good advice from people who knew the monetary situation. The three guys who were advising me each had over 40 years experience in Irish monetary policy and I was just lucky to have three guys of that experience.' The personal and political pressure on Ahern was significant. Interest reached 100 per cent, business was stretched and the farmers were up in arms.

'It was a straight case of the markets closing on Friday and waiting for the speculative hits to begin the following Monday morning. I'll always remember going in one Monday morning at 8 a.m. and meeting one of the fellows, I think it was Tom Considine (a senior civil servant in the Department of Finance), who told me we'd been hit for another £75 million. I said, 'Jeez, who's up so early? It's only about a quarter past eight on a Monday morning."

'Someone bought Irish punts in Japan – £75 million worth. There wouldn't have been 75 million pounds worth of Irish punts bought in Japan for the previous ten years and this was done early on Monday morning,' he says.

'At the end of the day, I didn't get much satisfaction about devaluing, but many of the speculators cancelled their options because they thought we would be forming the new Government and sticking with the same policy. They reckoned the Government would be sitting it out for another number of weeks. I tell you I got an awful lot of satisfaction out of that because we stung a lot of them.

'Some of them probably made a lot of money, obviously – you can when you're dealing with those kind of swings – we might have lost substantial sums but in the end we were only a small amount out. That's why Maurice Doyle said, "this is the time to go" because the hit on them was going to be bigger than it was on us,' Ahern says, rubbing his hands.

He has no doubt in his mind that some Irish banking institutions and foreign banks based here joined in the free-for-all speculation against the punt. 'There were financial houses involved but it's always the argument if it is speculation. I certainly thought what was going on at that time was sheer speculation and I always come back to the £75 million hit against the Irish economy in Japan. That was purely a person trying to make money on the exchange deal.

'Allied Irish Banks took a very supportive line. The Bank of Ireland didn't do anything big either way but if there was speculation you could never prove it,' he concludes.

Chapter 22

Oh, Sugar!

With the most advised Government in the history of the State bedded down, normal politic was resumed within Fianna Fáil. The Ahern faction didn't get a scratch in terms of Cabinet positions from Reynolds and had settled down for a long sojourn as backbenchers. This FF–Lab production, as Brian Lenihan was still enthusiastically saying, would run and run. Ahern was becoming detached from the day-to-day politics of government, contented to mind the Exchequer and do the figures.

The policy thrust of Government had dramatically turned from Social Partnership agreements and the routine scandal from the Golden Circle to developments on the Northern Ireland front and to the liberal social agenda which was being processed by the Labour Ministers. For once there seemed to be no crisis, foreign or domestic, in his bailiwick. Or so it seemed. The FF–Lab administration was committed to serious spending on high-spending programmes in the social and welfare areas which would be financed partly from a share sale programme of State assets.

The Labour party of 'nationalise everything' had perceptively changed and now appeared to be halted at a half-way house on privatisation issues and Fianna Fáil now, for once in its history, had the luxury of getting the rubber-stamp of the socialists for such fund-raising ventures. No sooner had the thought of coasting entered Ahern's mind, however, than his old friends in Greencore, the former Sugar company, landed him in another fine mess.

The project was simple. Sell the Government's remaining shares in the company. The sale of the shares was in the Budget arithmetic and the Government would ultimately decide on the matter, Ahern told the Dáil. Ahern recommended to the Government that Davy Stockbrokers, a Bank of Ireland company, and no amateurs at the game, should negotiate with the US food company, Archer Daniels Midland, on the sale of the government's 30.4 per cent stake in Greencore. Shortly afterwards, Ahern was forced to announce that the Arthur Daniels interest in the shareholdings had terminated but the shares would be placed with the financial institutions. But finding a sufficient number of buyers for 25.4 million shares at a price acceptable to the Government was not an easily accomplished task.

Davy Stockbrokers had assured Ahern that it had an undertaking with S.G. Warburg in London – Warburg would purchase any unsold shares (up to a maximum of 10 million) in return for a fee of £550,000.

Later that day, Davy informed Ahern that the shares 'had been placed with institutions in Dublin and London at a price of 275p per share'. QED. Job over. Nearly £70 million in the bag. Unfortunately for Ahern and the Government, that was not precisely what happened: Davy changed the plans, maintaining that if Warburg ended up with a lot of Greencore shares, the share price might weaken over fears of an early Warburg sell-off. Critics hotly disputed this version and questioned why, therefore, Davy ever entered into an arrangement with Warburg in the first place. It was also asked why Davy did not inform its clients – the Government – of such a significant alteration in the agreement between them. It later emerged that the 4.5 million shares were sold to Davy 'associated' parties including directors, a Davy pension fund and another investment company in which the Davy directors had a substantial share. In selling even 1 per cent to persons 'associated' with Davy there was a clear risk of transgressing Greencore's rules which forbids any individual or parties to hold more than 15 per cent of the shares (the Bank of Ireland, through its investment subsidiary, already held a 15 per cent share).

Davy was 90 per cent owned by the Bank of Ireland and had the largest share of government gilts and shares and was the official stockbroker to companies that make up over 60 per cent of the value of the Irish stock market. Its clients included Jefferson Smurfit, Independent Newspapers, Kerry Group, Avonmore Foods, Waterford Wedgewood as well as its own parent company, Bank of Ireland. It also emerged that Warburg were guaranteed by Davy that if the share price fell below 275p (the price sold to ordinary investors) and Warburg suffered a loss, then Davy would make good that loss. In effect then, the selling of the Greencore shares was artificial and unfair.

Because of these revelations, the Government announced it would have the Stock Exchange investigate the matter. Ahern told the Dáil he was seriously concerned and disappointed that important steps had been taken by Davy Stockbrokers with regard to the placing of Greencore shares without his knowledge or agreement. He said that before placing the shares, there was no indication from Davy that any question arose as to the appropriateness, under Stock Exchange rules, of the prearrangement that had been made with Warburgs of London to take up the shares.

'Davy Stockbrokers have informed me that any changes they made to the pre-agreed arrangement, which I became aware of for the first time yesterday, were made solely to ensure the success of the placing and that they were not done with the aim of securing a financial gain for any party having any association with them,' he explained at the time.

'They have also informed me that their decision to seek legal advice was taken solely on their own initiative and solely to clarify the matter and was not prompted by any questions raised by any other party.'

The expected receipt from the placings totalled over £69 million, which was due to be lodged with the Exchequer on 17 May.

'In view of what has arisen I am not in a position now to say categorically that these monies will be received in full on schedule,' he said then. 'I am awaiting legal and other advice on this.'

He also disclosed that the Exchequer had paid a grand total of £175,000 'for advice' on the sale of the shares. The opposition were up in arms at his admission that four million shares had been placed with Irish investors, Pat Cox of the PDs claiming that 'each . . . was connected to Davy'. Ivan Yates (Fine Gael Finance spokesman) again attacked Ahern over his handling of the Greencore saga and demanded that the Minister resign.

'The unavoidable conclusion from this entire sorry saga is that the Minister must take responsibility and take the only honourable course of action and resign from office,' Yates fumed. 'It is unacceptable that, due to a combination of circumstances, so many people were intentionally or otherwise misled.'

He said that competitors and opponents were citing the debacle on a par with the Blue Arrow financial scandal in the UK. Ahern retorted angrily that if anyone botched up the share sale it most certainly was not the Government.

During the debate, there was no Taoiseach or Tánaiste to give him support. His fellow Minister Brian Cowen sat beside him along with junior Minister Noel Treacy, but of the Labour Ministers 'in partnership' there was not a sign. His brother, Noel Ahern, loyally attended. Behind Ahern was former Minister Ray Burke, who got his word in when he 'congratulated' the Minister and lashed out at the 'shameful behaviour' of his stock brokering advisers and the 'unacceptable greed' of others. Ahern reeled off the people he had had discussions with – the Attorney General, the Stock Exchange, the stockbrokers, his officials, his colleagues in Government. 'I acted correctly.'

In an editorial entitled 'Deeply Disturbing', *The Irish Times* agreed with Yates's remarks that the Greencore debacle had 'brought the credibility of Irish financial institutions to an "all time low" and that 'his comment that Ireland might now come to be seen as "the dodgy market of Europe" is – unfortunately – no exaggeration.'

The Irish Times stopped short of backing up Yates's demand for Ahern to resign but insisted that Ahern 'does indeed have to carry the can' and 'this affair will further undermine confidence in him'. The newspaper said, though, that 'the place for resignations to manifest themselves may be in the offices of Davy Stockbrokers'.

Following the privatisation of Irish Life and Greencore, Ahern announced that the sale of all public assets was to be examined as a matter of urgency with a view to selling shares directly to the members of the public rather than transferring them via a golden circle in the financial world. It subsequently emerged that three directors of Davy's controlled almost seven million shares in Greencore, worth £19 million – close to 8.5 per cent of the total shares, following the sale of the Government's remaining 24.5 million shares towards the end of May.

One of the Davy directors maintained that they took up the shares only after institutional investors agreed to subscribe for only 17.5 million of the 25.4 million shares being offered.

Four companies directly associated with Davy and four of its directors acquired shares at a cost of £12.4 million while a further 2.5 million shares worth £6.9 million were held on their behalf by Warburg, which provided funds for their purchase.

Later that March, Ahern demanded that Davy's explain why it had been reprimanded and fined £150,000 by the London Stock Exchange. Ahern concluded that without a satisfactory explanation, he could not determine if the brokers were suitable for future Government work.

'I need to know why charges were brought and why the fine was imposed,' Ahern stormed. 'The bottom line is that Davy's have been reprimanded for something after a 12-month-long investigation and I don't know why.

'It is important for me to know. As Minister for Finance, I am the one who has to make decisions about whether Davy's are involved in privatisation or other work in an area where the Government does not have expertise. I need to know before I can make these sort of decisions.'

Ahern stressed that with the exception of the Greencore 'incident', Davy had a 'good record with successive governments as a competent company' and it was in the wider interests of the company to co-operate with his request. He emphasised that the Exchequer had suffered no loss arising from the placing of the shares and the full proceeds of nearly £70 million had been received.

Davy's later wrote back to Ahern with its 'explanation', which was examined by the Attorney General, Harry Whelehan. Ahern said that the Stock Exchange Bill he was drafting would be reviewed to ensure that the Stock Exchange would not be able to keep vital information from the public. He said he saw no further need for action in relation to Davy's following their response to him for additional information on the Greencore affair. He added that the Attorney General concluded there had been no breach of the criminal law nor had the State suffered any loss and he had been advised that legal proceedings were not warranted. The Stock Exchange committee concluded that 'the events giving rise to the charges were not a deliberate and predetermined course of action by Davy's but a result of the desire to complete the transaction efficiently early in the morning.'

'I consider the matter closed,' said Ahern.

Kyran McLaughlin of Davy's said: 'We're glad it's all over.'

It was a close run thing, as Ahern recalls it today. Certainly, the whole fiasco was a nightmare for Ahern.

'I gave them a job to do,' he recalls today. 'There should have been no problem selling the shares in the Sugar company. The market had improved, things were good, and all the advice was that this was a great time to go. I was informed that all the shares were sold and that we had done the deal. I went on the one o'clock news and said as much. I went to the Stock Exchange and was told everything was successful. A few financial guys were interviewed on financial programmes and they said everything had been successfully completed.'

Then everything went pear-shaped. 'The following morning, I found out that it was successfully done alright – a whole block of shares had gone into companies owned by Davy's, several companies owned by Davy's,' he explains. 'I interpreted the advice given to me – which is now profusely denied from all sides – and that was to let things be,' Ahern reveals.

'My accountancy training said, however, "ah, no, no you don't". We, the Government, said this was a sale. You're not telling me the people who were handling the sale have bought the shares.'

Ahern considered the stock placement by Davy's overnight and called the Stock Exchange early the next morning to suspend the shares.

'I knew what was going to happen. I was going to have a big lot of hassle, but very quickly people would see it was the right thing to do. I came out and made a public statement, went into the Dáil and, of course, had to listen to a lot of flak. But it had to be sorted out and we sorted it out. I stood up and blew the whistle.

'It wasn't a question of selling them or the £70 million we got for them. The issue was that you could not sell them to yourself or your replacement. I brought the world down on myself for 24 hours, but it was a very wise decision, a very wise decision indeed,' Ahern adds.

Chapter 23

Tax Dodgers' Charter

Bertie Ahern takes an uncomplicated view of tax evasion – Lester Piggott deserved to serve time. The view is out of kilter with the hero worship that the Irish reserve for the world's greatest jockey and the general ambivalence that surrounds the question of tax avoidance. Of all the EU countries, Ireland has yet to produce a Lester Piggott – a celebrity convict likely to jolly up the payment of taxes by those in default.

For Ahern, the idea of a tax amnesty was anathema but it was to be one of several off-centre measures which the FF–Lab administration would indulge in to generate Exchequer finance to fund their expanding programmes. The theory behind the amnesty was strictly from the carrot and stick school of economics: cut your losses on outstanding taxes by getting defaulters to pay a discounted 15 per cent of what they owned while at the same time getting the defaulters names on the Revenue Commissioners files for ever and a day. A short-term loss for a long-term gain. At a stroke, the Exchequer would receive a windfall funding bonanza and a continuous stream of income in future years. The netting of the defaulters would also eliminate the constant demands from the trade unions to tackle tax evasion because the perpetrators would once and for all be dragged into the system.

It was all an ingenuous Exchequer win and provisional estimates of the windfall suggested that £200 million was there in the offing which suggested, of course, that there was at least £1.2 billion. Ahern was not home for business when the amnesty was mooted and it appeared that the Labour Ministers were out for lunch when the memo was sent around.

'I was opposed to the amnesty for three reasons: one, the Fianna Fáil party was against it; two, the Revenue Commissioners were against it; and three, I saw the tax amnesty as unnecessary because I had given all this power to the Revenue Commissioners to go after these evaders in the 1992 Finance Act for which, of course, I got hammered in the so-called business media.'

'I just did not think there was any reason to give a massive discount and I underline it – a massive discount – to 15 per cent for evaders. We are talking about very substantial bills which involved very substantial people,' Ahern adds. 'I was just opposed and I fought the amnesty through five cabinet meetings. In the end I was left on my own. There was no Dick Spring or no Ruairi Quinn there to help me out. It was 14 to 1 all the time,' he reveals.

Ahern was so vehement about the issue that he considered the possibility of resignation. 'It got very near that. I didn't support it but in the end I was left with little alternative. Under the rules of collective responsibility, I had to go back to the Dáil and bring it in, which I did. That was my job,' he adds.

The 'Waiver of Certain Tax, Interest and Penalties Bill' was introduced by a Minister who showed the enthusiasm of a wet fish. The tax system had to be cleaned up, he said, and the amnesty was an attempt to do that. People guilty of tax fraud should go to jail: 'You cannot have a young lad getting six months for a minor offence and someone committing fraud getting away scot-free.'

Tax evaders were warned to avail themselves of the one-off opportunity to put their affairs in order and use the amnesty. Otherwise the Revenue Commissioners would move on them and hit them with potential eight-year jail sentences.

'It is time we started jailing people, and quite frankly, I look forward to that day,' he added pointedly.

During the Bill's second reading he pointed out that the amnesty was aimed at the thousands of people in small businesses whom everyone knew were suppressing their income for tax purposes year after year and it was not just a measure for the 'big operators'. Defending the amnesty and promising that suggestions made about its operation by the opposition would be taken into account when the scheme was formulated. Ahern noted that there were about two million people active in the economy, 'yet we have about 15 million bank accounts in the country'. He added that in some towns around the country the amount of 'foreign' accounts outnumbered domestic accounts. Impassioned speeches were made in the Dáil condemning the tax amnesty, to which Ahern listened impassively. He was accused of being against the amnesty by the opposition who detected his misgivings when he was still making vague statements about opposing the idea in the days before the Bill was introduced.

When the amnesty's deadline was subsequently extended by three weeks, Ahern publicly admitted that the fiscal trawl had failed to net the hot money owed by the big evaders.

'Some of the mortal sinners, the really big tax evaders – unlike the small fry – are not coming forward for the amnesty,' he noted. He warned that 'those who are foolish enough to ignore this opportunity' would be detected and pursued.

'They will deserve little sympathy when the day of reckoning comes,' he cautioned.

After the event, the Labour party suggested that they were against the amnesty and according to Fergus Finlay's book on the last two Governments, one of the party's main advisers, Willie Scally, threatened to resign the moment the Cabinet approved the amnesty.

Any rewriting of the episode was quickly put to bed by Albert Reynolds when he went out of Government: 'I must say I appreciated the fact, in fairness to Albert Reynolds, that he put it in the public domain that I was the only one opposed to the Tax Amnesty. In earlier meetings Dick Spring and Ruairi Quinn had reservations but in the end they reluctantly voted for the Amnesty,' Ahern adds today.

In an end-of-year stratagem aimed at concentrating the minds of the Social Partners on wage inflation within the economy which was running at substantially higher rates than our competitors, Ahern offered a carrot and stick solution by announcing he would abolish his controversial 1 per cent income levy in return for concessions in the area. The trade union side had been making a big song and dance about the levy which had been introduced the previous February and raised £147 million for the Exchequer. Ahern had yet again created a bargaining counter from nothing at all and would now proceed to abandon his unpopular measure for a substantially higher price in terms of economic productivity. It was a case of old tricks work best.

In another tidying-up operation Ahern announced that reducing the top rates of income taxes was no longer a Government priority and this would be reflected in his next Budget.

'When the quite generous discretionary reliefs which are available are taken into account, it is clear that a top rate of 48 per cent is by no means excessive,' he pointed out.

'Accordingly, the lowering of the top rate is not on this Government's short-term agenda.'

Chapter 24

We're in the Money

The tax amnesty which Ahern so vehemently opposed brought in an extra quarter of a billion pounds to the Exchequer as tax evaders rushed to get on side with the Revenue Commissioners at the never-to-be-repeated discount offer of 15 per cent. It had been like the New Year's sales at the tax offices throughout the country. The economic argument on the amnesty was over but Ahern was still smarting at losing the other billion had the evaders paid up like everyone else. Nevertheless, he used the amnesty money in his 1994 fiscal statement to produce what observers described as the 'biggest give-away' Budget of the decade.

Ahern announced that the inflow of cash from the amnesty was a conservative £150 million but he stressed that these funds would be applied to resolve 'a number of old issues' such as balancing the pension provisions for State companies like An Post and Telecom Eireann and with defraying the outstanding overdrafts of the country's Health Boards. He then went into William Carnegie mode and started to dispense tax concessions left, right and centre. The best part of £200 million in mainstream tax-relief would go towards the 200,000 lower-paid incomes to encourage jobs. His diverting 1 per cent income levy was abolished for all tax-payers, in a concession to the trade unions who could claim another victory for the Social Partnership approach to the national economy and, after all, there is a certain cachet in being able to show halls of trade unionists that Government policy can be influenced. Tax band and allowances were increased for the middle income group, welfare went up 3 per cent and disability payments by a remarkable 10 per cent. The old reliables of booze and cigs got hammered again.

The most controversial aspect of his Budget was reserved for householders who in future would have their mortgage and family health insurance reliefs scaled down. Thresholds for residential property tax were lowered which brought more of the more affluent households into this particular taxation net, but Ahern saw the tax as a socialist vanity tax which was hardly worth the money it was taking to collect.

It was raising around £5 million in a Budget running into billions and would not fund the refuse collections services of a small city for a year, yet the levy created acres of copy space in newspapers like *The Irish Times* and the *Sunday Business Post* who saw the property tax as an assault on the rights of the affluent.

The reaction to the 1994 budget by *The Irish Times* illustrates the point. On Budget day the newspaper ran an editorial under the headline 'TWO CHEERS FOR MR AHERN' which said, 'Overall, the direction this Budget takes deserves to be supported, as the Minister has reduced taxes on income and also started a long overdue process of reforming the tax code.'

The following day, in another editorial entitled 'A TAX ON PROPERTY', *The Irish Times*, having touched base with their ABC1 readers, attacked Ahern's property tax measures.

'By widening the property tax net in the way that he has done, the Minister for Finance, Mr Ahern, has exacerbated the irrational and inequitable aspects of an instrument which, from its introduction, has contained a large element of unfairness in its application. How, for example, can the Minister justify increasing the burden on a married couple with several young children, and thus with a relatively large house and mortgage, when a single person with a substantial salary in a comfortable and fully-paid apartment pays nothing?'

The tax affected significantly less than 7 per cent of the population as only 3 per cent of the residential properties were within the net on the valuation income rules, yet it led to lacerating attacks on the Minister and the Government. Fine Gael claimed the measure was 'anti-family and anti-home' while Pat Cox of the Progressive Democrats accused the Minister of being 'out of touch with the genuine anger and fear of householders'. Ahern even had to face his own Dublin TDs and Senators, including his brother Noel, who were claiming that all of the capital's middle-class constituencies – where property values were breaching the valuation thresholds – would be engulfed in the tax. Government backbenchers and the opposition, backed up by editorial writers and vested interest groups outside, forced three concessions in terms of income and evaluation thresholds and the duration of the tax on the Government during the Finance Bill. When the truncated tax was passed by the Dáil, *The Irish Times* noted 'may yet become a tax that costs more to collect than it yields'. Ahern finally lashed out at the 'hysteria' being generated on account of a minor fiscal measure like the Residential Property Tax. The Government was being 'scalded because a small minority of middle-class people were exerting a disproportionate influence on Irish society,' he said. It was a double standard at work, he added. Ahern said that there would be an outcry over fraud and abuse of the system if the unemployed were involved, but if the Government pursued another class of people, it was accused of destroying the incentive to enterprise.

'I am trying not to despair about the prospects for more fundamental tax reform, given that the property tax was the least radical measure available within the overall area of taxation,' he said then. Today Ahern is more emphatic.

A sequel to the Property tax would occur some months later when Taoiseach Albert Reynolds suggested at a business meeting in Kerry that it might make more sense from a Revenue perspective to merge the property tax with the controversial 'local charges' that were being levied by local authorities to fund refuse and water services.

Environment Minister, Michael Smith, immediately and publicly opposed the idea claiming that the charges were justifiable and needed to be bedded down in the public's mind. The Labour party were appalled that their vanity tax would be subsumed into what looked like a return of the hated domestic rates or the introduction of a poll-tax. The controversy over Reynolds's remarks lasted a week and the idea was quietly consigned to the 'out tray'. Ahern was sent into the Dáil to explain, 'there is no particular Government agenda about property and local taxes'.

Ticking away in the background was the Passports for Investments Scheme which was developed as a fiscal instrument by Haughey and thrived during two short-lived Governments headed by Albert Reynolds. Like the tax amnesty, it was a notable little earner for the Irish economy. Rich foreigners undertook to invest in Irish companies in difficulties, in exchange for an Irish passport. The offer was mainly taken up by millionaire Arabs and Far Eastern businessmen particularly from Hong Kong in the run up to the colony being returned to China. The scheme was administered by the Department of Justice and among the beneficaries from the scheme was the pet food business owned by the Reynolds family in Longford which an Arabian family called Masri invested in, in return for a passport. This investment was subsequently repaid by the C and D pet food company. The scheme, which is being probed by the Tribunal into Payments to Politicians, set up in the wake of revelations about the financial connections between former Taoiseach, Charles Haughey, and former Fine Gael Minister, Michael Lowry, with former supermarket tycoon, Ben Dunne, was partly regularised during the course of the Fianna Fáil–Labour administration of 1993–1994. Ahern was emphatically against the scheme and shelved the inward investment to be gained from foreigners in return for an Irish passport when he put together his present Government. His opposition to the scheme was vehement. He explains, 'When I looked at the passport scheme closely, you just couldn't stand over it. I certainly couldn't stand over it. It looked a good scheme at the time with all that Arab and Hong Kong money coming in for investment in Irish companies but there was no control over it whatsoever. It's one thing for a fellow to say he's coming here with £10 million and going to open a place in Sligo in return for a passport, but what happens when you go back five weeks later and find out it's a cowshed?' he points out.

One of Ahern's main problems with the scheme was the fact that there was no system of checks and balances between the person who was investing, the capital they were investing and what the foreigner was investing in.

'I think there is a case for a passport if a guy has been investing and building up an Irish company for over five or ten years. It wouldn't matter if he came from Outer Mongolia, but I don't see any case for a fellow coming here to St Luke's on a Monday afternoon to tell me he will do the world and all for Irish citizenship. I just have a fundamental objection to something like that,' he stresses, 'so having gone up and down the passport scheme at Cabinet when we came into power – and not everybody agreed with it this time either – we made a collective decision to abolish the scheme once we reviewed the outstanding cases and tidied up the few cases who were due to get citizenship.

'There's no doubt that many companies in this country are still alive today because of the passport scheme. There's an old rag place in this constituency that employs hundreds that nearly went until they got an investor. But I just think we are better rid of that scheme,' he emphasises.

The Beef Tribunal which had starred Albert Reynolds, Dick Spring and Dessie O'Malley, the main power brokers of the day, had reported at this stage, and the alacrity with which Reynolds got out his 'My name has been vindicated' message to the public caused friction with the Labour leader and graphically illustrated to Spring the bare essentials of his Taoiseach's *modus operandi*. The Tribunal uncovered all manner of income tax irregularities within the Goodman beef group and the beef industry generally but what mostly animated the public, as stated earlier, was the colossal legal fees that the Tribunal had generated. Ahern was not involved in the Tribunal and was conspicuous by his absence when Albert Reynolds grandstanded before most of his Ministers in Dublin Castle about his difference of opinion with O'Malley on the question of export insurance. As Minister for Finance, he had to deal with the financial implications of the Tribunal. He told the Dáil he was contesting the legal costs awarded by the Tribunal, particularly the costs of beef-related companies where large-scale tax fraud was found to exist. Ahern kept his best barbs for the legal profession who in the public's mind had all but squatted in Dublin Castle over the previous year.

'It seems extraordinary that in this age of deregulation and competition, there is what seems like a virtual cartel system applying to legal fees,' he said.

The tribunal cost over £30 million, with some legal fees stretching to £1,800 a day. There had been 226 sitting days, which were paid at the full fees, but these were renegotiated for the 419 non-sitting days, which had saved the Exchequer a considerable amount of money.

Instructions had been issued by the Department of Finance to all Departments in this regard with a view to minimising costs, he said. With regard to tax evasion, the report indicated that there was no evidence of the Revenue Commissioners turning a 'blind eye' to the activities of the Goodman group. The report found that evasion had taken place on a substantive scale but, like all evasion, it was difficult to detect in the ordinary course at the time. Referring to the application of the tax amnesty to some of the liabilities uncovered by the tribunal, Ahern said the Revenue Commissioners had to apply the amnesty in an even-handed way. 'They cannot exclude any individual or company which satisfies the conditions laid down by the Oireachtas,' he said.

As for the tribunal's recommendation to oblige accountants to report tax evasion to the Revenue, he said there would be discussions with the profession to come up with a sensible working arrangement. 'I don't think that the professional bodies can argue strongly against change in the light of all that had happened and has been noted in the tribunal report,' he added.

The first half of what was to become a dramatic political year was pretty pedestrian for Ahern who was now semi-detached from Government and concentrating on European Union downtable negotiations for the final net tranche of development millions from Brussels. Reynolds and Spring were deep into the Peace Process and developing the window of opportunity which the IRA cease-fire of 1993 provided and were virtually dealing with the Northern parties and John Major's Government on a full-time basis. Reynolds was all but beatified by Fianna Fáil and as far as Ahern's inner circle were concerned, the Longford man could look forward to a long stint as Taoiseach. Ahern took over the chairmanship of the OECD in Paris in Buggins-turn fashion which had a certain irony as the last Irish chairman was Ahern's old constituency rival George Colley 20 years previously. The job also gave him the pleasure of introducing an OECD report which showed that Ireland was one of the least taxed populations in Europe. Negotiations at the European Commission on the amount of funding which the country was likely to receive in money transfers from Brussels to 1999 was concentrating his mind. The previous December, during the hiatus between the FF–PD Government and the negotiation of the FF–Labour administration, Reynolds pulled off what appeared to be another of his exceptional fiscal coups, at the Edinburgh EU summit, where he shook his fellow European leaders down for £8 billion in funding over the '94–'99 period. The transfers when rolled over with private and Exchequer investment would produce an unprecedented investment in the country's infrastructure and create the conditions for the economic boom of the late '90s. A National £20 billion plan, which included investment in a new Light Rail system for Dublin (LUAS – which just recently got the go-ahead), more development in the Shannon region and the construction of a state-of-the-art peat-based electricity station, was underpinned by the EU Funding, but suddenly the Government

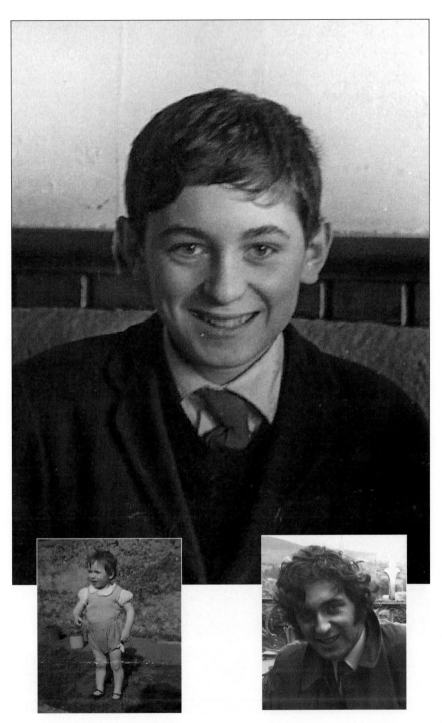

Ahern as a toddler (*above left*); as a pupil at St Aidan's CBS Secondary
School (*main picture*); and in 1970, at the College of Commerce
at Rathmines (*above right*)

Ahern with his late parents, Con and Julia, shortly after his election as Lord Mayor of Dublin in 1986

Pictured in Limerick with partner Celia Larkin (left) and Hillary Clinton during the American President's visit to Ireland in early September 1998

Flanked by his daughters, Georgina (left) and Cecilia

Miriam Ahern and her daughter Cecilia pictured at the funeral of Julia Ahern, the Taoiseach's mother, in April 1998.

Bertie Ahern's constituency team: (*back row from left to right*) Noel Ahern, Chris Wall, Tony Kett, Martin L'Estrange, Frank Worley; (*front row from left to right*) Cyprian Brady, Jimmy Keane, Bertie Ahern, Liam Copper and Paddy Reilly

Bertie Ahern's first cabinet portfolio was as Minister for Labour in Haughey's minority administration in 1987. Front row (left to right): John Wilson, Gerry Collins, Brian Lenihan, Charles Haughey, Ray MacSharry, Mary O'Rourke, Albert Reynolds. Back row (left to right): Brendan Daly, John Murray (Attorney General), Bertie Ahern, Michael Woods, Padraig Flynn, Michael O'Kennedy, Ray Burke, Michael J. Noonan, Rory O'Hanlon.

Albert Reynolds, Dick Spring and Bertie Ahern at the launch of Fianna Fáil's national plan in October 1993

Ahern with former Fine Gael Taoiseach John Bruton at the start of a TV debate on RTÉ before 1997's General Election

The General Election campaign in June 1997: Ahern visits St Patrick's, his old primary school in Drumcondra

An admirer in Galway provided a humorous talking point during that same campaign

Sinn Féin leader Gerry Adams visited the Taoiseach in Dublin in early '98

During the peace process: the leader and deputy leader of the UUP, David Trimble and Ken Maginnis, make a joint statement accompanied by Ahern

Bertie Ahern and John Hume pictured outside Ahern's constituency office, St Luke's, in Drumcondra, Dublin early in 1998.

The culmination of months of negotiations: Tony Blair and Bertie Ahern sign the Good Friday Agreement

were short-changed by the European Commission and left £800 million light. Ahern had to moderate this ambitious investment programme and outline where the '£800 million adjustments' would fall. Neither the Dáil or the Labour party leader and Tánaiste were over the moon. Spring was not party to the Edinburgh negotiations and had taken Reynolds's word that £8 billion in Euro cash was in the bag. The former was furious when he and Ahern were accused by the former Fine Gael leader Alan Dukes of misleading the Dáil. He dismissed the national plan as a 'rag of a document' with £800 million missing. All Ahern could do was promise intensive negotiations to retrieve the funding once the Mid-term review of the EU funding tranche came round. The department would maximise funds from various EU Community initiatives but additional Exchequer funding to make up the shortfall would depend on annual budgetary positions.

Back at the ranch, in Dublin central, Ahern's car was robbed again. The £30k Opel Senator was stolen from outside his Garda driver's home in the Cabra area of Dublin when Ahern was away in Russia at a European Bank conference. The thief evaded the pursuing Gardaí in a high speed chase which ended when the Minister's car careered into the Neilstown housing sprawl on the West side of the city, famed as the capital's Bermuda triangle for stolen cars. The Opel Senator was found four days later in Malahide with only minor hot rodding damage.

At this stage, Ahern decided he needed a make-over and dumped his anoraks and jackets for sharp Louis Copeland suits – Copeland being yet another of his constituents who ran his tailoring business from Chapel Street. He put his anorak up for a charity auction in the constituency and Kennedy's pub promptly bought the garment. It put an end to the 'slagging I got for wearing anoraks and jumpers,' he says. As things would develop later in the year, an armoured plate suit might have been more appropriate.

Chapter 25

Nuts – Absolute Nuts

The beginning of the end for the Reynolds–Spring government came on the day that the Cabinet decided to go ahead with the appointment of the Attorney General, Harry Whelehan, as President of the High Court.

The appointment had long been fingered through the summer and into the autumn because objections from the Labour party could not be overcome and at one stage it looked as though the matter was resolved as word got out that the Attorney General was not going to be promoted to the bench. However, when Dick Spring was out of the country that autumn on State business, the question of Whelehan's appointment resurfaced at Cabinet when his name was again put forward for the job. The remaining Labour Ministers withdrew from Cabinet and spent three hours negotiating with their Fianna Fáil counterparts to have the appointment deferred until it was sorted out personally between Reynolds and his Tánaiste Dick Spring. Both men, at a meeting in Baldonell airport, agreed to revisit the High Court appointment once legislation on court reform was published.

Why a judicial appointment which was causing such friction in Government was allowed to permeate into everything the Cabinet did that autumn still perplexes Ahern.

Ensconced at the Department of Finance and outside the Reynolds inner circle which at that stage included Michael Smith, Noel Dempsey and Maire Geoghegan-Quinn, Flynn having long since departed for the EU Commission, the row over Whelehan concerned him.

Ahern says today: 'Harry Whelehan is a nice guy but it was very unfortunate that from September to November of that year everything was dominated by whether Harry Whelehan was going to the High Court. The row was worrying me at the time. I'll put it to you this way. If Mary Harney today said to me that she wouldn't agree with so and so being appointed to the High Court then I would try to resolve the matter amiably.'

The first near disaster over Whelehan was narrowly averted by the Baldonnel meeting but when it started to emerge that his office (Attorney General) had not expedited an arrest warrant for a paedophile priest, Fr Brendan Smyth, to Northern Ireland and when the explanations of a perfunctory nature came forth from the office, a series of bizarre incidents was soon unravelled which none of the main participants seem to have put back together since. Labour Ministers would not be supporting Whelehan's High Court appointment except in the event of the Attorney General or Reynolds himself giving a satisfactory explanation. Reynolds pressed the appointment of Whelehan immediately. Labour withdrew and Harry Whelehan was on the bench by that weekend. The only way of saving the Government was a full explanation to the Dáil of the Brendan Smyth affair and, although a deal to secure the Reynolds administration was clinched before the Taoiseach entered the chamber, it would be blown apart by the emergence of another extradition warrant for another paedophile monk – the so-called Duggan case.

At this point, the Fianna Fáil–Labour coalition led by Albert Reynolds and his leadership of Fianna Fáil effectively ended, though it would take another week to play out in the Dáil. Reynolds resigned on 17 November with a speech that is remembered for his horse-racing metaphor regarding his three years at the top: 'You get over the big hurdles; it's the little ones that trip you up.' Later that day when he resigned as leader of Fianna Fáil he said, 'I simply wish to state that it was never my intention to mislead the Dáil or withhold any material information from it.' Harry Whelehan resigned as President of the High Court on the same evening and Ahern began his campaign to become the next leader of Fianna Fáil.

As Ahern says, the idea that the Government should collapse in the end over extradition warrants for paedophile priests was 'nuts – absolute nuts'.

'It's a pity the way that Government ended. But in terms of what really ended the Government, that stuff about the priests was absolute nuts; Albert was totally innocent of that. We knew nothing about it; we knew absolutely nothing about it,' he says today.

The tension in Dáil Eireann was such that over the days throughout which it took the Government to collapse, Ahern threw his first, and so far only, wobbler in the Dáil. Asked by Gay Mitchell where the Taoiseach was, he rounded on the deputy lambasting him as a 'waffler'. Mitchell, he said, was coming in and out of the Dáil for the past 20 years and all he ever did was waffle. 'You're a waffler, a waffler – and you've always been a waffler.'

The outburst was like a tension release.

'I lost my head with Gay Mitchell because he was trying to order Albert back into the chamber. He gave me half an hour to produce Albert. I'll tell you, if he had been near enough to me that day . . . so I ended up calling him a waffler.'

It was suggested at the time, mainly by die-hard Albert loyalists, that Ahern failed to pass an important file to Reynolds while he was on his feet in the Dáil fighting for his political life which may have got the Taoiseach out from under the Doghan paedophile case. The letter involved was a note from the new Attorney General, Eoghan Fitzsimmons, outlining precisely that the Doghan case was a precedent of the Smyth paedophile case.

'It's the one question I am always asked. In terms of me holding back anything, I didn't. In terms of us not copping the importance of the letter, I have to say I've read that letter many times since and if I read it today I still wouldn't cop the importance of it.

'There are those who say that if Albert had read the Fitzsimmons letter he would be all right today. To be honest with you, from my point of view, I wish he had read the letter, but he didn't read 90 per cent of the other stuff I gave him either. I said I'd bat for Albert when he took over the leadership and I did. I did my utmost to help Albert in those weeks. I was the one doing the fighting on radio and TV when people closer to him weren't doing it,' he recalls.

Ahern was not party to the inner meetings which the Taoiseach held during those crisis days. The cabinet Ministers he relied upon were Michael Smith, Maire Geoghegan-Quinn and Charlie McCreevy. Smith had just returned from the by-elections in Cork (where the Labour party were pasted by the electorate on a polling scale of a political Alamo) when he got a call from Maire Geoghegan-Quinn effectively telling him they were 'in the shit now' and suggesting a meeting in Smith's house in Donnybrook.

'Nobody thought anything about the second case. There was no reason to hide anything about it. The paedophiles were not the issue, though that's the way it played publicly,' Smith says. 'There were a fair lot of accidents over those days and changes to the scripts in the Taoiseach's office and very desperate attempts to remain in power. It was like going to see a play in a theatre where everything that can go wrong goes wrong,' he adds.

Smith, who always believed the Harry Whelehan issue could have been resolved over a cup of tea between the coalition leaders, says he was convinced that Labour was going from Government anyway: 'There was no chemistry between Albert and Dick. Neither took account of the other's sensitivities. Spring was particularly annoyed that he was not getting his due credit for what was happening on the Northern peace process and the ceasefire.'

Chapter 26

No Contest. No Problem

A traumatised Fianna Fáil parliamentary party convened the following weekend to elect a leader, with Ahern the overwhelming favourite. Maire Geoghegan-Quinn, the then acting Justice Minister, threw her hat in the ring. Both candidates, according to Ahern, decided to 'keep things friendly and helpful' over the short and sharp four days of the campaign. 'There was no backbiting or any of the stuff that went on during previous leadership elections,' he adds.

Geoghegan-Quinn attempted to rally the support of the 'Country and Western Alliance' which brought Albert Reynolds to power but their ranks were scattered because of the Government upheaval. Charlie McCreevy did his best to muster the Alliance but with mixed results. On their first tally they had Geoghegan-Quinn with only 14 backers against Ahern's 49. Even Michael Smith wasn't biting and told McCreevy, 'The job is Ahern's. It's no contest.'

Geoghegan-Quinn persevered with a radio and television campaign while Ahern kept a low profile running his campaign from his constituency headquarters at St Luke's. His best canvasser turned out to be Brian Lenihan, who was hospitalised up the road in the Mater Private for routine tests on his transplanted liver. He regularly kept in contact with reporters covering the leadership election, giving the latest tallies for Ahern and asking in return if there were any signs of Maire Geoghegan-Quinn 'getting off the pitch'. He even sent out a typically enthusiastic and laudatory pro-Ahern call from his hospital bed on the eve of the election to his colleagues which said, 'Having served under all five Fianna Fáil Taoisigh, I would urge the Parliamentary Party at this critical juncture to select Bertie Ahern as leader of the party. He has the right balance of ability, age and experience. Electorally he is ideally located to strengthen party support and personally he has the negotiating and consensual skills that are so required for national leadership in the modern age.' Ahern couldn't have got better copy from a retained PR agency.

When the majority of Fianna Fáil deputies on the Western seaboard came out for Ahern, the game was up for Maire Geoghegan-Quinn but she did not decide to get off the pitch until after Brian Lenihan sent his vote overnight to the party parliamentary chairman, Joe Jacob. The Lenihan vote was the only one actually cast for Ahern that day as Geoghegan-Quinn had packed in her challenge before the full parliamentary party convened.

'I still appreciated her withdrawing,' Ahern says today. 'It was nice because it helped me in terms of getting on and uniting the party, and needless to say Sean Lemass got the job unopposed.'

'Our party had such a great name but by the time I came in, in 1977, things were grand for about 18 months and from 1979 it was all just haggling. Now nobody checks who said what; even my brother can get up and have a go at me most weeks,' he says today.

On Saturday, 17 November 1994 Ahern was elected the youngest-ever leader of Fianna Fáil at the age of 43. The vote cast by Brian Lenihan from his hospital bed remained sealed and when 'no contest' was declared, party officials went to shred Lenihan's envelope but remarkably the machine refused to work. It was decided to place the still sealed envelope in the party archive. Ahern says it was opened for him at the end of the meeting and is now in the party's archives.

He immediately told reporters that his wife Miriam had been fully supportive of his leadership bid. 'She knew I wanted to have a run. She wanted me to get it. She could not have been more helpful and I am very grateful.' He said his partner, Celia Larkin, would accompany him to formal functions.

Ahern, in his first press conference as Fianna Fáil leader that evening at the Burlington Hotel, identified the Northern peace process as his first priority, whether in or out of government, while other priorities included public accountability, freedom of information and tackling of unemployment.

Ahern said he ran an unobtrusive campaign: 'I simply rang all my colleagues and asked them to take into consideration my record. We've had 25 years of heaves and counter-heaves, of hassles and controversies. We've recovered from all of them, but we've lost focus at times. We have lost market share with the electorate.'

He warned it was time 'Fianna Fáil won back those members who had been alienated by the arms trial, the Haughey heaves and that type of thing. I suppose there will be many more good days and bad days. All that I can say is that I will do my honest best to do a good job for the party, for the people that I represent and for the whole country in whatever capacity I serve Fianna Fáil.'

Asked if Dick Spring was correct in pulling out of government the previous Wednesday, he replied: 'We did not do anything wrong – we made an error. We left out something. We regret that but we can't change it now. We can't do any more.'

Asked about coalition, he replied: 'I believe I could work with the Labour party.'

After the press conference, Ahern went immediately to see his mother, Julia, made a television appearance on the *Kenny Live* television show and then adjourned to Kennedy's pub in Drumcondra for celebratory drinks with a couple of hundred supporters.

'Sure there's everything in Drumcondra now,' smiled local shopkeeper Jim O'Neill. 'We have an archbishop up the road and now we're going to have a Taoiseach as well.'

Chapter 27

'Hell!'

Renegotiations between Ahern and Spring for a renewal of the Fianna Fáil–Labour Government got underway soon after he was elected party leader.

The chief Labour demand was a truthful explanation of the extradition fiasco and a further explanation as to why the political correspondents had been briefed on the Attorney General position of the Smyth extradition cases. Specifically, Ahern was asked by Spring to get the Attorney General to give the full facts about any contacts he made with Harry Whelehan, any discussions that took place and the context of his approaches. Inquiries were immediately set in motion.

Ahern later replied, 'Based on what the Taoiseach [Reynolds] has told me – and I believe him – he did not ask the Attorney General to request the resignation of Harry Whelehan on Monday, 14 November. Neither did Fianna Fáil Ministers speak to the Attorney General on that Monday with a similar purpose.'

The question hinged on exactly when the Fianna Fáil members of Government knew that there was a precedent case involving the monk Duggan in the Attorney General's office which pre-dated the Smyth extradition case – a case which had been delayed so long as to create misgivings about the manner in which Harry Whelehan ran the office of the Attorney General. For the Labour party, the answer to this question was vital because it would prove or disprove whether the Fianna Fáil Ministers from Albert Reynolds down were being open and transparent with their partners in Government.

Ahern and Spring met face to face at the beginning of December having earlier appointed negotiating teams to deal with the housekeeping issues. Labour demanded the abolition of university fees, the rescinding of controversial pay hikes for politicians and the appointment of a Labour Party Minister for Finance for which they were pushing Ruairi Quinn. Meanwhile, Fianna Fáil's requirements for a resumption of the coalition were largely based on the Programme for a Partnership Government. Ahern showed a willingness to draw up structures to permit greater accountability and transparency in government, especially at the Attorney General's office which he remarked would be best located in a glasshouse. There was a view within Fianna Fáil that the decision rested with Labour, but many FF backbenchers expressed concern that there was a limit to how much the party could give away. The Albert Reynolds Cabinet was still in place and Ahern assuaged Spring's fears about the estimates for the following year by guaranteeing that these estimates would be a matter for whoever formed the incoming government.

At this point the story about accountability becomes relevant. Sufficient agreement had been reached for both men to begin considering the formation of a new Fianna Fáil–Labour Cabinet.

As Ahern remembers it, 'On the Sunday night I was with my people in my office in the Dáil. We were finalising things. There were two or three bits and pieces to finalise and we left them to my programme manager, Gerry Hickey, and his [Spring's] manager, Greg Sparks. They knew each other well so there was no problem. I had to get ready to go to a European finance meeting, where there were resources available for the peace and reconciliation fund the following morning, so I was not going to miss that. I even suggested that both myself and Dick Spring should go because there was £30 million involved – so it was a worthwhile trip.

'I was on my way to the State jet and as we were driving along the Naas road, I was reading the Geraldine Kennedy article on the front page of *The Irish Times*. I just wondered what it was all about.'

Kennedy had reported that the Fianna Fáil Ministers knew of the precedent case on the Monday rather than the Tuesday of the week in which the Government collapsed.

'I didn't see a lot in it but I still wondered, what is it? All the political correspondents had been on the *Farrell* programme on

RTE the previous night saying Bruton would be gone as Fine Gael leader before the week was out and that Ahern was going to be Taoiseach,' he adds.

'During the morning I got a call from Spring wanting to know this, that and the other and I got on to the Attorney General and told him to give Spring whatever he wanted. Then I had to get Reynolds – he was in Budapest, I was in Brussels and the Attorney General was in Dublin. Reynolds was still Taoiseach; I was only leader of Fianna Fáil so we couldn't get everything cleared until Reynolds came back late that night. I then got the phone call from Spring saying the deal was off.

'When Dick Spring called at 2 a.m. on Tuesday, 6 December to break it off, I was left shaken. For about four minutes I dropped myself back down on the pillow and said "hell". Within about five minutes I was down in my office and back on the phone ringing around the ministers.'

When he met his inner circle, whom Emily O'Reilly described as the Drumcondra machiavellis, he was very sanguine about the whole affair. Tony Kett said he couldn't believe Ahern's attitude. He just said 'That's the way the chips fall. Forget about it.'

What started off as reservations from Dick Spring and the Labour party about the appointment of the Cabinet's Attorney General to the High Court had weaved its way through inefficiencies in the Attorney General's office which allowed a warrant for a paedophile priest to lie around unexecuted for seven months, which in turn uncovered another case involving another paedophile priest. These three separate events, whose only common denominator was their association with the office of the Attorney General, led to one Taoiseach being forced to resign, one President of the High Court tendering his resignation, one would-be Taoiseach missing out and a Government which made the breakthrough in the Northern Ireland peace process collapsing. According to the Labour party's spin doctor, Fergus Finlay, it was all down to Fianna Fáil's lack of accountability.

There had been speculation that several politicians from both parties had been ear-marked for various ministries and that O'Rourke was offered Environment.

'Environment was mentioned but I was not offered that position,' O'Rourke says. 'We had a very, very brief conversation, perhaps for half a minute and yes, Environment was mentioned, but not as saying that's what we're going to give you or anything.' She denies that there was a list of proposed ministers and has no knowledge of it.

'It was a very difficult time,' she recalls. 'We had Brendan Howlin, Ruairi Quinn, myself, Brian Cowen, Noel Dempsey and Mervyn Taylor. We were the negotiating team and we had worked quite long at it and drawn up lots of papers and we got on well and on the Saturday night we finished about 9 o'clock and we went down to the Davenport hotel. We had a drink and talked and all went home to bed and the present Taoiseach met Dick Spring the following afternoon to tidy up things on that document and we thought our work was complete.'

Ahern was now the leader of the opposition whose members were openly warring with each other over who was responsible for casting them away from power. There were demands for heads to roll and for full accountability from Albert Reynolds and his inner coterie. It was all too late. They had gone away.

Meanwhile, Ahern was left with crumbs of comforting news from the polls. Following Ahern's selection as Fianna Fáil leader, he brought his party's opinion poll rating up from 35 per cent to 44 per cent in the latest *Irish Times*/MRBI poll, while in the capital, FF rallied from a low of 24 per cent just two weeks previously to 42 per cent (eating heavily into support for the PDs and Democratic Left).

Chapter 28

Bit Player in Sorry Saga

Power was whisked from under Bertie Ahern's nose just 12 hours before the Labour party were due to go into the Dáil and support his nomination as Taoiseach. Only three minor issues – mere housekeeping matters within the Programme for Government – remained and were left by the two leaders to their respective Programme Managers, Gerry Hickey and Greg Sparks to sort out. Overnight, *The Irish Times* published a Geraldine Kennedy exclusive about the foreknowledge of the Fianna Fáil Ministers of all the events surrounding the hysterical attempts to shore up the Reynolds Government, including the overture to Harry Whelehan to resign as High Court President just days after his appointment. The story ran a coach and four through Fianna Fáil claims that Ministers were unaware of these approaches and the story was based on a significant leak that could have only come from Fianna Fáil or Labour insiders. A Labour source was, nevertheless, unlikely as none of their people were near the scene of the events reported and Labour were still in negotiating mode when *The Irish Times* report was published.

Considering the scale of the headless chicken operation mounted by the Fianna Fáil Ministers to save the Reynolds administration, the lack of clarity on the subject might have been entirely understandable except that the Labour party had given Fianna Fáil every opportunity to straighten matters out over the previous six weeks and Fianna Fáil were now coming up on the fuzzy side of transparent yet again. The options for the Labour party were squeezed. Spring went through the procedure of asking Ahern, who was in Brussels, to clear up the new mess but Ahern in turn was dependent on Reynolds who was in Budapest. The matter took all day to clarify and the clarification was a confirmation of the Geraldine Kennedy news report. The Government deal was off and the Labour party was off. The source of the leak has always been a matter of contention for Fianna Fáilers who immediately jumped to the conclusion that the 'prima donnas' in the Labour party were at it again. Although the precise source will remain, like the Third Secret of Fatima, a mystery, a betting man would have to put his wager on a Fianna Fáil source. The only people privy to what was going on within the Reynolds inner circle and on its margins were Fianna Fáil and the only offices of State dealing with the issues concerned were Fianna Fáil held.

'I never criticised Geraldine Kennedy and she wrote the story. I don't know who gave it to her. There are still stories doing the rounds that it was a Fianna Fáil colleague. Who knows. Ask Geraldine Kennedy. I took the view soon afterwards that it was time to move on,' Ahern says today.

However he still maintains that the anti-coalition views of the Labour party spin doctors like Fergus Finlay did little to facilitate the renewal of Government between Fianna Fáil and Labour.

At the subsequent enquiry into the collapse of the Government he said that Fianna Fáil Ministers in that Government, including himself, were deeply suspicious of the role played by Labour advisers in the Whelehan affair and that this role contrasted with the more co-operative attitude of the Labour ministers with whom they had been in daily contact. Ahern added that he found Spring to be 'a good politician and a fair man' but criticised Labour programme manager Fergus Finlay, claiming that they played a part in bringing down the Government.

An issue in Fergus Finlay's book *Snakes and Ladders* subsequently brought to light the contention that Fianna Fáil were willing to sacrifice party heavyweight, Ray Burke, to clinch a renewal of the Government but Ahern dismisses the suggestion as rubbish.

'Ray Burke was not an issue. If we had gone into government with Labour, clearly it was going to be something like 9–6 or a 10–5 scenario as far as Cabinet seats were concerned,' Ahern explains. 'I would have been working around the Ministers that I had because we were talking about the people who were already at the table.

'It was probably unlikely that Burke would have been considered because I was going to be dealing more or less with the Ministers that were there. It is written by Finlay as if Burke was on the Fianna Fáil front bench for a few years. That was not the way it was in November of 1994. Burke was out in the cold then. Spring never asked me about Burke, as I recall. We would have been asking each other who was likely to be put into the Cabinet, but the way Finlay writes he makes it sound as if Burke was on the front bench. He wasn't there.

'In fact, some of the Fianna Fáil people at the time were very narked with Burke because he was going around hassling Albert. They were probably saying that if Labour didn't want Burke then it was fine by them. I myself didn't agree with some of the things Burke was doing at the time. I never agree with in-fighting,' Ahern adds.

Burke had bluntly said, 'Whoever is in any way responsible for what has apparently been going on, let them pay the price.'

Another matter raised by the Finlay book concerning Ahern's fears that his telephone calls were being bugged is also played down by Ahern.

'The phones have been interfered with at St Luke's a good few times, by whom I don't know. Once or twice, journalists tried to show they could change the tapes. There were a few other times we were worried but I think it was probably interference or somebody on the line. I'm not into that sort of paranoia,' he says.

Ahern, still acting Minister for Finance and Tánaiste, addressed the Dáil on 6 December in the by then familiar Fianna Fáil 'Penitence at Canossa' style. After going through the most excruciatingly detailed statement about the extradition warrants for the paedophile priests, the conflict of legal advice they received from their law officers, the unread memo and files and the overtures from Reynolds to overturn his decision on Harry Whelehan and get the Judge to resign, he cut to the quick of the matter.

He told the Dáil:

'We [the Fianna Fáil Ministers acting alone] should not have appointed Harry Whelehan until after the Tuesday Dáil debate. That was a mistake. It negated the idea of a partnership government.

'We did not refer to the Duggan case in the Dáil because the question was not asked of the Taoiseach and because the two appointed Ministers did not get around to saying it.

'We did not keep the Labour party informed of events, confused as they were, as they unfolded. That was a mistake. We have paid a price for these mistakes but we will not carry the can for the misrepresentations and slanders with which others, for their own agenda, may wish to lumber us. I have shown that we have tried to do the right thing at all times. When we get it wrong, we accept the blame.'

As the Labour party entered negotiations on a Rainbow Coalition with Fine Gael and Democratic Left, the Fianna Fáil Ministers prepared their statements for the Dáil Committee, set up to investigate the reasons why the Government had collapsed. Wisely, the acting Government decided not to throw good tax-payers' money after bad by setting up a judicial Tribunal with all the attendant opprobrium not least because of the potential reaction from the public still reeling from the Beef Tribunal Bill. The Inquiry was carried out in house by Oireachtas members colleagues.

Ahern was grilled for six hours during which time he lashed out at the spin doctors of the Labour party. His old adversary, Tony Gregory, asked him: 'Are you saying that the whole crisis that ultimately brought down the Government was orchestrated by people in the background who were not elected?' to which Ahern replied, 'I am afraid that is my conclusion. When I left for Brussels at six o'clock in the morning of Monday, 5 December, I had no reason other than to be optimistic that I would be Taoiseach the following day. I am still a bit bewildered about what changed so much.' Asked if he knew what changed, Ahern replied: 'If you can find out in this committee, I would be very interested.'

He reiterated his ignorance of the significance of the material he handed Reynolds in the Dáil – the definitive letter from the new Attorney General Eoghan Fitzsimons on the Duggan precedent – and confirmed that he had no knowledge of the first visit by Fitzsimons on behalf of Reynolds to Whelehan on 14 November asking the latter to consider his position as President of the High Court. In addition, the secretary of the Department of the Taoiseach, Paddy Teahon, had passed this letter to Ahern in the Dáil with a note drawing his attention to a vital passage in the letter which was to be used if the relevant question was asked (in the event the Opposition had failed to ask the question). But Ahern admitted he did not take any notice of Teahon's communication.

It also emerged that Reynolds had turned down six requests by Ahern to obtain an account of events complied by Fitzsimons, which were later shredded. Reynold's excuse was that he disagreed with much of Fitzsimons's version. Ahern claimed he never saw the document signed by Spring on Wednesday, 17 November, in which he agreed to stay in government with Reynolds, which followed a night of negotiations between Charlie McCreevy for Fianna Fáil and Brendan Howlin and Senator Pat Magner for Labour and finished off at a meeting in Reynolds's home, attended by Geoghegan-Quinn.

He was curt in his references to the Attorney General Eoghan Fitzsimons at the committee's investigation. He had no particular difficulty with the law officer apart from his assertion that Fianna Fáil Ministers were kneeling down thanking him profusely for stating that they were very tired and confused at a time of crisis. 'It is hard for me to get down on my knees. Anyone who knows me knows that. But I certainly didn't that night,' Ahern said.

Asked if he would regard Fitzsimons as a decent and honourable man, Ahern replied that he didn't know him well enough. But he later emphasized that Fitzsimons, to his knowledge, had always acted in a professional and honourable manner. From his evidence at the Inquiry it was plain for everyone to see that Ahern was totally outside the loop within the Reynolds administration.

The Irish Times remarked in its editorial the following day: 'For a man who has put the word "waffle" into the Irish political dictionary, Mr Bertie Ahern gave a good account of himself at yesterday's meeting of the Dáil Select Committee . . . there was a sense that he was endeavouring to give the committee the full, unvarnished facts as he knew them about the Smyth–Whelehan affair. The unspoken message from the Fianna Fáil leader to the committee – and the country – is that he was no more than a bit player in the sorry saga which led to the collapse of the last government. If he is a sinner, his are only venial sins.'

Chapter 29

Opposition

The Opposition bench for a politician is truly a miserable place and all the more miserable when you don't know why you are there. Fianna Fáil had miraculously hung onto power for seven years with a set of diminishing general election results. Haughey blew an unchallenged minority Government in a last shot for his elusive overall majority and was reduced to pleading his case with the Progressive Democrats. Albert Reynolds was so sure this 'temporary little arrangement' with the PDs could be jettisoned that he forced a general election and came back to the Dáil nine seats lighter for his optimism. Fianna Fáil then grabbed victory from the jaws of defeat with the fluke of Dáil numbers and negotiated a Government with the Labour party with the biggest overall majority in the history of the State which was promptly blown out of the water in due course.

On top of that, the party was scraping votes at the lower 40 per cent end of the scale and sometimes less, in successive general elections. A couple more election victories like the previous three, and Fianna Fáil would be heading to the political boon docks of the 30 per cents. The only policy that Fianna Fáil had enunciated with any conviction over those seven years was power.

In parallel to their Houdini-like ability to hang on to power, the three Fianna Fáil-led administrations became inveterate begetters of Inquiries and Tribunals as Stock Exchange ethics became *de rigueur* in Leinster House. The party felt and looked tired and, in the opinion of most political observers, required a long, most said prolonged, period of rest and recreation on the opposition benches. The 20 years of haggling, to use Ahern's phrase, had to come to an end.

As the third Fianna Fáil leader in four years, Ahern's first task was to unite his party, a coalition of opposing leadership manifestos, and his first hurdle would be the construction of his shadow front bench which would even up the competing claims – it was a typical attempt to unite the competing factions within the party. Mary O'Rourke's seniority, proven Cabinet and political ability and closeness to Ahern both personally and through her brother Brian, was the obvious deputy leader. In her infectious enthusiasm for politics, O'Rourke said of being in opposition, 'I like the idea of being on probation. I loved opposition but I like government better. It was very, very difficult for those who had been in cabinet and for us who felt we were entering into a cabinet with Labour and particularly being on the negotiating team, signing off on the Saturday night and going happily to bed. But going into opposition, I just feel it's an honour to be elected and trusted by the people and you have an important job if you're a good opposition and I think it did the party good.

'Bertie toured the country and met people and that's his real forte, with people of all walks of life, and he worked very hard in that two-and-a-half years. He visited every town, village, city, met so many people who were, and are, very taken by his natural manner and then we got to do our policies. He's a very strong leader. Everything that he has to decide on, he has thought about. It's not just that he has read what's put to him but he will bring up angles when he's talking about things to you which show clearly that he has reflected a lot on that subject.

'I do think that he has united the party. Find me a political party where everybody is bobbing their heads at the one time. Political people are opinionated I suppose, but he has done a very good job at parliamentary party level.' As for her own appointment as deputy party leader she admits she was 'surprised but very honoured'.

'The Taoiseach and I have a very good relationship with regard to the party and work and talk over matters when needed,' she adds.

The surprise appointment of Finance spokesman was Charlie McCreevy, the right-wing accountant who revelled in the controversy caused by his so-called Dirty Dozen cutbacks when he was Social Welfare Minister. Ray 'Rambo' Burke was brought back into the sunshine in the Foreign Affairs portfolio and although commentators thought that Maire Geoghegan-Quinn and Noel Dempsey had to be placed, lest it be thought that omitting them would be interpreted as impugning them prior to the Committee report on the collapse of the previous Government. Ahern says that was never the case – they were obvious choices.

Another Reynolds loyalist, Brian Cowen, was slotted in. Ahern believes Cowen is a natural for any Cabinet while Síle de Valera, who had been banished to exterior darkness when she argued with Haughey in the '80s was also brought back to the front line. Political veterans like Michael Smith, Seamus Brennan, Joe Walshe and Michael Woods got their berths as did David Andrews, arguably the most talented politician to be serially overlooked in the Haughey years. Solicitors Dermot Ahern and John O'Donoghue, whose talents impress Ahern, and Micheál Martin, the youngest of the gang, made up what most of the commentators regarded as a cautious line-up. His 'junior ministers' with special responsibilities were Eamon O'Cuiv, Eoin Ryan, Tom Kitt, Jim McDaid, Mary Coughlan, Liam Aylward, Chris Flood, Willie O'Dea and Mary Wallace.

Ahern concluded his appointment of shadow junior ministers, bringing in John Ellis, Senator Marian McGennis, Senator Dick Roche, Dr Tom Moffat and Brendan Smith. Altogether, he gave a vigorous Dáil performance during a short period in opposition.

Ahern also shook up the party's backroom staff, bringing in Paddy Duffy, his friend and press officer at the Department of Finance as his chef de cabinet while Mary Kerrigan, Reynolds's press officer, was retained as his deputy. Martin Mansergh, the special adviser to Haughey and Reynolds on Northern Ireland and the man seen as critical to the evolution of the Northern Ireland press office, modestly turned down an invitation from the incoming Government to remain in a special advisory capacity and returned to the Fianna Fáil backrooms. Three other significant appointments were made by Ahern to beef up the party's research and policy development capacity. Jackie Gallagher, an industrial correspondent with *The Irish Times* along with Catriona Mullaney, industry group executive with the Federation of Irish Chemical Industries, were appointed senior advisers while Marty Whelan, former research officer with the National Youth Council, became press officer.

Over in the Dáil, the new Fine Gael Taoiseach, John Bruton, retained Padraig Flynn as Ireland's European Commissioner in a generous concession to the former Fianna Fáil Minister which Ahern cordially described as a gesture in the national interest. But when

Bruton moved to unseat the Leas Ceann Comhairle (a State car and an extra salary went with the job) Fianna Fáil jumped up and down like affronted judges and started smacking Bruton around the ears with the tomes of precedents in Dáil Eireann.

The Fianna Fáil incumbent, Joe Jacob, was livid and wondered how he was suddenly unsuitable for the job. He memorably remarked that 'There is precedent to consider here. It is not as though I am being accused of amatory walking.'

The new Fine Gael Defence and Marine Minister, Sean Barrett, said Ahern and Fianna Fáil could rant and rave about Dáil precedents but the Fine Gael man was getting the job. A couple of days later, precedent prevailed and Jacob held on to the post.

By Budget Day, Ahern was back on sure ground telling the Government that budget deficits could be abolished forever. He noted that the commitment to eliminate the Budget deficit had been deleted from the new Government's programme. It was Ruairi Quinn's first Budget and the first of a Labour Minister but it was an unmitigated PR disaster for the Rainbow Government, with every measure apart from the immediate excise increases leaked before the Minister got onto his feet in the Dáil. The level of taxation breaks were known to the public through the Sunday newspapers three days previously and the entirety of the Welfare sections of the Minister's speech were reproduced by the *Irish Press* on the morning of the Budget.

By that stage, Murphy's law set in when a junior Finance Minister, Phil Hogan, resigned his post immediately after his press service prematurely faxed 'his reaction to a positive Budget' to the evening papers. Finance Minister, Quinn, had yet to rise to his feet in the Dáil when the contents of his Statement and the comments of his junior Minister were splashed all over page ones.

Ahern demanded a comprehensive statement to the Dáil on all breaches of Cabinet confidentiality, and although Minister Hogan had taken the honourable course, more senior Ministers had a case to answer. The actual contents of Quinn's financial statement was what Ahern described as a blow to future tax reform – 'If I had remained Minister for Finance I should have insisted on running a much tighter ship. The Labour party know that. Perhaps that's why they jumped ship.'

For the first time, Ahern was also speaking daily on the North, warning against allowing an impasse over the disposal of weapons. The British Government would be 'wrong', he said, to unilaterally insist on preconditions that are not clearly and explicitly set out in the Downing Street Declaration. He also called on the British and the Unionists to face up to the necessity of sitting down to talks with Sinn Féin 'who have a clear mandate, given to them by the people they represent'. He added: 'It would be a serious mistake for anyone to attempt to treat Sinn Féin, and even more importantly the communities that they represent, as second-class citizens.'

'This is what caused the conflict in the first place. It is difficult to think of anywhere in the world where governments and parties would refuse, on principle, to treat each other for all purposes across the table, even after four-and-a-half months of a complete cease-fire.' He pointed out that the nationalist community was entitled to full representation at the conference table 'of which it has been deprived for far too long, first by discrimination, then by violence and conflict.'

The whole demilitarisation agenda should be dealt with in parallel with political talks and not as a precondition for participation in dialogue, he said. Ahern, whom one Unionist described as welcome, since he was not a man overburdened with ideology, set up a special Northern Ireland Committee and was accompanied by Martin Mansergh, Brian Lenihan, Ray Burke, Jim McDaid and Dermot Ahern. Albert Reynolds was excluded from the committee because his presence would be incompatible with Burke's. Suddenly Ahern, whose major speeches on the North over the previous 20 years could be counted on one hand, was being called green by many commentators and deep green by others. Noting that the IRA cease-fire had lasted 150 days, he remarked: 'I read carefully what Mr Major is saying – that there cannot be any inclusion of Sinn Féin in the round table talks that are required unless the IRA decommissions its weapons. The question that must be put to Mr Major is this: "Is this the end of the peace process?"'

By the end of January he had wound-up his involvement in the North by visiting the Unionist headquarters in Belfast where he was welcomed by Ken Maginnis, Jeffrey Donaldson and Chris and Michael McGimpsey. He later visited Belfast city hall to meet Progressive Unionist Lord Mayor of Belfast, Hugh Smyth. It was a frank and blunt meeting, according to the Unionists.

In a frenetic and driven start to his leadership, especially as it affected the North, Ahern predicted that a United Ireland would take a generation to achieve, adding, 'I intend to live that long'.

His reaction to the publication of the Framework Document in its final form that February was predictable. It contained no important variations on the document in place before the last Government left office and the compromises reached were reasonable and sensible. 'We may not have achieved everything that we sought but the final outcome represents perhaps all that we could reasonably expect to achieve at this stage.'

If the Republic could no longer contain what the Framework Document described as the 'territorial claim' over Northern Ireland in its Constitution, it was reasonable to ask that the British do the same.

Fianna Fáil's clear political intentions were to out-manoeuvre the Rainbow Coalition on the North and remain the guardians of the Pan Nationalist interest in the Republic and launch a sustained, and at times insulting, campaign against the then Taoiseach, John Bruton.

By February of his first year in office Ahern was dismissing Bruton as being a PR Taoiseach. Bruton was being 'totally handled' according to Ahern, who painted a picture of Sean Donlon, Shane Kenny and other Bruton advisers spending 'extensive' time with Bruton each Friday, planning the following week. 'He's not carrying out official engagements; he doesn't attend the Forum most of the time. He takes as few Dáil questions as possible . . . I don't know what he's doing,' sneered Ahern at the time.

By the end of his first session as Fianna Fáil leader, an *Irish Times* poll indicated that Fianna Fáil's support had shot from a low of 35 per cent up to 47 per cent, with Labour down from 21 per cent to 15 per cent. Fine Gael had gone up one point to 23 per cent.

Ahern's satisfaction rating was at a high 69 per cent against Mary Harney at 64 per cent, Dick Spring at 56 per cent, Proinsias De Rossa, 54 per cent and John Bruton, 54 per cent.

Chapter 30

The Transfers Will Do It

The tragic death of independent Wicklow TD, Johnny Fox, from a heart attack at a GAA function in the county gave Fianna Fáil an early opportunity to test the political waters for Ahern's leadership. The by-election, held late in June, was an opportunity to kick start Ahern's leadership with a much needed Fianna Fáil victory having already gone through a run of four by-election defeats under Reynolds, including the sensational defeat in Co. Mayo of Beverely Cooper Flynn, the daughter of the EU Commissioner, Padraig Flynn, by Fine Gael's Michael Ring. The by-election also provided a testing ground for Ahern's drive to unify the party after 20 years of haggling and an opportunity to assess the political value of Ahern's face on an election poster.

In the event, as an exercise in party unity, the Wicklow by-election was a total and abysmal disaster while the notion of gauging Ahern's poster marketability might have been interesting if there was any real effort to put the posters up in the constituency. Wicklow Fianna Fáil is a large organisation divided into two parts – three parts when you consider that most of the late Johnny Fox's organisation was originally in Fianna Fáil. Both parts can be mutually exclusive and it is not unheard of that each can vote in opposite directions on Wicklow County Council. The predominant part was run by Joe Jacob who was the Leas Ceann Comhairle of the Dáil at the time while the lesser part was headed by Senator Dick Roche, who was given a front-bench position by Ahern when he took over the Fianna Fáil reins. At a stormy convention in Aughrim to choose a candidate, it was widely predicted that Roche, whose political base was in Bray, would be 'screwed' for the nomination by the rural delegates. Roche's wife Eleanor, a driving force within his organisation, was all but in tears in the hotel even before the convention got under way. After a fraught and contentious convention which Ahern attended, Roche scraped home by one vote from Michael Lawlor. There were immediate suggestions by disgruntled delegates in the hotel bar afterwards that more than one vote was inexplicably strewn around the convention floor. Ahern instantly put his foot down, demanding that the whole organisation should put its campaigning and canvassing weight behind Roche to regain the Wicklow seat from the Independent Fox organisation who had decided to nominate the late TD's daughter, Mildred, a 24-year-old just out of university.

With the Labour party having its internal problems and Fine Gael a good distance from the required 50 per cent of the Wicklow electorate, the game was between Senator Roche and Mildred Fox. Ahern put his full shadow cabinet into the fray but half way through the election it became abundantly clear that there was something amiss. Deputy leader, Mary O'Rourke, noticed that the postering along the main commuter artery in the constituency – the N 11 – was bereft of Fianna Fáil election posters, as were many of the towns in the county. Whatever was happening, it was becoming pretty clear that the entire Fianna Fáil organisation was not breaking into a sweat in Wicklow; Fox, on the other hand, simply avoided controversy especially in relation to her contrary views on the introduction of divorce which was beginning to animate the electorate again: her organisation was playing the sympathy vote in the fashion of a political orchestra.

Also effecting the Roche campaign again was the candidacy of Nicky Kelly, who had revived his personal fortunes after being cleared of any involvement in a robbery, by building up another solid political organisation in Arklow. Roche started off the campaign being the bookies' slight favourite over Fox, and by midway was being quoted as an outside 7–2 by the Paddy Power chain of bookies, run, coincidentally, by Sean Power, a Kildare Fianna Fáil TD.

The campaign was a shambles for Fianna Fáil and the university rookie, Mildred Fox, headed the pool with nearly 2,000 more votes than Roche with the help, it was alleged, of dissident Fianna Fáil activists. She won the seat on the eighth count with over 8,000 votes to spare over her rival. Such was Ahern's fury over the electoral debacle that he disbanded the entire Fianna Fáil organisation in Wicklow and replaced it with an eight-person Commission. He said that he was determined to put in place a unified Fianna Fáil organisation before the next general election and intended to put an end to the in-fighting in Wicklow. The Commission failed to reconcile both Wicklow factions but, organisationally, matters did improve sufficiently in the following year to ensure a critical additional Wicklow seat for Roche and Fianna Fáil in the 1997 General Election.

The following April, Fianna Fáil would pull off two stunning but close by-elections: in Donegal, to fill the seat caused by the death of Independent Fianna Fáiler and Arms Trial defendant, Neil Blaney, a close friend of the late Johnny Fox; and in Dublin West where Brian Lenihan, Ahern's forever optimistic PR man, had succumbed to his liver problems.

In Donegal the Fianna Fáil candidate, Cecilia Keaveney, faced Neil Blaney's brother Harry and the legendary Blaney organisation which had produced the seat for the family down the decades. In Dublin West, Brian Lenihan's son, the barrister Brian jun., was out into the fray against a sheaf of candidates, mainly left wingers who between them commanded the majority of votes in the Constituency. Party strategists decided that the best card for Fianna Fáil to play was Bertie Ahern himself and kept him on the campaign trail for the duration of the two simultaneous campaigns. They believed that transfers would clinch the seats for either side and deliberately moved to maximise first preferences and then canvass for every transfer available. Ahern spent the campaign perpetually between both constituencies, flying to Donegal in the morning and back to Dublin West in the evening and vice versa. The entire shadow cabinet was again dragooned in the campaign.

Ahern wanted the Donegal seat, which had been outside Fianna Fáil since the Arms crisis, at all costs, and if he could get parts of the Blaney organisation back inside the Fianna Fáil tent, so much the better. And there was no way he was going to give Brian Lenihan a seat without a fight to the last vote. Dublin West was personal for Ahern. When the first counts of the two by-elections were announced, the seats were delicately poised between Keaveney and Blaney in Donegal – a mere 900 in favour of Keaveney but with the transfers of Fine Gael, Labour and Sinn Féin, the vote was said to be favouring Blaney.

In Dublin West, Lenihan jun. got just over 200 votes in front of

Socialist Joe Higgins on the first count and with the gaggle of left wing, Green and independent transfers the vote was said to be going Higgins's way.

In Donegal, Keaveney slipped on the Sinn Féin transfer of party vice president, Pat Doherty, but maintained a lead of less than 150 votes. She held her own on the Labour transfer but her margin was reduced to 10 votes. On the final count, however, she stretched ahead to win the seat dramatically and remarkably when she received over 2,500 Fine Gael transfers to Blaney's 1,500.

In Dublin West, the tension at the count was palpable and so close that Fianna Fáilers conceded defeat to Higgins at one stage. In a nip and tuck contest, Higgins had drawn ahead of Lenihan by 140 votes when on the ninth count the votes of Tomás MacGiolla, the Workers Party veteran, were distributed. With a Fine Gael transfer left to distribute and just over 60 per cent of it still live, the remarkable happened again – Lenihan outpolled Higgins by 2,084 to 1,574 to win the seat by 370 votes.

To Fine Gael's dismay, their traditional political enemy Fianna Fáil had won two famous by-election victories in two completely dissimilar constituencies on Fine Gael votes. It was unprecedented.

The three by-elections decided the precise electoral strategy that Fianna Fáil were to pursue in the summer election later in 1997 – organisational unity even in fractious Wicklow, transfer plunder left, right and centre and Bertie Ahern gladhanding and grandstanding throughout the 42 constituencies.

Chapter 31

Turning the Cards

Fianna Fáil had always espoused conservative views on social issues. Its founder, Eamon de Valera, had even enshrined into the 1937 Constitution the special status of the Catholic Church and its doctrines were mirrored in much of 'Bunreacht na h-Eireann'. Throughout the subsequent years, Irish governments had to throw an uncomfortable look over their shoulders as to what the attitude of the hierarchy was to any upcoming social legislation. Matters became so fraught in 1950 between Church and State that Health Minister Noel Browne was forced to abandon the 'Mother and Child' scheme, whereby he proposed that in a crisis pregnancy the mother had more right to life than an unborn child if both lives were threatened due to medical complications. The fall-out precipitated the collapse of the then Inter Party Government.

During the 1960s, the Archbishop of Dublin, John Charles McQuaid, was almost seen as the Minister for Religion and Social Affairs in Cabinets, such was his influence. In 1979, the then Health Minister, Charles Haughey, brought in what he called an 'Irish solution to an Irish problem', when he allowed contraceptives to be sold, but only through prescription. It is hard to imagine now, but contraceptives were effectively illegal in Ireland until then. It was only five years later that further legislation was brought in which allowed contraceptives to be sold in vending machines and over the counter in pharmacies.

In 1983 the government of the time brought in a Bill enshrining into the Constitution the absolute right to life of the unborn child, subject only to the equal right to life of the mother, due to enormous pressure from organisations like the Society for the Protection of the Unborn Child (SPUC). It led to a hateful atmosphere between the pro- and anti-camps and still did little to solve the contentious abortion problems facing the country.

Homosexual practice, too, was illegal up until 1993, when the then Justice Minister, Maire Geoghegan-Quinn, brought the law into line with the rest of Europe following a victory by Senator David Norris at the European Court of Human Rights on the issue.

Geoghegan-Quinn said the straw that broke the camel's back was when a mother of a gay man came to her office, amid a long line of gay rights groups, and asked if the Minister was telling her that the son she loved was a criminal just because of his sexuality.

The abortion crisis again blew up in the early 1990s when a 14-year-old Dublin girl, who was raped by a neighbour, was legally disallowed from travelling to England to terminate her pregnancy. The girl's family had contacted Gardaí telling them they were in England and asked them if DNA samples from the aborted foetus could be used in the prosecution of the assailant. Word went up through the various offices to the Attorney General of the time, Harry Whelehan, who successfully obtained an injunction stopping the girl, 'Miss X', from having the right to travel to have the abortion. Even though they were in England at the time, the girl and her family returned to Ireland.

The case was brought to the Supreme Court, which found that there was a real and substantive threat to the life of the pregnant girl, as she was believed to be suicidal. The Supreme Court gave her 'permission' to terminate the pregnancy within the realms of the existing Constitution. She then travelled to England again, where the abortion was carried out. This became known as the 'X' case and horrified not only liberal elements within the then Coalition parties, but also fair-minded politicians unnerved that anyone should be kept in the country against their will if they wanted to have an abortion.

Three referenda were drafted and held on the same day as the General Election that November 1992. Two of them were passed – the right to travel abroad for an abortion and the right to information on abortion services. The third, the allowance of abortion in Ireland in limited circumstances, failed, with both anti- and pro-abortion camps voting against it. The pro-abortion camps voted against it because they claimed there was a loophole in it which excluded a threat to the life of the mother.

The 'Right to Travel' Bill was quickly passed in the Dáil but there was more contention over the 'Information' part throughout the Fianna Fáil–Labour Government, with the law enshrining the passing of that referendum still being formulated. Due to the collapse of that Government, however, it was left to the Rainbow Coalition to push through the 'Abortion Information Bill'. It would allow doctors and nurses to give pregnant women the addresses and details of abortion clinics abroad if they asked.

Ahern always held left-of-centre views on social issues, and had made clear his own views on the likes of divorce, maintaining that he was in favour of it, and that was regardless of his own marital difficulties. In the late '80s he said he would be in favour of divorce being granted but only after a period of five years. One of the reasons which appeared to influence him on holding such a view was the case of one of his friends, who had been separated from his wife for almost five years but got back together again and had a further two children.

At first Ahern decided to keep an open mind on the 'Abortion Information Bill', despite strong opposition within FF, particularly from the Des Hanafin wing of the party. Ahern and the party's health spokeswoman, Geoghegan-Quinn, initially met the then Health Minister, Michael Noonan, to discuss the upcoming legislation. Ahern said he was determined not to 'oppose for opposition's sake' and told the parliamentary party there was 'no percentage in stroke politics'.

At a highly charged four-and-a-half-hour meeting of the Fianna Fáil parliamentary party in March 1995, only 10 members spoke in favour of the Bill and a massive 42 speakers against. Among those who supported the Bill were Mary O'Rourke, Charlie McCreevey, David Andrews and Geoghegan-Quinn. Ahern, in his opening and closing speeches, gave the impression that he was not coming down on one side or the other, although the party Whip, Dermot Ahern, later said Ahern supported the Bill. It was noted later that Ahern had only himself to blame for the split in the party over the issue as he had thrown it open to the floor without giving any guidelines. He had given the impression initially that he was opposed to the Bill and this encouraged the wavering middle ground within the party to grab the huge anti-abortion vote.

The blitz on the bill was spearheaded, ironically, by his brother, Noel Ahern. He was strongly supported by John O'Donoghue,

Michael Martin, Sean Haughey and Senator Anne Ormonde, among others. The majority of other speakers opposed the Bill at second stage and tabled a range of motions for committee stage, ranging from a ban on the release of the names and addresses of abortion clinics to extra support for agencies such as CURA, which supports pregnant women.

It was one thing to propose amendments at committee stage, as that was normal practice, but to oppose the principle of the Bill would have been seen to side with the defeatist elements of the 1992 referendum. At first, Geoghegan-Quinn was against the notion of referral names for abortion clinics but then opted out of that issue. Yet she tried to mollify the anti-abortion elements within her own party by saying: 'We do not wish to see abortion made legal in Ireland. We do not wish to see abortion facilities made available in Ireland.' In the aftermath of the 'X' case, the party came suspiciously close to demanding another referendum on abortion.

The amendments then sought by Fianna Fáil included the insertion of a special opt-out conscience clause for doctors, greater restrictions on television and radio broadcasts about abortion clinics and statutory provision to provide resources for counselling agencies.

The controversy over the Bill was seen as the first real test of Ahern's leadership. *The Irish Times,* in an editorial titled 'NON-DIRECTIVE LEADERSHIP', criticised him for showing 'little social inclination to address critical social issues like abortion and divorce in any considered way'. It added: 'The choice is clear: he can seek to shore up his party's traditional, conservative vote or he can attempt to carve out a new relevance for Fianna Fáil in the thinking of a rapidly changing Ireland.'

But Ahern told his parliamentary party that the controversy over the abortion issue should not colour their attitude to progression on other social issues and that his attitude on divorce was 'well known'. He said that the party would support the referendum on divorce and there would be near unanimity on the question. Ahern then announced after a rally attended by 2,000 people at the National Stadium that Fianna Fáil were likely to oppose the second stage of the Bill, although Noonan said he was receptive to amendments.

When the vote on the Bill in the Dáil finally arrived, Fianna Fáil took the official line whereby they would 'not challenge' the Bill and abstained from voting. The Bill was passed.

To this day, the whole issue of abortion has still to be sorted out. A

Cabinet sub-committee is currently drawing up a green paper on the matter. It has received 10,000 submissions and will address the problems raised by the 'x' case and the other anomalies.

After his on abortion, Ahern then used the divorce issue to lay down the law for Fianna Fáil and even upstage Fine Gael by agreeing to Mervyn Taylor's proposals. Fine Gael backbenchers had been huffing and puffing during Taylor's solo run, in which he said he proposed to write divorce changes into the Constitution, when Ahern sliced through the Fianna Fáil anti-divorce element. It was seen as giving those conservatives in the party who had locked him into an opposition mode on the abortion information issue, their comeuppance. He was turning the cards. The Government were in disarray on approaching the November referendum and the appeal of a pre-emptive strike by Fianna Fáil seemed irresistible. There was a near-revolt in Fine Gael over lack of consultation over what should and should not be placed in the Constitution and Ahern swung his party into 'unanimous support for the principle of changing the Constitution to allow for remarriage'. He further committed them to the view that 'at least the period of separation required before the remarriage could take place would be specified in the Constitution'. Fianna Fáil published its position on divorce in early September, saying it would impose a whip to secure parliamentary party support for the Bill.

But they had not ruled out the possibility that TDs might vote for it in the Dáil and then later campaign against it in the constituencies. Ahern said on the television show, *Questions and Answers,* that if the Government brought in a constitutional amendment which allowed couples to divorce after three years separation, FF would oppose it. If the measure proposed four years they 'would look at it' but his own preference was for five years. Dissident Michael J. Noonan from Limerick abstained in the vote on the Bill to hold a divorce referendum.

'The party rules are quite clear,' Ahern said. 'He automatically loses the Whip. I strongly believe people have the right to a referendum to state their views; there's nothing more democratic that that.' But he added: 'I'm not going to push a vote on the right to remarry down the necks of anybody'.

He said he himself would not be canvassing. 'I never canvassed like that in my life, except in 1972 for Europe and the Good Friday Agreement,' he stressed.

Neither did he have any problems with the deeply conservative views of his brother. There were open divisions on the floor at the Ard Fheis in November regarding the divorce issue. Ahern's unambiguous call for a 'Yes' vote received a warm round of applause – 'Divorce is not something that any of us feel enthusiastic about,' he pointed out. 'But our considered view as legislators is that on balance, a 'Yes' vote is the most realistic and compassionate response to the extent of the problem of broken marriages.'

Some hours earlier, the Ard Fheis had barely passed a motion affirming the right of the Irish people to decide in the referendum the issue of the right to remarry. The pro- and anti-divorce contributions from delegates, including Des Hanafin, head of the Anti-Divorce Campaign, were outspoken, often acrimonious.

Garret FitzGerald's coalition had failed miserably in 1986 to bring in divorce, when a referendum on the 'Dissolution of marriage' issue then was comprehensively defeated (by 63.48 per cent of voters to 36.52 per cent). It also opened up large wounds between the pro- and anti-camps, and the pros were determined to have another go – 1995 was seen an opportune moment for another try. The FF front bench now seemed at odds with the grass-roots at their Ard Fheis, with an apparent 60–40 majority of the latter, holding an anti-divorce view during the equality and law reform debate. Michael Woods, who was the party's spokesman on Equality and Law Reform at the time, was badly barracked and broke down during the debate when responding to attacks.

Ahern later admitted FF co-operated with the Government in 'rushing' important family legislation through the Oireachtas in the run-up to the referendum. 'We rushed very important legislation through, to be helpful and constructive and get on with having a referendum,' he explained.

He got his way in demanding from the Government that there must be a period of five years of separation before a couple were allowed to be divorced. This was good news for the 70,000 separated couples in Ireland (although few have availed themselves of the opportunity to divorce since). Almost all the front bench turned up at the party's press conference to support the Divorce Bill, including Michael Woods, Mary O'Rourke, Michael Smith, Ray Burke, Brian Cowen and Maire Geoghegan-Quinn. Ahern claimed his party started campaigning for a 'Yes' vote weeks before the Government did. He warned that if the referendum failed then the basis for many of his statements calling for parity of esteem at the Forum for Peace and Reconciliation would also fail.

He deplored the 'intemperate statements' made by both sides during the campaign and said the referendum represented a 'defining moment in our history'.

Calling on the people to be caring and compassionate and recognise the reality of marital breakdown, he said the situation in other countries was that divorce had been accepted. 'I am not aware of any authoritative or reputable academic study which recommends or finds that divorce should be prohibited,' he noted. 'I know of no country that wants to abolish its divorce legislation. If legislation was so self-evidently damaging to the common good, as it is claimed, it is very difficult to understand why no other country even contemplates reintroducing a ban on divorce.'

Divorce was finally legalised when the majority of the voters passed the referendum – but despite all the main Government and opposition parties advocating a 'Yes' vote, it was only a bare pass. Out of an electorate of 2,628,942, some 1,633,942 (62 per cent) voted. A total of 818,842 voted in favour (50.28 per cent) while 809,728 voted against (49.72 per cent). Spoiled votes amounted to 5,372.

Irish conservatives had lost a telling victory. The fact that it was sunny in Dublin and raining in the West on the voting day may also have played a part. As the result came in, Ahern accused Labour, particularly Education Minister, Niamh Bhreathnach, of 'triumph-alism'. She denied clenching her fist on television and said she was simply pleased with the result.

Ahern said FF had not 'closed the file' on divorce and would ensure that appropriate protections for the family would be included in legislation on divorce and other issues. It was an obvious move by him to pacify the large wing in his party – and almost half the country – who were vehemently opposed to divorce under any circumstances. Noel Treacy from east Galway expressed concern that the party's core support would slip because of its support for divorce, a view which was backed up by John Ellis from Sligo and Senator Michael O'Kennedy.

But Fianna Fáil – and Ireland – had finally crossed a monumental Rubicon.

Chapter 32

Et tu, Bertie?

Ahern has an uncomplicated opinion about politicians taking money – 'You don't have to have a law against it to know it is wrong'. The passing of money would twice engulf the Fianna Fáil Party shortly after Ahern took over. First through a straightforward gift to Charles Haughey from supermarket king Ben Dunne, which unfortunately for everybody amounted to over £1 million and came to light during a do-or-die litigation between the supermarket tycoon and his siblings over control of the retail billions. The second was a straightforward brown envelope job which came into the public domain after Ahern won the 1997 General Election and involved his Minister for Foreign Affairs, Ray Burke. This, however, was small change by comparison – a mere £30,000 given by a group of developers towards the advancement of Fianna Fáil, especially in Burke's North Dublin constituency.

The discovery of the Ben Dunne gift to Haughey when he famously replied, 'thanks a million big fella' after trousering the largesse, hit the headlines in the lead-in period to the General Election. The Dunne money trail led to Haughey's accountant, the late Des Traynor, which in turn led to the discovery of substantial accounts held by Irish citizens, including Haughey, in off-shore bank accounts in the Cayman Islands. The revelations hit Ahern and Fianna Fáil with the force of a Scud missile.

They had been indulging in a spot of *schenefreude* at the financial entanglements which the former Fine Gael Minister, Michael Lowry, shared with Ben Dunne, an entanglement which led to his resignation and the initial political moves to set up a public enquiry into the Payments to Politicians.

The Fianna Fáil reverie was short-lived as details of the gift to Haughey gushed forth including what was seen by the public as the comic meeting between Margaret Heffernan, the winner of the Dunnes litigation row, arriving at Kinsealy's door to demand the repayment of the monies. The general public and politicians like Bertie Ahern often wondered how Haughey could live his Gatsbyesque lifestyle at the baronial Kinsealy with its stables and horse-breeding operation, the island at Inishvichullan off the Kerry coast where summers were spent, the yachting and fine wines and all the rest of the splendour which Haughey had become accustomed to. Ahern believed, up until the Dunne revelations, that Haughey's wealth was sourced in conspicuously lucky land deals in the '60s, the sale of a prosperous accountancy practice in the '70s and shrewd and regular winning investments.

The Dunne revelations showed that Haughey was being kept by at least one of the wealthiest people living in the country. And this was not pub talk – this was evidence given to a preliminary tribunal. There was only one option left to Ahern and that was to politically bury Haughey, a task he carried out in a cold and clinical speech delivered to a largely receptive Fianna Fáil Ard Fheis audience where he cast Haughey adrift.

It could not have been a pleasant task for Ahern who admired Haughey above most politicians with the exception of Haughey's father-in-law, Sean Lemass, who defended Haughey in the numerous heaves against his leadership, including the final one with Reynolds where Ahern himself nearly got a comeuppance from the victorious Country and Western Alliance. He went into that Ard Fheis to put serious distance between himself, his party and Haughey and came out of that Ard Fheis well beyond microphone distance of his former leader and mentor. His speech that evening to Fianna Fáil rank and file certainly had its desired effect.

It was a classic speech – 'You can have Haughey but you cannot have Fianna Fáil' – which left Haughey paddling his own canoe while Ahern returned to his office to get on with the business of returning Fianna Fáil to power. A cry of 'Et tu, Bertie?' could almost be heard from Abbeville, Haughey's house at Kinsealy.

Ahern says today: 'The rules may have been different then, but a politician does not need a law to know you can't take money. I can do a lot but I cannot change what other Fianna Fáil politicians did in the past,' he adds.

The Haughey debacle, which will eventually be played out publicly before the Moriarty Tribunal into Payments to Politicians, along with Michael Lowry's tribulations, involved a retired leader whose manner of financing a private lifestyle would never have become public unless a multi-million-pound family of fast turnover supermarketeers did not have a falling-out.

The Ray Burke case, as we shall see later, was a horse of a different colour for Ahern.

Chapter 33

The Starship Enterprise

Having applied a political guillotine to Haughey, Ahern felt safe enough to spend the spring of 1997 goading the Rainbow Coalition into a General Election. It seemed at first glance to be a rush of optimism over experience: John Bruton's Rainbow administration was popular; it was announcing huge tranches of new jobs every week, sometimes by the thousands as the economy boomed and it was keeping faith with the Social Partners by reducing income tax levels by the not-immediately-noticeable mechanism of expanding bands and allowances. This eschewed the more showy instrument of reducing tax rates. When Finance Minister, Labour's Ruairi Quinn, actually reduced rates it was only by a penny in the pound, though this was in addition to the expansion of rates and allowances.

Northern Ireland, however, was not progressing to schedule with the IRA no longer in cease-fire mode after the Canary Wharf atrocity. Politically, there seemed to have been a realignment of Government attitudes to the Peace Process now that the IRA and Sinn Féin were out of the loop and progress was being impeded by impositions of conditions on decommissioning and viable cease-fires. If a cease-fire were to be reinstated, it would not be on the basis of the similar rhetoric coming from the Rainbow Government, the Unionists and John Major's dying administration.

Ahern continued his meetings with Sinn Féin to get the cease-fire back in place through his senior adviser Martin Mansergh and his network of contacts on both sides of the divide in Northern Ireland.

The traditional Dáil bi-partisan policy on the North held in name only.

The Rainbow Coalition could have panted on to the autumn but Dick Spring at his party conference that year tightened their options to a summertime election. The polls were as good as the Government were going to get, the economy was booming and the Haughey card was there to bait Fianna Fáil with. They called the election for 6 June.

The Fianna Fáil campaign was effectively based on the two successful by-election campaigns of 1996 writ large. Bertie Ahern's door-stepping campaigning style would be played for all its worth; election candidates would stick rigidly to the vote management decrees from party headquarters and transfers would be sought from every opposing candidate. Policy-wise, the party was in good shape as an internal committee had been researching and costing programmes for over a year and these would be released daily throughout the campaign. Everything from policy to paper clips would be decided by headquarters and everybody would sing off the same song sheet.

Party strategists believed Fianna Fáil could win 79 seats or an additional 11 seats on the disastrous Reynolds showing of 1992 and, with the help of the Progressive Democrats, could wrest power from the Rainbow Coalition.

The strategy team included Director of Elections P.J. Mara, the urbane and well-liked former Government press secretary from Haughey's time, Gerry Hickey, Ahern's studious programme manager, Pat Farrell, the party general secretary, Paddy Duffy, Ahern's chef de cabinet, Martin Macken, the party's European parliament spokesman, and Sean Fleming, who was a candidate. They called the shots. Des Richardson, another of Ahern's inner circle and chief fund-raiser for the party, located a Georgian building near the Shelbourne hotel for a campaign headquarters – a one-stop shop for policy, press and promotional matters which Labour Party backbencher Pat Upton remarked was lit up '24 hours a day like the Starship Enterprise'. Martin Mansergh was on hand throughout the campaign but operated mostly from the Fianna Fáil offices at Leinster House where 'his files' were. Two mysterious American academics who were reputedly friends of Gerry Hickey, and answered to the names of Tod and Ted, arrived occasionally to peruse polls and study speeches. They looked like CIA agents; they did not socialise a great deal and were last heard of flying to London to board a flight to Columbia. The inner circle (all of the above, minus Tod and Ted) met each morning and at intervals during the afternoon and evening to meticulously organise campaign details.

Back at the 'Starship Enterprise', the party research team of Jackie Gallagher, Catriona Mullaney, Mandy Johnson, Martin Long, Gerry Howlin, and Sinead McSweeney toiled away on speeches and policy spins and generated the reactive element from election HQ to whatever the Government were saying. As often as not, the statements and speeches were written and sent out in a TD or Minister's name before the politician was informed of what pearls of wisdom he or she was imparting to the nation. If the media did not bite on this politically partisan material, the research team would shamelessly harangue the various media news desks about bias and unbalanced reporting. Co-ordinating this part of the campaign was Martin Macken and Jackie Gallagher. Both would drill shadow cabinet members, even the likes of Mary O'Rourke and Brian Cowen, on possible pitfalls before they went to any of the press conferences they were assigned to. In the evening they would often ruthlessly put these senior party politicians through their paces before speaking on TV or radio.

Macken, a former school-teacher from Dundalk, now the general secretary of the party, had a passion for lists and would create political concoctions like the Ten Biggest Cock-ups of the Rainbow, Nora Owens' Greatest Flops and Ten Questions Labour Cannot Answer which when completed would be duly faxed to every candidate for mention in any local radio or press interview he or she might be involved in the next day. It was also suggested they might circulate the lists among the wavering constituents. Macken would also choose and tutor party activists that he would be planting on RTE television and radio shows like *Questions and Answers*. These campaign workers would leave the Stephen's Green complex each evening with a mission to kill the enemy and Macken would not be enthused if any of his troopers missed their target.

In short, all the party candidates were treated by headquarters like four-year-old children. It made life uncomplicated and maximised campaign time. The candidates were spoon fed policy on a nightly basis and warned not to deviate from the script. HQ did not exist to sort out the mess caused by over-anxious candidates who strayed from the party text. Every morning they were faxed the latest campaign information and their thoughts for the day.

The third part of the back-up team and by far the most exhausting or exciting, depending on your physical condition, was out on the campaign trail with the party leader. Eileen Gleeson, an experienced PR company director and now the press spokeswoman for President McAleese, Marty Whelan, a party press officer, and Denise Kavanagh, a seconded civil servant, took care of Ahern's itinerary from his speaking engagements to laundry, make-up and food. His booze-free diet of fruit and health foods was meticulously adhered to. The campaign kicked off with a photo opportunity with Ahern and Sylvester Stallone, pulled off by P.J. Mara as payment of a personal bet with showbiz accountant, Ossie Kilkenny, that Mara would give up smoking cigarettes.

In media terms, Fianna Fáil got the best breaks on television with Charlie Bird assigned to cover Ahern. It was not that Bird was better than the other RTE reporters covering the election or that he was particularly favourable to Fianna Fáil but he could certainly be relied upon to ensure his story got top coverage.

Bird later said of the election: 'I have been with most of the political leaders over the years and I have seen nothing like the response Bertie Ahern got all over the country. It was "Bertie, give us a hug" or "Bertie, give us a kiss". He never seemed to flag. I must have around 50 minutes of film just of him kissing people.'

Ahern's ability at the kissing game was remarkable and got the page one treatment in full *Irish Times* colour when he was photographed wrapped around a teenager in a crowd in Galway. A media chase to find out who she was and how old she was immediately followed: she turned out to be a student and an enthusiastic Fianna Fáil supporter, as well as the daughter of a local councillor.

Garret O'Connor of Dublin independent radio was also regarded in the same professional vein as Bird by Fianna Fáil. Regarding the print media's coverage, Macken and Gallagher were wont to complain about the lack of balance – Macken was able to trot off a comparative list of copy lines among the main papers, although generally none of the national papers were overtly hostile to the Fianna Fáil campaign, while the *Examiner* paper in Cork was adjudged the fairest of the nationals. In terms of policy coverage, however, and publicity, particularly photographic, of the party leader, there was little scope for Fianna Fáil to complain.

The campaign quickly became a battle of personalities between Ahern and Bruton rather than policies between Fianna Fáil and Fine Gael. On the economy, the only difference between the parties was methodology and the North was an electoral no-go area in percentage terms. Bruton decided to go around the country on a train which produced few photo opportunities while Ahern was glad-handling crowds in shopping centres and cattle marts everywhere. The man on the ground was beating the man on the train in the photo battle.

In an attempt to generate controversy, Bruton labelled Ahern the 'most over-estimated man in Irish politics', to which Ahern replied, 'God bless him. I hope he doesn't get too distracted.'

Early in the campaign, P.J. Mara, still bragging about his brand-new green Jaguar ('like driving around in your living-room'), was convinced that Fianna Fáil's trump card was Ahern himself and his ability to work the crowds.

'They just love Bertie. This campaign is for Bertie and about Bertie. Keep him out on the campaign trail,' he declared.

Polling information showed that Fianna Fáil was holding steady at around 40 per cent, which would be adequate on the day if the Progressive Democrats vote held up. An FF–PD agreement on government looked as if it was on the cards: the election outcome was predicated by the PDs holding most of their Dáil seats which turned out to be the only miscalculation of the Fianna Fáil campaign. The PDs produced a convoluted policy idea about single mothers and the need to encourage them to stay at home for economic and social reasons. The statement sent shock waves through Fianna Fáil TDs like Michael Woods, who represented a constituency with huge tracts of working-class suburbs which proportionately had greater percentages of single parents. Fortunately, the idea was not pressed by the PDs and just slipped out of the campaign.

The pronouncement threw a lifeline to the Labour Party which was hardly the intended point of the exercise. They were now fully aware that they were going to be mauled by the electorate and were keeping their heads down in their constituencies. In the middle of the campaign the Progressive Democrats came up with another election turkey claiming that 25,000 jobs could be shed in the public sector over the lifetime of the FF–PD administration. The PD calculation was based on a crude piece of mental arithmetic which multiplied the 5,000 jobs shed in the public sector the previous year – mostly through exceptional on-off restructuring in the semi-state sector at a cost of half a billion – and multiplied by the presumed five years of the Government. The figures were a mess and the idea was worse. The PDs were obviously launching a fleet of lifeboats to help the beleaguered left-wing parties as distinct from throwing them a lifebuoy as had been their norm formerly in the campaign.

Gerry Hickey and his PD counterpart, John Murray, quickly arranged a get-together between the two leaders at the Green Isle hotel where their policy differences were ironed out, or in the memorable words of P.J. Mara: 'The contretemps over public sector jobs had been discussed by both leaders and amicably settled on Bertie Ahern's terms.'

Apart from taunting Dick Spring and Ruairi Quinn for their 'miserable penny-in-the-pound reduction', PD leader Mary Harney had a quiet campaign afterwards.

In the last week of the campaign, with Ahern still traversing the country looking for preferences, it was becoming clear that the left-wing parties were in for a drubbing as the electorate were simply deciding to return to the 'centre'. It showed scant regard for the Labour Party, in particular, who had delivered on all its promises on the social agenda.

The polls in the final week showed that the Fianna Fáil numbers were holding up as were the Fine Gael numbers while all the other parties were struggling. The special TV debate between Ahern and Bruton was billed the election clincher. News of an Irish Independent poll which showed Fianna Fáil nearly at 43 per cent of the poll would, with proper vote management, see Fianna Fáil back into power. The poll news as well as the fact that the *Irish Independent* was coming out in favour of an FF–PD coalition in a page one editorial, was conveyed to Ahern before he went into the TV studio.

Chapter 34

At Last – Taoiseach

Negotiations between Fianna Fáil and the PDs took less than an hour and a half in which they produced the outline sketch for Programme for Government with Fianna Fáil careful not to include some of the PDs exceptional vote-losers like the public sector jobs cuts. The Progressive Democrats nevertheless got a fair shake-down with a good deal of their taxation and privatisation policies taken on board. They also achieved two Cabinet places – Mary Harney was appointed Tánaiste and Minister for Enterprise, Trade and Employment while Bobby Molloy got a seat at Cabinet and a job as super junior Minister. Liz O'Donnell went to Foreign Affairs as a junior Minister.

The deal also gave the PDs four guaranteed Senators on the Taoiseach's panel provided they did not contest the Senate elections and mandated their votes to Fianna Fáil. It was an untypically generous package for the political party that was virtually wiped out at the preceding polls: 75 per cent of their Dáil party had portfolios. Ahern then moved quickly to deal with the independents and targeted Jackie Healy Rae, Harry Blaney and Mildred Fox, all of whom had Fianna Fáil connections and were amenable to supporting Ahern.

The colourful Healy Rae was the election manager for Fianna Fáil in Kerry for years but went independent when he failed to win an election nomination and saw a window of opportunity for his candidacy because he said the party 'hadn't their ducks in a row' in Kerry South. He was right and he clinched a deal which would see him take a joint chair on an Oireachtas committee on the Environment as well as various developmental concessions for his constituency. He said the deal he struck was good for Kerry and Ahern knew what that deal was and he would also know when he had broken it.

Harry Blaney was also given Oireachtas committee status and constituency concessions while Mildred Fox not only did a deal on constituencies issues in Wicklow but proceeded to itemise each aspect of it to the Dáil before voting for Ahern as Taoiseach. The three independents agreed that they would act in consort – one for all and all for one. They agreed that if any of them were at odds with the Government over their deals the three of them were at odds. The votes to make Ahern Taoiseach were sealed.

Ahern met all the other independents as a matter of courtesy to outline his proposals for Government and seek their support. His old constituency friend, Tony Gregory, made breathtaking demands, according to the Taoiseach.

'He came in and told me he wanted to be Ceann Comhairle and in the Cabinet. I knew he couldn't be serious. He wanted a super junior position like (Pat) Rabbitte. I offered him a job as chairman of the Drugs committee in which he says he has an interest and knowledge, but he turned down the job,' Ahern says.

The aid given by the two Green TDs, Trevor Sargeant and John Gormley was of a perfunctory nature; before outlining the Green concerns, the soon-to-be-Taoiseach replied, 'Come on lads, we don't want another election.' (Although Ahern had, at the time, worked out a programme for government with the PDs and as Sargeant explains today, 'he wanted our bodies, not our minds'.)

The Government was formed on 26 June with Ahern bounding up the steps of Aras an Uachtaráin to get his seal of office from President Robinson. 'It's a beautiful day in Aras an Uachtaráin. It's a beautiful evening and I could not be happier,' he told the pool of reporters. Later, he remarked, 'My biggest fear was the last night. It was the eleventh hour and I had been in that position before. It was the only time in the last few weeks that I felt nervous. I'll give it my best shot.'

No sooner had Ahern announced the formation of his Cabinet than the rumbles of controversy began. He appointed Ray Burke as Minister for Foreign Affairs and extended the brief of the previous Foreign Minister, David Andrews, to cover European Affairs so that at any time he had two Ministers fully *au fait* with the Northern talks.

When Dick Spring and John Bruton pointed out in the Dáil the possible Constitutional implications of having a Minister of equal standing subordinate to another, the idea had to be abandoned. The awkwardness of the move got the Burke tenure off to a shaky start from which it never recovered.

Throughout the summer, newspaper reports from named sources suggested that a senior Fianna Fáil figure was involved in alleged bribery in the planning process in Dublin and the name of the individual was shouted from the tree tops in the region. Burke, whose family held a Fianna Fáil seat since the '50s, had always been associated with the fast and loose approach by the Fianna Fáil party in general to planning and re-zoning matters and during one alleged round of irregular re-zonings he, along with politicians from Fine Gael and Independents, was interviewed by the fraud squad. Nothing, however, came of the investigation.

Nevertheless, this investigation irrevocably linked Burke's name in the public mind to dodgy re-zonings, even when he was not a member of the Planning authority passing these lucrative designations. This was the background to the appointment of Burke.

'When I called in the people I was appointing to Cabinet individually, Burke was the last one I spoke to,' Ahern discloses today. 'He had worked very hard on the North but I had to check around here, there, and everywhere to see if there was anything in the story from the old man in Clontarf, James Gogarty, who was making the allegations about Burke.

'We were worried, but Burke always told us that there was nothing in it. There was no problem. We were still worried about it, but at the end of the day I did appoint him as Minister for Foreign Affairs. We were in the old dilemma – if I didn't appoint him I was declaring him guilty. I had checked with everyone, including the Gardaí who had completed their enquiries, and the Garda Commissioner. I was checking where the wrongdoing was and I was doing it within a limited amount of time. We were checking with our councillors in North Dublin and with GV Wright [Burke's fellow constituency TD] and we couldn't get anything.'

Ahern then sent Cabinet Colleague, Dermot Ahern, to London to check the allegations out with an associated company: 'We assumed we would get it there but that just made our position worse.'

The rest of the Cabinet went more or less to plan. Mary Harney took the Tanaiste's role over the party deputy leader, Mary O'Rourke, which was described as an expensive bauble for partnership, but Brian Lenihan's sister held on to the key department of Public Enterprise where she took over responsibility for the entire commercial State sector. Charlie McCreevy was promoted to Finance and a one-time favourite for that job, Brian Cowen, went to Health. Other Ministers appointed included Cabinet veterans, Michael Woods and Joe Walsh. John O'Donoghue, the Zero Tolerance campaigner of the General Election, got the Justice portfolio while Síle de Valera was brought in from the cold and younger talents like Michael Martin, Noel Dempsey, Dermot Ahern and Dr Jim McDaid were appointed to senior portfolios. David Byrne, a senior counsel and personal friend of Ahern's was appointed Attorney General while Seamus Brennan took over as Government Chief Whip.

Ahern and Harney immediately abolished the Office of the Tánaiste, which was a bureaucratic super-structure put in place to facilitate the formation of the FF–Lab Government of 1992 and which remained in place during the Rainbow Coalition. Both the PDs and Labour kept the appointment of non-civil service advisers down to a minimum in contrast with previous administrations. The planned regional educational boards by the previous administration was shelved while new Health Minister, Brian Cowen, promised a new look at the McCole case and the scandal uncovered over the Blood Transfusion Service. In another housekeeping measure, the new administration abolished levies paid by independent radio stations to the Independent Radio Commission. Before the Dáil adjourned for its summer recess with the down-playing of a Peace Ambassadorial role for the former Taoiseach, Albert Reynolds – his Fianna Fáil successor publicly said Reynolds had the 'right credentials' to succeed President Robinson in the Presidential election due for the job the following Autumn. He refrained, however, from endorsing his former leader.

Overshadowing the appointment of his first Cabinet were rumours about Ray Burke and his connections or otherwise to developers in North Dublin. Rumours about the politician had abounded and in the late '70s he was questioned by others in relation to alleged irregular re-zonings in the region. By September, the Burke affair was intensifying and the politician was forced to make a full statement to the Dáil about the allegations. It was an unprecedented move by the politician who said he was 'drawing a line in the sand' over the affair. He said he received £30,000 in two brown envelopes during a meeting held in his house in 1989 with representatives of Bovale

Developments and JMSE – the money was intended to go towards the expenses of the General Election of that year. No favours were asked or given for the donation, he claimed. Burke explained that he remitted £10,000 to party headquarters and the rest of the cash was used for the party's election expenses in his constituency.

The entire Cabinet, including Mary Harney, supported Burke and argued that they believed the Minister's explanation. The rules which govern political donations now on the Statute book did not apply then, they added. Within weeks, more speculation about Burke's dealings with prospective donors to the party's coffers was spreading which was making his critical role at the Northern Peace talks, then at a crucial stage, almost untenable. He was being further questioned, even by his Cabinet colleagues and pre-emptorily resigned both his Cabinet seat and his Dáil seat, thereby precipitating a by-election.

It subsequently emerged that Burke asked for, and received, another £30,000, this time from Rennicks, a Tony O'Reilly associated company, and it further emerged that the £10,000 he remitted to party headquarters of which he spoke in his Dáil speech came from this tranche of funds.

Ahern has already pronounced his views on politicians taking money. He reveals today that he too has been offered money during his 20-year political career. 'I was offered money twice. Once I nearly clocked the guy and the other time there was a group of Fianna Fáil councillors lobbying us about the law on one-arm bandits which we were against because they were causing havoc, especially in my constituency,' he recalls.

'The first one involved warehouses in the docks area. There were a lot of guys operating around the centre of the city at the time and they were into big buildings or crime. This is the guy I nearly clocked. You always had to stand up for yourself around my constituency and you still do. If you don't, you may get set up,' he adds.

On the general question of taking unsolicited donations Ahern is equally emphatic: 'When you co-operate with these guys they have you. If someone comes along to you and says, "Listen, I'd love to support the party; here's £20,000" – sure you know bloody well they're going to be back to you. I mean, I was occasionally slagged off about my anorak and not looking the best or having a few pints or whatever, but I'd rather have that life. Who wants to have islands, helicopters, boats? It's grand, once I can get into Croker or Dalyer,' he adds.

The other question that arises in relation to the Burke appointment, especially considering the level of worry created by the appointment within his inner circle is whether Burke, in the colloquial sense, had 'something' on Ahern.

'Burke has bugger all on me. Anyone who's been around the political scene would know that. Of course we were political buddies, but while Ray Burke was a political ally, I wasn't part of his social scene.'

The allegations which led to the two pending Tribunals have done damage to Fianna Fáil, he said.

'All that stuff, I think, has harmed Fianna Fáil but we have been trying to handle it as best we can. I am not afraid of the Tribunals – I just wish they would get on with it and find out everything that has to be found out. The only thing that is a bit tedious is who knew what, when and where. Our people are trying to remember things and every week another guy in our place remembers a bit more. That's bound to happen because some people remember and others don't.'

Burke's farewell visit to Fianna Fáil was the by-election which they promptly lost and left them with tighter numbers to support the FF–PD coalition. During the by-election campaign, Burke and Ahern met on the hustings at the Lord Mayor's pub in Swords where a bitter verbal row erupted between the two politicians. Urban myths about the mêlée which followed with pints of Guinness being flung all over the pub are exaggerated according to Ahern. It wasn't like that, but drink had been taken, he adds.

Ahern's autumn of discontent also saw the Presidential election and the final fling in politics for Albert Reynolds. Reynolds was assumed to have the majority support of the Fianna Fáil parliamentary party who would decide the issue and also the endorsement of the party's new establishment. His main opponent for the prize was the relatively unknown Mary McAleese, a law professor from Belfast who was on the Board of Channel 4 on one hand and was known to be close to the Irish Catholic hierarchy on the other.

McAleese approached Ahern during the summer asking to canvass for the Fianna Fáil presidential nomination. He had no problems, but pointed out the likely predominance of Albert Reynolds at the convention. For Reynolds it was a poll too many. He lost the nomination to McAleese who was comfortably ahead on the first count. Too many of the people he discomforted in Fianna Fáil during his tenure lay in wait for him at the convention which was held in the party's offices in Leinster House.

Ahern gave Reynolds his No. 1 vote and made a point of showing it to him before he put it in the ballot box.

As a disillusioned Albert Reynolds crossed the road from Leinster House to the prearranged press conference at Buswell's hotel, the word immediately went out that Ahern had screwed Reynolds. Ahern's position today is clear-cut.

'I stayed out of the thing. I came to the conclusion, having listened to the Cabinet the day before, that the people Reynolds would have thought were definitely voting for him would do so. I didn't speak to Cowen, Dempsey, McCreevy and Smith [thought to be Reynolds supporters] about the thing.

'My own friend, Tony Kett [Senator] asked me the night before, "What am I going to do?" and I said, "Do whatever you like Tony". So he said, "I'll vote for Albert, then."

'Everyone made a big thing about Albert getting shafted but McAleese ran a good campaign and she won the election afterwards with few problems,' Ahern adds.

Chapter 35

Phoenix from the Flames

The teenage boy who surveyed the rows of ravaged and burnt-out houses in Bombay Street in south Belfast could scarcely believe his eyes. Hundreds of Catholic families had been forced out of their homes as sectarian pogroms by Protestant mobs ran rife through the city. It was August of 1969 when civil strife engulfed Northern Ireland as Catholics demanded proper voting and housing rights, of which they had been disenfanchised for decades from a stoney-faced, Unionist-led quasi-government. The Unionists sent in their armed thugs, the B-Specials, to put manners on the 'Taigs'. 'Down croppy, lie down.' Only this time the 'Taigs' would not take 'No' for an answer. London was forced to send in the British Army. The seeds of Catholic discontent led to the formation of the Provisional IRA.

What was odd about this particular 18-year-old boy who surveyed the chaos was that he was neither a Belfast Catholic nor a Protestant. He was a young Dubliner, who had travelled up North for his brother's wedding to a Co. Down girl living in Belfast. The name of that boy was Bertie Ahern. Little did that boy – or the rest of the country – realise that over three-and-a-half thousand people would be slaughtered in Ireland, Britain and Europe for nearly 30 years in a struggle over who owned six small counties in the north-eastern part of Ireland. Little, too, did that boy know he would later become leader of his country, and become a catalyst which would help bring about a cessation of war after 30 years. He would be instrumental in creating an opportunity for peaceful harmony among all sections in

Ireland and between Britain and Ireland after over 700 years of suspicion, conflict and bitterness. Ahern would emerge phoenix-like from the flames of Bombay Street.

He was from a deeply Republican family; Padraig Pearse was one of Ahern's idols. Despite immersing himself among trade unions in his young adult life, he chose Fianna Fáil as his party rather than Labour because he considered himself a Republican. Fianna Fáil, after all, considered itself the 'Republican Party'.

Bertie Ahern was a man thrown into the Irish political cauldron of domestic matters and twiddled away his time dealing with industrial relations and financial matters for the best part of 20 years. For a man who had little to say about Northern Ireland during most of his career, he was extremely well versed on the matter when he took over the Fianna Fáil leadership in November 1994. Until then, his only publicised pronouncements on the North included an emotional Republican speech at the Liam Lynch commemoration ceremony at Fermoy, Co. Cork in September 1983 and an insightful probe into his Northern outlook in a *Hot Press* magazine interview in July 1986. At the Liam Lynch ceremony, he said: 'We share the deep frustration of Northern Republicans at the discrimination, oppression and denial of national rights which they have suffered.

'We would like to work hand-in-hand with the entire Nationalist community to create a new, free, united independent and sovereign Ireland, separate from Britain . . . It is the political weakness of Northern Ireland, not the military strength of its defenders, that must be challenged. Let it be clearly recognised that violence cannot achieve the political objectives which we all desire.'

In his *Hot Press* interview he said that while Sinn Féin represented a large section of the Nationalist community in the North, he himself did not support the 'armalite in one hand and the ballot box in another'.

He said that he could not understand how shooting and blowing people up could achieve anything. When asked, 'What about shooting a British soldier?' he replied: 'Well, I think violence is totally wrong. But if that was the only action they [the IRA] were involved in, in a war position, they would have an argument. It's an argument certain people will vote for. It's not an argument I agree with.'

Fast forward to November 1994, and Ahern had finally taken over the leadership of Fianna Fáil.

In the North, Ahern's elevation got a mixed reception. Dr Philip McGarry, chairman of the Alliance party, described Ahern as 'a realistic politician who does not become excessively preoccupied with ideology'. But Ulster Unionist deputy leader John Taylor claimed that Ahern had once predicted that a United Ireland was not far off. 'This negative approach by Mr Ahern, in which he even held out the possibility of a united Ireland in five years, causes instability within the political framework of Northern Ireland and will have a detrimental influence on the peace process.'

A number of attempts to solve the Northern Ireland impasse had failed miserably in the past: Sunningdale 1973, which collapsed after Ulster Workers Council general strikes the following year and the purge of Ulster Unionist leader, Brian Faulkner; and the Anglo–Irish Agreement in 1985, which incensed Unionists into more mass demonstrations.

In 1988, Charles Haughey started putting out feelers to the Republican side in the North through intermediaries, particularly Father Alec Reid, a Belfast priest, and Dr Martin Mansergh, Haughey's Northern adviser. Haughey had a private meeting with John Major in 1991, where he outlined the possibility that Republicans may be ready to put down the gun and talk peace.

On entering Government in 1992, Albert Reynolds confided that SDLP leader John Hume had been in secret talks with Sinn Féin leader Gerry Adams and believed there was a chance that the IRA would abandon their campaign of violence if an acceptable political settlement was available. At the time, few believed him. Dublin's *Sunday Independent* made Hume out to be a 'Bête noire' in a series of unforgivable attacks for having the audacity even to talk to Adams. The talks process culminated in the Downing Street Declaration on 15 December 1993.

The document accepted the right to self-determination consistent with the principle of consent to any constitutional change and promised to encourage the achievement of agreement between the two traditions in Ireland. The Unionists were assured that Articles 2 and 3 of the Irish Constitution, which lay territorial claim over Northern Ireland, would be changed and their political aspirations within the United Kingdom safeguarded, but demands by Sinn Féin for clarification of the Declaration delayed an IRA cease-fire.

Nevertheless, the IRA finally did call a 'cessation of all military activities' on 31 August 1994 and it was a truly historic moment. The announcement was greeted by hooting carloads of flag-waving Republicans on the Falls Road, as like a victory. Over on the Shankill Road, graffiti beamed 'We, the Protestant people of Northern Ireland accept the unconditional surrender of the IRA.' The British kicked up a rumpus over insisting that the IRA should state that the cease-fire was 'permanent' while Unionist demands for arms decommissioning stalled the talks process and Reynolds's Government fell in November 1994.

In January 1995, in a strongly worded warning against allowing an impasse on the subject of weapons disposal, Ahern said the British Government would be 'wrong' to unilaterally insist on preconditions that were not clearly and explicitly set out in the Downing Street Declaration.

He also called on the British and the Unionists to face up to the necessity of sitting down to talks with Sinn Féin. 'The British Government and the unionist parties have to face up to, and should do so sooner rather than later, the necessity of sitting across the table with Sinn Féin who have a clear electoral mandate given to them by the people they represent,' he said.

'It is obvious that there will be no progress towards a peace settlement as long as attempts are made to exclude Sinn Féin from the table. A complete lack of progress, based on continued exclusion, must not be allowed to undermine confidence in the peace process.'

He said that the whole demilitarisation agenda should be dealt with in parallel to political talks and not as a precondition for participation in dialogue. He welcomed the removal of British troops from accompanying RUC patrols in Belfast during daylight hours as this represented progress; 'but I look forward to the day when the army is removed from the streets of Northern Ireland altogether.'

Ahern also set up a special Northern Ireland Committee and was accompanied by Martin Mansergh, Brian Lenihan, Ray Burke, Jim McDaid and Dermot Ahern. Ahern met Adams for the first time as Fianna Fáil leader and said that the issue of decommissioning weapons should be taken 'in parallel' with direct talks between Sinn Féin and the British Government. 'We do not see the necessity or the value of it being a precondition,' Ahern said. 'Preconditions in the current period are not helpful. The talks about talks have gone on for a long time.'

Noting that the IRA cease-fire had lasted 150 days, he remarked: 'I read carefully what Mr Major is saying – that there cannot be any inclusion of Sinn Féin in the round table talks that are required unless the IRA decommissions its weapons. The question that must be put to Mr Major is this: 'Is this the end of the peace process?" He added that the British had been denying Sinn Féin's democratic mandate by not involving them in talks and that the deterioration of Republican prisoners in Britain was also a matter for concern.

Ahern later told a meeting of the Irish Association at the Mansion House in Dublin in early February that almost no one believed it is either feasible or desirable to attempt to incorporate Northern Ireland into the Republic or into a united Ireland against the will of the majority there, either by force or coercion. He said that in his view they had to leave behind the territorial claims of the British and Irish states and view the future exclusively in the hands of its people 'North and South' in keeping with the principles of the Downing Street Declaration:

'In keeping with our principles, it is the people of Ireland who are sovereign, not the State, be it British or Irish,' he said.

He pointed out that North–South institutions with executive powers were a fundamentally different concept from joint authority, which he said Fianna Fáil had never advocated as realistic. Consent, he said, was a two-way street between Nationalists and Unionists in Northern Ireland, and that the irredentism was dead. In a telling *Irish Times* interview also that month, he said: 'Nobody can ask us to accept in our Constitution that Armagh, Derry or Antrim are British and not Irish. The understanding has to be that a part of Ireland may be under British jurisdiction, but that does not make either the territory of the North or the people of the North any less Irish.'

By the end of February 1995, Bruton and Major had agreed a Joint Framework Document, which among other recommendations espoused co-operative North–South bodies with executive powers. It was rejected as a template for a political settlement by Unionists, the details having been leaked earlier in *The Times*, and was given only conditional support by Sinn Féin.

Ahern welcomed it and pledged support for constitutional changes in the Republic if there were appropriate changes in British law. He said that maintaining the integrity of the nation as set out in Article 2 was vital.

'We were not prepared to accept a 26-county based definition of the Irish nation, which would exclude Northern nationalists,' he pointed out. 'Anyone born on this island, or of Irish parentage, is entitled to be regarded as a member of the Irish nation, regardless of borders. Equally, we are committed to the idea of one nation; in Tone's words, "substituting for Protestant, Catholic and Dissenter the common name of Irishman". That is our ideal, even if not everyone accepts it.'

Ahern maintained that when Fianna Fáil secured government it would not force anyone in the North to accept Irish citizenship if they did not want to, adding that if the Republic was to no longer contain what the Framework Document described as the 'territorial claim' over Northern Ireland in its Constitution, it was reasonable to ask that the British do the same. He pointed out the Government of Ireland Act must be updated and said he was heartened to hear John Major say that the future of Northern Ireland rested with the majority there and that 'provided that it translated clearly and unambiguously into British constitutional law, following an overall agreement, we will have no complaint. British territorial sovereignty over Northern Ireland will be gone. We will have helped to place sovereignty unequivocally in the hands of the people.'

Sir Patrick Mayhew made a speech in Washington that March where he called on Sinn Féin and the IRA to demonstrate their good faith in the peace process by undergoing a number of tests. The third test, now known as Washington Three, called for the decommissioning of weapons. Bruton backed up the call in spite of earlier assurances by him that the British Government's position did not require the decommissioning of weapons as a precondition for Sinn Féin's participation in all-party talks.

'People, not just Republicans, feel cheated by the absence of all-party talks that were publicly promised,' Ahern blasted.

The obstacle later became a mountain and would ultimately lead to the collapse of the IRA cease-fire.

Ahern strongly criticised the British in a speech at the 1916 leaders grave at Arbour Hill that April for failing to open ministerial talks with Sinn Féin in the wake of the cease-fire as the cessation was complete.

'The British Government have not a shred of justification for slowing down the peace process or for continuing to discriminate against Republicans who have opted definitively for the democratic path,' he said.

At the Forum for Peace and Reconciliation at Dublin Castle, Ahern was accused of flippancy when he proposed that 'A Nation Once Again' might be a suitable choice for a new national anthem at sports fixtures which attracted a large 'non-nationalist' attendance. John

Lowry of the Workers Party said he did not know whether Ahern was being flippant or not, while Mary Harney said it was associated with the IRA: the current anthem, she said, while she could understand the emotional attachment, had militaristic lyrics which were not compatible with peace and reconciliation.

That May, Ahern made a three-day visit to the US where he met Al Gore and leading politicians and businessmen. After a meeting in the White House he urged the US to 'keep a close watch' on the continuing negotiations in Northern Ireland.

'We need our political friends,' he said. 'We are going to need support to keep the pressure up.'

The same month he made a two-day visit to Belfast where he met Loyalists and representatives of the Unionist business, social and church community. He and Ray Burke met Gary McMichael of the Ulster Democratic Party, which has links with the UDA, and David Ervine of the PUP, which has links with the UVF. Ahern described the talks as frank, open and useful, although there was no 'meeting of minds'. He indicated that Fianna Fáil in Government would be prepared to make unspecified changes to Articles 2 and 3.

When Private Lee Clegg – jailed for killing a girl joyrider – was released, Ahern accused the British of double standards and said prisoner releases were a vitally important confidence-building measure.

'Most of the English politicians sent over to govern Ireland, or part of it, go on making the same mistakes, year after year, century after century,' he noted. 'They do not understand the sensitivities on which they tread.'

John Major was becoming increasingly dependent on Unionist votes to bolster up his slim government majority at Westminster, while UUP leader James Molyneux was replaced by David Trimble, a perceived hardliner who had gained cult status among Unionists for his confrontational attitude towards the RUC at the Drumcree stand-off the July before. With the talks becoming increasingly stalled, Ahern accused Bruton in July of 'no longer playing a central role in the peace process as its predecessor did under Albert Reynolds'. He said there was frustration that 'the political process seems to be reduced to stand-off between the British Government and Sinn Féin'.

In an open letter to Mayhew in the *Irish News* he said that nowhere else in the world had there been so little political movement at the end of a long-standing conflict. He said if Mayhew's policy was to move the peace process forward as slowly as possible without causing its collapse then 'the risk of failure is too great'. Nobody should test the process 'to destruction'.

Ahern said one of the key elements in the peace process was the preservation of the 'united stance adopted by nationalist Ireland' and called on Bruton to 'ensure that the clear and demonstrable unity of purpose underpinning the peace process since its inception is maintained'. Complete cessation of violence must be maintained, 'even in circumstance of a manifest and persistent breach of faith by the British Government, or of a persistent refusal by other parties to enter negotiations'.

Attempts to force a political humiliation of the IRA was entirely contrary to the spirit of honourable compromise, he added, and accused the British of trying to 'put the cart before the horse' in the area of decommissioning of paramilitary weapons.

'They also tried to divide the nationalist consensus, which brought about and has sustained the cease-fire,' he claimed. 'Leaders of the Irish government have not always been as clear or consistent as I would have wished. But I am glad the Government pulled back from the brink of accepting something that might have caused a serious crisis.

'I am quite certain that there is no danger to the permanence of the cease-fire provided that its basis is not undermined.'

In November he even went so far as to demand an apology from the British for the Great Famine.

'I think a frank acknowledgement and expression of regret about the shortcomings of the then British Government's response to the Famine would contribute to a better climate of relations between Irish people, or people of Irish stock across the world and the British, who after all have intertwined experiences in so many respects.

'A little bit of British humility towards this country, which has not been much in evidence in recent times, would greatly assist the process of reconciliation.'

(British Premier Tony Blair would, in 1997, issue the official apologetic declaration which was demanded).

At the Fianna Fáil Ard Fheis that November, Ahern ruled out an elected Northern Ireland assembly or convention on its own. He devoted one fifth of his speech to the North. He said it would neither be 'sensible nor acceptable' and to take such a course would be to return to a proven cul-de-sac.

'Indeed, it would cause further delay and it would inevitably revive and further embitter old antagonisms.'

He added: 'We hear repeatedly about Unionist fears. I genuinely understand those fears and I understand the need to allay those fears. But both the British Government and the Unionist leadership must acknowledge the fears of the Nationalist community – fears that are based on 75 years of bitter experience.'

Senator George Mitchell had been chairing the International Body on Decommissioning along with leading experts from Canada and Scandinavia who had been deliberating over recommendations about the decommissioning of weapons in the peace process. The body was set up in December and at the end of January 1996 delivered its report. They addressed the issue of decommissioning at the level of principle and recognised that it was an issue which defined victory or defeat for the protagonists.

The British Government's reaction was bluntly negative. They replied with an announcement of a new Northern Ireland assembly and an election to precede, something the Unionists had been baying for. Ahern was incensed at Major's dismissal of Mitchell's report.

'The report provides the means for breaking the log-jam over decommissioning which has stalled the peace process for over a year and it should be grasped,' he stressed.

'The body listened to the different positions on the decommissioning issue, and has produced, in our opinion, an excellent compromise formula, which deals fairly with the legitimate concerns of all parties and recommends a system that will pave the way for all-party talks in the near future.

'Fundamental to participation in all-party talks is an absolute and unqualified commitment to the principles of democracy and non-violence. The six principles put forward by the body involve an absolute commitment to democratic and peaceful means of resolving political issues. They also involve a commitment to the total disarmament of all paramilitary organisations in a veritable way: it is in effect, a disbandment and a renunciation of the use of force which must influence negotiations.

'They are committed to abiding by the agreed outcome of negotiations and to seek to alter anything disliked in that outcome by peaceful methods while also involving a pledge to make best efforts to stop and prevent punishment killings and beatings, which are not consistent with the absolute commitment to democracy and non-violence that is required.'

Ahern then announced that his party was prepared to accept an election in the North if it led to all-party talks immediately afterwards. But he stressed he saw 'no guarantee' that talks would follow an election and was worried that Major was already talking about the 'nuts and bolts' of an assembly.

On 9 February 1996, the IRA finally decided that the British had done enough pussy-footing with Sinn Féin. After 17 months, Sinn Féin were still being told they could not take part in any all-party talks unless the IRA began decommissioning, and so their reply was swift and deadly. At 6 p.m. that evening they announced their cease-fire was over. Minutes later, a huge bomb ripped through the Canary Wharf section of London's Docklands, killing two people and causing £100 million worth of damage.

Ahern noted that when the IRA called their cease-fire they announced that there would be a 'complete cessation of military operations' and a 'definitive commitment' to the success of the democratic process. While they did not use the word 'permanent', he said the word 'definitive' meant fixing something or 'conclusive'.

'I am very disappointed that the present IRA has not kept its word and in practice have ignored the principle of national self-determination,' he said. ' The people of Ireland have over and over again expressed in unmistakable fashion at elections their will that their profound differences have to be resolved by exclusively political means.'

While Fianna Fáil considered partition to be 'a grave injustice and contrary to the principle of national self-determination', they could not ignore Northern Ireland and while most Irish people would like to see a United Ireland he said it could only be brought about 'by peaceful means and agreement' and that they had 'no wish to coerce an unwilling Unionist majority into a united Ireland against their will.'

He said Major was more concerned with the political arithmetic at Westminster than the peace process. As for Sir Patrick Mayhew, the Northern Ireland Secretary: 'I believe he bears more responsibility than anyone else for the prolonged impasse in the peace process up to last Friday.' Ahern said the 'excellent' Mitchell Report paved the way for all-party talks, yet had been 'cast unceremoniously aside by the British Prime Minister for an idea that came from only one side of the divide'.

'We must at all costs avoid being drawn back into old arguments about permanence and decommissioning,' he added.

He said the six Mitchell principles should be used as a cornerstone for the peace process and that there should be no preconditions and found no difficulty in John Hume's call for a referendum on both sides of the Border to underscore the principle of self-determination in relation both to violence, to put it beyond all argument or doubt, and all-party talks.

'At that point the IRA and the political parties would be directly confronted by the wishes of national democracy,' he explained. He said the proximity talks proposed by Dick Spring before the end of that month would be a demonstration of the two government's good faith in keeping to their previous communiques.

'The idea gets over the problem of parties that will not talk to each other,' he added. 'I believe that either the appointment of a US peace envoy or the proximity talks or a combination of both would provide a good way to sort ideas on the way forward.'

Later that month he met Mo Mowlam, Labour's Northern Ireland spokeswoman, for the first time. She was given a copy of Ahern's Dáil speech in which he sharply criticised Labour. 'I robustly defended our position as an opposition party, as Bertie did his,' she said.

Gerry Adams had said the peace process was now a spent force and needed to be rebuilt from the ground up, while Ahern admitted that he felt the best prospects for peace lay with Adams. The two made contact by telephone and met in Dublin and Ahern proposed George Mitchell become peace envoy to Ireland.

In another broadside at Mayhew, Ahern accused him of operating a 'patronising colonial style approach' towards Northern Ireland and a 'failure to show any empathy' towards the nationalist community in the North, which was in stark contrast to his predecessor, Peter Brooke.

The date set for all-party talks was 10 June and the workings of the Joint Framework Document were resumed, following their suspension after the Canary Wharf bombing.

Ahern used the annual Arbour Hill oration for an attack on the Government. He slammed Bruton's attitude to the peace process and said his refusal for a joint meeting with Hume and Adams the previous October was a 'serious mistake'. He also criticised Bruton for suspending the Forum 'at a time when it was most needed.' He then admonished Spring for replacing a leader of Fianna Fáil for 'an admirer of John Redmond'.

Bruton launched a counter-offence and criticised Fianna Fáil's 'ambiguity' on the North. He said Ahern's 'views differ radically from the inclusive and balanced approach of previous leaders of his party, like Sean Lemass and Jack Lynch, who went out of their way to reach out to both traditions in Northern Ireland. By contrast, Deputy Bertie Ahern seems to want me and the Government to reach out only to one tradition.' He added that Ahern's views were very much out of touch with that of Wolfe Tone's pluralist views.

Ahern met Adams that June to encourage an IRA cease-fire to allow for all-party talks. He said that since March 1995 it was a 'tragedy' that decommissioning had been allowed to dominate political discussions and preparations for all-party talks. The marching season was in full flow in the North and Ahern dismissed a 'review' of Orange parades as 'inadequate'. He said 'nobody in nationalist Ireland' believed Mayhew's recommendations as the RUC's reputation was 'worse than it has been at any time over the years'.

He explained that it was no longer realistic to insist upon early parallel decommissioning as an absolute precondition to the progress of meaningful negotiations and that Sinn Féin must be admitted to all-party talks once a new cease-fire was called. Following a bomb attack in October on a British Army barracks outside Lisburn, which killed two soldiers, Ahern insisted the IRA must restore the cease-fire and the two governments should establish a time-frame for talks. Decommissioning should be part of the peace process and not something on which prior agreement was required and there should be a 'liberal regime' for the release of all politically-motivated prisoners, he said. The British government should act, independently of the talks process, to enhance equality and parity of esteem to build confidence and economic and social progress. Ahern also believed that the talks process should also be moved to a 'neutral' location such as Washington.

'The British government, who have been prepared to talk to Sinn Féin themselves after a cease-fire, have no right to disenfranchise 40 per cent of the nationalist population in respect of their participation in talks, or deny Sinn Féin's full democratic rights as a party, once it is prepared to make an irrevocable commitment to peace and democracy by signing up to the Mitchell principles on behalf of the Republican movement, as soon as it is able to enter talks,' he said.

'Unionists have no right to be given, by any government, a political veto over the presence in talks of those who have been freely chosen by a substantial section of the nationalist population to represent them.'

The following January, Ahern pressed Bruton to call in the British ambassador and demand a new inquiry into Bloody Sunday, when 14 unarmed civilians were shot dead in Derry in 1972 by British paratroopers. The murder of a British soldier at Bessbrook Co. Armagh in mid-February was repudiated as 'senseless and brutal' and a killing which had endangered peace on the island.

'It's long past time for Sinn Féin to show some political leadership and declare whether they are seriously interested in a peaceful settlement and playing a useful part in the ongoing negotiations,' he pointed out.

Ahern later said at a meeting in Belfast that the Republican movement should stop blaming the British Government and face up to its responsibilities to rebuild the peace process and restore trust. He called for an immediate IRA ceasefire and said that if Sinn Féin didn't 'make the best of what is currently on offer', it would face increasing political isolation.

At a meeting of the Campaign for Democracy, a small Northern-based cross-community group, he remarked:

'The Republican movement needs to address seriously without waiting any longer how it rebuilds peace and restores trust. The onus for building peace rest with everyone, including them. The entire responsibility cannot be shifted on to someone else. Failures by the British Government are no excuse for the continuation of an IRA campaign which is rejected by the overwhelming majority of both the Irish people in general and Irish nationalists in particular.'

He claimed that Republicans could not make preconditions as the IRA violence made their position 'untenable', but that the difference between London and Republicans over a new cease-fire was 'small enough' and could be bridged. He urged the British to signal that inclusive talks would commence once a new cease-fire was declared, a cease-fire which must be 'real, not a sham' and not conditional or tactical. What would not work was an in-between approach to on-off violence as an à la carte option to be resorted to whenever difficulties or blockages arise in the peace process, he added.

Once again he urged the British to make an inquiry into Bloody Sunday, possible miscarriages of justice and the 'callous conditions of imprisonment' of Roisin McAlliskey (who was wanted by Germany for allegedly bombing a British Army base there).

Writing in the *Irish News* that March, he called on people voting in the British General Election in Northern Ireland not to vote for candidates who were prepared to see a repeat of Drumcree or to vote for Sinn Féin if there was no IRA cease-fire.

Ian Paisley responded: 'The people of my constituency are very angry that here we have the leader of the opposition party in a foreign country directing them how to vote.'

But Ahern was relentless in his campaign for peace. Launching another attack on Major, this time at a function at Boston College, he said: 'John Major, unfortunately, is more concerned to keep the Ulster Unionist party on side, on whom his Government has increasingly come to depend, than to move the peace process forward.'

Weeks later, again at Arbour Hill, he said that Fianna Fáil, as a party representing Nationalist Ireland, was best placed to reach a 'historic compromise' with Unionism. He said the vision of peace created by Albert Reynolds and John Major had faltered not only because of difficulties with the unionists, but because there was 'not the same passionate conviction coming from the new Government in Dublin.'

'Peace was declared unconditionally by the IRA on the understanding that after a few months and post-Framework Document, Sinn Féin would be admitted to talks. The Taoiseach permitted a fatal prevarication by the British on that commitment, using the red herring of decommissioning.'

He added: 'The Taoiseach boasted in 1994 that he was the best person to make peace with the Unionists. Two-and-a-half years on, he has made no progress. The Downing Street Declaration was the first Irish-inspired initiative to win widespread unionist and loyalist support.'

He claimed that no party had condemned the resumption of violence more than he had, saying that 'Continued IRA activity, even if less lethal than in the past, makes the task of rebuilding the peace process harder and fosters huge distrust that is a real barrier to progress.'

Justice Minister Nora Owen said Ahern was 'making a dangerous error of judgement – consciously or unconsciously providing excuses for gunmen and bombers who returned to violence.' She added: 'His criticisms display a lack of understanding that it is the duty of all democrats to seek the decommissioning of arms held by paramilitary organisations that have never recognised the State. He also seems to believe that the Irish Government should, as a matter of course, hold symbolic meetings to line itself up in some sort of nationalist front with Sinn Féin and the IRA. His views are wrong on both counts.' She said his criticisms 'uncannily echo almost word for word those of Gerry Adams'.

Despite the killings of two RUC officers in Lurgan in the middle of that June, Ahern said he would leave the door open for Sinn Féin to come into talks – provided there was a new IRA cease-fire. A proposed meeting with Adams was called off and Ahern said it would be 'meaningless' unless the IRA called an unequivocal restoration of their IRA cease-fire.

The elections of Ahern as Taoiseach and Tony Blair as British Prime Minister within weeks of each other injected fresh momentum into the peace talks. Their first major problem was the Drumcree march on 6 July, at which a third year of a major stand-off was a strong possibility. The so-called proximity talks at which the new Northern Ireland Secretary, Dr Mo Mowlam, and her officials had tried to broker a compromise between Orangemen and representatives of the Nationalists on the Garvaghy Road in Portadown fizzled out.

Ahern met Mowlam in early July, as well as Brendan Mac Cionnaith, spokesman for the Garvaghy residents. 'Clearly nobody wants to see the march forced through as last year,' said Ahern. 'Nobody wants to see people "ringed in" as last year.' He suggested that the handling of Orange Order parades should be seen in the context of 'the bigger picture' of Northern Ireland. And as for Garvaghy Road, 'I am going to do all that I can not to get sidetracked by one event on the road to getting to the bigger picture.'

Jeffrey Donaldson, deputy Grand Master of the Orange Order, accused Ahern and Foreign Affairs Minister, Ray Burke, of 'damaging' the prospect of reaching an accommodation over Drumcree by coming in 'with their clodhoppers'.

Donaldson referred to comments made by Ahern and Burke that the march should not be forced down the Garvaghy Road.

'Their intervention this week was most unhelpful. These people came in from the Irish Government and hadn't really been involved in the situation. They weren't aware of all the nuances and came in with their clodhoppers and really just walked all over the situation and increased tension at a time that was very, very critical indeed.'

At 7.30 a.m. on the morning of 6 July, Ahern received a courtesy call from Tony Blair.

Blair told Ahern that on the advice of RUC Chief Constable, Ronnie Flanagan, for security reasons he had no alternative but to force the march down the Garvaghy Road. Television pictures of heavy-handed RUC men batoning bloodied residents protesting in vain at the decision were beamed round the world.

Northern Nationalists had felt let down by the new Labour Government, and Mo Mowlam in particular. Ahern said the Garvaghy Road decision had made life difficult for everyone and the Irish Government had an obligation to understand the Nationalist position and the sense of disappointment within that community. He admitted that he was aware the previous weekend of what was likely to happen.

'Now we are in a position where it has happened,' he said. 'I certainly am disappointed with that. I regret it. But I want to see these matters dealt with with respect and dignity so that we can move on, because the greater issue is the ultimate political solution and that is what I am going to continue to work for.'

He said the Government's response would be to pressurise the British for legislation providing for new ground rules and a code of practice for parades in Northern Ireland. Mo Mowlam promised such legislation in the autumn, but Ahern's unwillingness to offer unqualified political support for the future efforts of Dr Mowlam in relation to both contentious parades and the multi-party talks reflected tension between the two governments. Ahern felt there had to be some sort of recognition from the British of the hurt and disappointment felt by the Nationalist community when it came to consider future contentious Orange parades. He said he accepted the 'good faith' of Blair, despite the decision to allow the march to go ahead.

'At the end of the day, the Prime Minister said to me that he had to make a decision based on security considerations,' he explained. 'I think it is regrettable that some other alternatives he had before him were not used. But I do not believe that he was involved in anything other than spelling out the position as it was.'

He refuted an accusation from Bruton that the pronouncements from Ahern and Burke before the march made it inevitable that Orangemen would not voluntarily abstain from the use of the right to march. In spite of an on-going ban on Ministerial meetings with Sinn Féin, informal channels of communication had been used since the Government took office.

Later that month, Blair had a 20-minute telephone conversation with Ahern in which the former thanked the Taoiseach for his positive reaction to the Orange Order's announcement that they would re-route contentious marches. Both leaders welcomed the announcement and said there should be an equally positive response from the Nationalists.

On 15 July, Ahern and Clinton had a 15-minute phone conversation about Northern Ireland. A White House spokesman said the call had been made on the initiative of President Clinton and it was the first contact by telephone the two men had had since Ahern became Taoiseach. The White House said the two leaders had discussed how to get the peace process moving and their hopes that the Northern Ireland talks could 'move into substantive stage'. They both wanted this to be on the basis of Sinn Féin at the table following 'an unequivocal IRA cease-fire'.

Three days later, Ahern confirmed that contact was reopened with Sinn Féin. It was understood that his Northern adviser, Dr Martin Mansergh, had renewed contact with the Sinn Féin leadership because of the prospect of a new cessation of violence.

Government representatives had also had private meetings with leaders of the UUP over the previous two weeks to offer clarification of the Irish position on the decommissioning of arms. One of the meetings was held in Belfast between Burke and Trimble. Ahern said he understood that Adams and McGuinness had given the IRA a detailed assessment of the current situation and believed that the conditions for a cease-fire were in place.

The clarification documents amounted to 20 pages and were as long as the decommissioning paper, which had been published a month earlier. These 20 pages of clarification, and also assurances on parity of esteem, confidence-building measures, the structure of the talks and the issue of prisoners, made a difference: the single most important development to secure a possible second cease-fire in Ahern's view was the unanimity of the positions adopted by Blair, Clinton and himself about the road to the talks table which lay ahead for Sinn Féin. Ahern acknowledged his belief that the IRA were driven out of the peace process in 1996 and on Sunday, 20 July 1997 the IRA declared a new cease-fire – one which has turned out to be permanent. Several more phone calls followed that weekend between Ahern and Blair which were to ensure that all parties would attend the inclusive talks scheduled to begin on 15 September.

Ahern also spoke to Adams by phone on the Saturday night. 'The message was that we must make this permanent,' Ahern said.

He also told RTE's *This week* that Articles 2 and 3 were on the table in the forthcoming negotiations and stated that he guaranteed the right to consent.

'Anything negotiated will be put to the people, North and South, on the same day requiring the agreement of both communities,' he pointed out.

'The Republican movement's attitude to the cease-fire was that they will never say the matter is permanent. Where they are coming from, they want a 32-county Republic. They want to see the British administration out for good, so they are not going to use the word permanent.'

Nevertheless, he added: 'All we want to do is to try and replace killing, murder and mayhem with political, democratic dialogue. That happens in every democracy around the world and I invite them to join with us in that.'

As for the cease-fire, 'We could all sit back and watch the cease-fire break down. It is easy to do nothing, but harder to get up every morning and work through complex issues and try and see what parity of esteem means, or see how to deal with the prisoners issues, or how we try to find our way through the three-phase process, find ways of building accommodation within Northern Ireland, find a new relationship between Belfast and Dublin, and a new relationship between Dublin and London.'

He said that he could see a new form of administration evolving with David Trimble, as leader of the largest party, leading Northern Ireland – a new system which would have a North–South dimension.

Outlining the Government's approach to all-party talks, he said that if they were to be successful they must involve 'a radical renegotiation on a three-strand basis, not just of the Anglo–Irish Agreement, but of the 1920–21 settlement'.

Then, for the first time as Taoiseach, Ahern met Adams, along with John Hume. The latter said: 'Don't be looking at the picture of the three of us. Look at what we have said because we have made very clear that our objective is agreement among our divided people. We make it clear that the problem can't be resolved without the agreement of the unionists.'

However, UUP leader Trimble effectively ruled out an early meeting with Ahern because he said he wanted to see a 'clear statement' from the Government in relation to the decommissioning of paramilitary weapons:

'What I want to hear from Mr Ahern at the minute is a clear statement that the Irish Government will support the Mitchell compromise on the decommissioning of weapons: that is, decommissioning will take place during talks.'

Chapter 36

The Long Good Friday

E aster 1916 has gone down in history as one of the defining moments in the birth of an independent Ireland. Sixty two years later, the events of another Easter week would pave the way for a monumental leap in finally bringing peace to the island. Serendipity is a word used to describe an enormous but fortuitous coincidence and it is a word that could apply to the blossoming Irish peace process. The seeds for cultivating a new hope for the future of the island have been sown.

A more enlightened government in the shape of Labour had taken over in Britain. Prime Minister Tony Blair had an open mind on Northern Ireland and was not at the beck and call of the Unionists, unlike the Tories who had ruled the six counties like a colony for much of its previous 18 years in power. Blair appointed Dr Mo Mowlam as his Northern Ireland Secretary. She was a no-nonsense grafter from the north of England who took no prisoners on either side when dealing with the testosterone-fused parochial politics of both traditions in Northern Ireland. Bertie Ahern had just been elected Taoiseach and, unlike John Bruton, he was trusted by the majority of northern Nationalists and as leader of Fianna Fáil could deliver any changes in Articles 2 and 3 which facilitated peace.

Bill Clinton had kept an avid interest in Northern Ireland affairs since he became President in 1992, an interest which stemmed from watching nightly television bulletins of unrest in the North while he was a student at Oxford in the late 1960s. He also had the ear of the powerful Irish–American lobby in Washington and considered himself part-Irish. His visits to Belfast, Derry and Dublin in December 1995 have stood out in his memory as one of the highlights of his career. Clinton appointed Senator George Mitchell, a skilled negotiator, and also an expert in conflict resolution, as a type of 'special envoy' to Northern Ireland to oversee the proximity talks.

Meanwhile on the homefront,Gerry Adams had successfully fought off the hawk elements in Sinn Féin and the IRA to deliver the majority of the Republican movement on the road to peace. David Trimble, while showing early signs of reactionarism during Drumcree 1995, was a pragmatic Unionist who had come to realise that the future of Northern Ireland needed to be finally resolved once and for all before a future British Government lost patience with the 'not an inch' syndrome. The spokesmen for the Loyalist paramilitaries, Gary McMichael and David Ervine, saw sense in a non-violent future. And there was John Hume, the courageous leader of the SDLP, whose initial contacts with Republicans had laid the groundwork for IRA cease-fires which would pave the way for all-party talks. These people were the ingredients who would produce the recipe for a final resolution.

The ice was soon broken in the Autumn of 1997 when Ahern and Trimble began talking and the two started a working relationship. Proximity talks began on 15 September and despite initial stumbling blocks about decommissioning, parties got their views aired. Ahern made room for Trimble's sensitivities on East–West structures, and to a lesser extent on North–South bodies. Following months of proximity talks, chaired by George Mitchell at Stormont Castle, involving all parties with the exception of Paisley's Democratic Unionist Party and Robert McCarthey and Conor Cruise O'Brien's UK Unionist rump, the scene was set for one of the most dramatic weeks in Irish history – the week leading up to Good Friday in April 1998. After frenetic weeks of discussion, two key issues proved to be the stumbling block to the multi-party talks meeting the deadline which was due to expire on Thursday of that week – the operation of a new Northern Ireland assembly and cross-Border implementation bodies.

Ahern phoned Trimble on the afternoon of 5 April and told him there would be no alteration in his approach to Strand Two. Strand One concerned the internal government of Northern Ireland, on which progress had been made, although problems at that stage did exist on proposals for cross-community decision-making in the assembly. Strand Two concerned some 10 North–South bodies (such as tourism and fishing), their executive powers and their relationship with the new assembly. Gary McMichael of the UDP said that an agreement might not be reached if the Irish Government did not compromise on Strand Two. He said it was quite clear that Nationalists wanted the creation of bodies which would 'take on a life of their own and in some way become dynamic and in our view undermine the primacy of a Northern Ireland assembly,' which was unacceptable. Sinn Féin at that stage looked set to sign on the dotted line, as the package seemed to suit them well – policing, prisoners, North–South arrangements and changes in British constitutional legislation.

During these tumultous negotiations for which Ahern had fought so relentlessly, his mother, Julia, passed away in the early hours of that Monday morning in Holy Week. She had been an active member of her local Fianna Fáil cumainn up to her death and was said to have been particularly close to Bertie, to whom she gave birth at the age of 40. Despite his huge emotional upheaval, Ahern found time to continue the round-robin phone calls and meetings in a bid to crack a deal.

There had been signs that the UUP were prepared to offer the SDLP a better deal on Strand One, coming close to a power-sharing executive, in the hope of weakening the Nationalist stance on the powers of North–South bodies in Strand Two. But the UUP said they had no room whatsoever to manoeuvre in relation to Strand Two and that if they did, it would lead to a Sunningdale-type disaster for Trimble.

The draft settlement paper, which was meant to be given to the parties the previous Friday but was delayed, was finally presented at 12.30 a.m. on the morning of Tuesday, 7 April.

Disagreements centred on the Irish Government and the SDLP arguing for a power-sharing, cabinet-style executive to run Northern Ireland but the UUP stood by its plans for a loose structure of committees to operate Government departments without an executive holding overall control. The other major disagreement was on the question of establishing the North–South Ministerial Council by legislation in Westminster and the Oireachtas, and whether the Council would begin to function at the same time as the assembly or even in advance. In relation to Strand One, Unionists feared the thought of Sinn Féin being assigned one of the portfolios in the aforementioned power-sharing, cabinet-style executive.

Later that Tuesday, it emerged that changes in Articles 2 and 3 of the Irish Constitution, which lay territorial claim to the whole of the island, would only be implemented if the potentially historic agreement was passed by referendum in Northern Ireland. Clinton rang Ahern that afternoon to offer words of encouragement and said the US still believed there was enough on the table to fashion an agreement. On Tuesday evening, Ahern attended the removal of his mother to the Church of St Vincent de Paul in Marino in Dublin and early on Wednesday morning, he flew to Hillsborough Castle where he had breakfast with Tony Blair.

Unionists and Loyalists had rejected Mitchell's first draft. The Alliance party also reacted unfavourably to what Mitchell called his 'synthesis for a settlement' paper, particularly over what they saw as two-tier or community-policing plans for the RUC. Ahern and Blair discussed the Unionist concerns about North–South bodies and Unionist demands that they derive their authority directly from a Stormont-based assembly. The two leaders considered a possible compromise which would result in the North–South Ministerial Council and a specified number of implementation bodies being defined in the legislation establishing a Northern Ireland Assembly, then rooting them in the authority of the Assembly once it came into being. Blair met Trimble and went through Mitchell's text line by line.

'I feel the hand of history on our shoulder in respect of this – I really do – and I just think we need to acknowledge that and respond to it,' said Blair.

Up to this stage, the UUP and Sinn Féin had not had a bilateral encounter and there were suspicions among Unionists as to why Republicans reacted favourably to Mitchell's draft.

Ahern flew up to Belfast on Wednesday evening, following the funeral of his mother, at which the Archbishop of Dublin, Dr Desmond Connell, told Ahern that this 'heavy burden of grieving' had come in a week in which he was exercising the responsibility of his high office for the sake of the entire community. He had tripartite talks with Blair and Trimble and signalled that the Government was ready to seek the compromises and accommodation necessary to bring the multi-party talks process to a successful conclusion. He said the Mitchell draft was 'certainly the basis for an agreement' and said everyone would have 'to move a little bit'.

There appeared to be progress on the crux issue of Strand Two, whereby a compromise appeared to be taking shape around a proposal to have the Assembly and the North–South Council established by legislation, with a new British–Irish agreement incorporating a prior commitment by the parties to establish cross-Border implementation bodies in a specified number of areas after the Assembly would come into being or in parallel with it. Dublin government officials stressed they were 'not going to start rewriting the document' and that if Blair wanted to rewrite the draft 'we'll be here for the next 21 months' while they 'still don't know what Trimble's bottom line is'.

At 1a.m. on Thursday morning he flew back to Dublin but returned North eight hours later. The full text of the changes to Articles 2 and 3 of the Irish Constitution emerged that day. Article 2 had stated: 'The national territory consists of the whole island of Ireland, its islands and the territorial seas.' It would be replaced by: 'It is the entitlement and the birthright of every person born on the island of Ireland to be part of the Irish nation. That is also the entitlement of all persons qualified by law to be citizens of Ireland.'

Article 3 had stated: 'Pending the re-integration of the national territory, and without prejudice to the right of the Parliament and Government established by this constitution to exercise jurisdiction over the whole of that territory, the laws enacted by that Parliament shall have the like area and extent of application as laws of Saorstat Eireann and the like extra-territorial effect.' It would be replaced by: 'It is the firm will of the Irish nation in harmony and friendship to unite all the people who share the territory of the island of Ireland in all the diversity of their identities and traditions, recognising that a United Ireland should be brought about only by peaceful means with the consent of the majority of the people. Until then, laws enacted by the Parliament established by the Constitution shall have the like area and extent of application as the laws enacted by the Parliament that existed immediately before the coming into operation of this Constitution.'

Sinn Féin sent signals that it was unhappy with what was happening. 'We will be here until the process either succeeds or collapses, but I think we are coming very close to the point of collapse,' said party chairman, Mitchell McLaughlin.

It has now emerged that the major stumbling block was the Unionists' refusal to allow a Sinn Féin Minister to take part in the governing Executive, even if Assembly elections gave them that mandate (the subsequent election in fact allows them two

Ministers). Today Ahern gives a new insight into the deadlock.

'The principal difficulties towards the end of the negotiations related to the coherence of the proposed Executive and the number and effectiveness of the North-South implementing bodies. We were being pushed very hard to water down our essential requirements. My job all along had been to bring my party and Northern Nationalists along with an Agreement, including fundamental constitutional change, which I could only do if there was a comprehensive, balanced and far-reaching political settlement that provided real partnership and equality on an inclusive basis in the North and meaningful North-South institutions.

'Early in April, before going out to a Summit in Assam, I had to put down a marker that we had made enough concessions. I put my foot down and said 'our compromises are over'. Over the weekend, we concentrated on providing Senator George Mitchell with a draft Agreement which he would be able to table, to bring the negotiations to their end phase in the last week before Easter. The British proved willing in the end to underwrite a pretty strong position from our point of view, which gave me some room for manoeuvre in negotiations at Hillsborough the following Wednesday.

'It was necessary for both myself and Tony Blair to be present for most of the last week, to concentrate minds and bring the negotiations to an issue. He and I were the only ones who already had power and who could exert the necessary influence and call the more difficult decisions. For me, it was not a very difficult week, but I felt I had to be there.

'Unionists, Loyalists and Alliance revolted at sight of the draft text, mainly because of our very elaborate and ambitious section on North-South bodies, but also because of the section dealing with fundamental reform of the RUC. Sinn Féin on the other hand wanted to harden up the text in many different places, relating to rights, judicial and police reform and prisoners. Now, I had an absolute right to say to the British in Hillsborough, that you negotiated this with me last Friday, that I didn't have to change. But both Tony Blair and I kept on talking, both with each other and with the parties, sometimes in long bilateral sessions where great reserves of patience were required. What was important was to protect our essential requirements and to try and improve the text in every way we could, so that we could carry everyone with us. It helped that the focus of some parties was mainly on the institutions, where they would have responsibility, while others were more focused on rights, and the justice and equality sections, some of which would remain the responsibility of the British Government. We were able to secure Sinn Féin participation by right in the Executive, and the SDLP were able to negotiate an effective system of partnership government with the Ulster Unionists. The First Minister and the Deputy First Minister were effectively equals, which was very important to the SDLP, and the whole system was interlocking and based on parallel consent. The SDLP were delighted.

'We had also won a critical number of North-South implementation bodies and an equivalent number of areas for close co-operation. The principle of North-South co-operation was clearly established, and we were being given the chance to demonstrate its potential for further expansion. Working closely with the Secretary of State, Mo Mowlam, we did our best in long night-time sessions to bring Sinn Féin on board, by going as far as we could to meet them on the many points of concern that they brought up. We were not sure of their final position that night, but at dawn it appeared to our great relief, after Mitchel McLaughlin gave a more positive interview than he had done the night before, that everyone was on board. There were, however, further delays, as there was something of a crisis of conscience in the Unionist camp, which only firm leadership by David Trimble with the encouragement of Tony Blair and President Clinton was able to overcome. But eventually everyone was on board, and Senator George Mitchell wrapped up the Agreement around 5 p.m. Everyone was utterly exhausted, and the enormity of what we had achieved only slowly began to sink in.'

The death of his mother could not have come at a worse time.

'What a week,' he sighs.

Immeasurably close to his mother, even to this day he cannot bring himself to go back to All Hallows, the house in which he was reared and where his mother died.

He is also certain a deal such as the Good Friday Agreement could not have been made if the Conservatives were still in power in Britain. 'Because of their party and what they stand for,' he insists.

On the afternoon of Good Friday, 11 April 1998, the historic multi-party document was finally signed after negotiators stayed up all that night and into the latter part of that day to come to an agreement. At 5.36 p.m. George Mitchell declared: 'I am pleased to announce that the two Governments and the political parties in Northern Ireland have reached agreement.'

Ahern said: 'This is a day we should treasure – a day when

agreement and accommodation have replaced days of difference and division.'

The main points of the deal were: a Northern Ireland Assembly with 108 seats, to be elected by proportional representation; the Assembly would elect a 12-strong executive committee of ministers; the Assembly's first task would be to set up a North–South Ministerial council within one year (which would have responsibility for cross- border bodies such as tourism and fisheries); the Council would be accountable to the Assembly and the Dáil; amendments to Articles 2 and 3 of the Irish Constitution would establish the principle of change but only consent and the repeal of the (British) Government of Ireland Act.

Strand Three included an Inter-Governmental Council (Council of the Isles) to be set up, with members drawn from the Dáil, Assembly, House of Commons and the new assemblies in Cardiff and Edinburgh; Rights, safeguards and equalities of opportunity including the establishment of a new Northern Ireland Human Rights Commission; accelerated mechanisms to be placed for the release of political prisoners; and an independent commission to make recommendations for future policing arrangements in Northern Ireland.

After all the bloody days down through the years – Bloody Sunday . . . Bloody Friday, this was truly a Good Friday. Several members of the negotiating teams wept openly, particularly members of the Womens' Coalition. Seamus Mallon said it was the highlight of his political career. Ahern said that the magnitude of the event really struck home when friends of his in Dublin told him that pubs and bars all over the city had switched over their televisions from compulsively viewing an English premiership football match between Liverpool and Manchester United, to see history being made.

On 23 May, a total of 676,966 (71.2 per cent) people in Northern Ireland voted in favour of the agreement and 274,879 (28.8 per cent) against. Out of an electorate turnout of 81 per cent, it meant that both a majority of Unionists and a majority of Nationalists had backed the peace accord. In the first All Ireland vote since 1918, the result in the Republic was even more decisive: those in favour, 95 per cent; those against, 5 per cent. Ahern had delivered. A couple of weeks later, a newspaper poll gave him a satisfaction rating of 83 per cent, the highest ever recorded by any Taoiseach. A later poll taken in October showed him still riding high with a remarkable satisfaction rate of 80 per cent.

Today, Ahern admits there are still problems over decommissioning but expects them to be ironed out – and ultimately he sees a United

Ireland in his lifetime.

'Based on the principle of consent and based on the powers of persuasion, I think it's still a political goal and a political aspiration worth working for,' he remarks.

'I'm heartened to see every day now that more and more bodies and more and more groups are becoming more All-Ireland-minded. As you know, within the Agreement, this basis, this arrangement, and hopefully all these institutions will be put together but in 10, 15 years, if a small proportion of Unionist people vote whenever there's another vote . . .

'I think peace has to be followed on economic, sport, cultural and religious grounds. I was at a thing the other night where purchasing managers were going to have a big conference in Newcastle, Co. Down, to look at the economy of the island; medics are getting together, engineers are getting together, farmers are working very close together – Republican farmers and Unionist farmers, Republican and Unionist fishermen, all of these things. Everywhere there's an All Ireland body.

'I can see a United Ireland. Remember, if there's peace, there's stability, if the institutions are working, if all the groups and organisations are working within the country. You don't need an enormous amount of people to change. It is a principle. I'm saying it is democratically fought for, peacefully fought for, and requires the powers of persuasion that we *can* run this thing better on our own and I think that's as real as it ever was on the other side of the Good Friday Agreement, far more real than it ever was.

'It's for us to persuade people. I think it's us who believe in it, and we have to work so that this island, as part of a block which is going to be 400 million people in the EU, can work it together. And I think you're going to see more co-operation across every kind of area.

'All those things were hindered because of violence and now they're blossoming.

'They're blossoming in a huge range of areas. It won't happen overnight, but I think the vote will come back again. It can't be a nationalist vote. It must be a majority vote within the North; that's now conceded, but I don't go with this thing that the Nationalists will outbreed them either (laughs). It is a question of the Nationalist and Unionist vote, whether it's a soft or hard Unionist vote.'

Chapter 37

Don't Shatter our Dream

O n a warm, sunny Saturday during summer in the bustling Co.
Tyrone market town of Omagh, the afternoon was spent by
shoppers out looking for groceries and clothes, and mothers with their
children searching for uniforms and books for the upcoming school
term.

It was 15 August and the feast of the Assumption in the Catholic
calendar. A carnival was being held in the town to celebrate the peace
process. A group of children from Buncrana, Co. Donegal, and their
friends from an exchange group of Spanish students who were staying
with them visited the town to see the Ulster American Folk Museum
and to take part in the carnival atmosphere.

Omagh is a mainly Nationalist town and at one stage had a Sinn
Féin majority on its local council. But relations between the majority
Catholic and minority Protestant communities in the town were
excellent and across the counties as a whole, the peace process was in
full swing. The Good Friday Agreement had allowed the people of
Ireland to hope that the violence which had claimed the lives of nearly
three and a half thousand people in the Troubles during the previous
30 years was a thing of the past.

Nevertheless, a small fanatical wing of Republicans had broken away
from the main body of Sinn Féin over that party's policy of pursuing
a peaceful settlement in Northern Ireland and of maintaining the IRA
cease-fire. An embittered hard core of men and women wanted to

continue the 'war against the Brits'. They did not care that 95 per cent of the voters in the Republic and 71 per cent in the North had passed the Good Friday Agreement. They still wanted the Brits out of Ireland, no matter what the cost, and to hell with any mandate. They set up a group called the 32 County Sovereignty Committee to push forward its 'political' views. It tried to distance itself from a terror group which called itself the 'real IRA'. Its leader was the former Quarter Master General of the IRA, who based his operations near Dundalk.

Although mustering less than 100 devotees, the group was determined to wreak havoc with the peace process through its bombs. The Gardaí had successfully thwarted their operations several times by seizing explosives and shooting one of its members dead during an attempted armed heist in Co Wicklow. But the 'Real IRA' continued its campaign and it was only a matter of time before tragedy struck.

A caller gave a message to the offices of the UTV newsroom and the Samaritans warning that a bomb had been left outside Omagh courthouse to explode just after 3 p.m. Yet the bomb had been left in Market Street, almost half a mile away, where shoppers, visitors and workers had been herded. The car bomb exploded at 3.10 p.m. The result was total carnage.

'I was here in St Luke's on the Saturday evening in the middle of August, which was unusual enough,' Ahern recalls today. 'I probably would have still been in Kerry until the following day, but the reason I was here was because I came back to meet the leader of the US Republican Party, Newt Gingrich.

'So I came back here to do a bit of work and my security guy picked it up from the Guards that there had been an explosion in Omagh. My brother Maurice then rang, having seen it on Sky News. At first they told me it was five, then it was eight dead.

'Immediately, I got onto the Guards. I got onto the Department of Justice; I got onto Foreign Affairs. It was very interesting that here for once was the Taoiseach ringing everyone and nobody knew. I got guys on golf courses; guys in sailing clubs; guys everywhere, but I got them. So within a few hours we had everybody. It was devastating. I was on to Clinton, I was on to Blair, I was on to nearly everybody. It just stemmed from there: it was non-stop.'

Some 29 people lost their lives in that explosion. It was the worst loss of life in Northern Ireland in a single atrocity. Dozens more were injured. The bomb killed Catholic, Protestant and dissenter. Most of the victims were women, including a pregnant mother of twins, her mother and her grandmother – three generations. Many of the other victims were children, teenagers and young adults. Three boys from Buncrana, a Spanish student and a Spanish teacher were also killed. The bombers appeared not to have cared who they killed or maimed.

At first the outcry of grief was immeasurable. It soon turned into a searing fury of anger and hate towards the bombers and their supporters. Ireland, north and south, was united in its revulsion towards the 'Real IRA' ringleaders, whose identities were well known by now. The town of Dundalk held a public protest to show its sense of outrage at the evil in their midst while the country held a communal one minute's silence the following Saturday at the same time of the explosion in memory of the victims. 'Never again' was the cry.

Ahern had appeared on RTE's television news on the evening of the bombing and stringently declared that he was going to 'crush' the organisation that was behind it. He now reveals for the first time, that he was formulating a piercing policy to be brought in to counter the terrorists.

'I had already formulated that type of legislation in my head,' he discloses.

'Back in July, I had told the Cabinet at the last meeting before the summer break that I really feared this group, unfortunately, if that's the way you might think of it. But I really thought this group could do something massive, and since February or March we had put a huge amount of surveillance on them. Like everything, we got them seven or eight times, we caught them so many times – we were so lucky. I mean, it was good intelligence, but there was a fair bit of luck, I can tell you.

The 'draconian' measures subsequently passed by both the Irish and British Parliaments in a bid to thwart terrorist groups like the 'Real IRA' included the removal of the right to silence during questioning by the police about their activities; they could be imprisoned on the word of a senior police officer that they were a member of a terrorist organisation; and anybody who helped them, by allowing them to use property such as land or the likes of garages, would have that property confiscated.

'We had been looking at these measures,' Ahern reveals. 'I had asked back in May or June to look at our legislation, to see what more we could do to really get after these guys and that review had started in

June. It was going on in two ends: it was going on in the AG's department, and it was going on in John O'Donoghue's Justice department, and at the last meeting on the 28 July, both of them had told me that their guys were going to continue working on it during the summer and they would have it for the first week of September for me.'

But the emergency legislation had to be railroaded prematurely in light of the Omagh atrocity. Ahern immediately knew that he had to recall the Dáil and bring in this type of legislation. He also needed Tony Blair to do likewise.

'I told him what we were doing,' he says. 'I told him we were recalling the Dáil, we were bringing in tough legislation, we were going to step up working with the RUC on this kind of stuff. He was still indicating for another ten days that they weren't going to do any of this for two weeks and then they had this thing in the British papers about the civil libertarian stuff and all that.

'I went to Belfast on the Sunday. The reason I didn't go to Omagh on the Sunday was that the President went instead. She asked me – she has to get approval – so I gave them the approval. And the Lord Mayor [of Dublin] asked. So the President went in the morning and the Lord Mayor in the evening and I went to Belfast. I did, however, go to the memorial ceremony later in Omagh.

'This was so devastating, I decided to go upfront and I went on every programme. Then I got all the security people in on the Sunday morning. We had the security meeting, and we got all that together. I went up to meet Blair and I told him what I was going to do on the Sunday night in Belfast and we prepared all the stuff and I announced it on the Wednesday.

'I don't think they had thought about bringing back their Parliament. I had announced on the Sunday we were bringing back the Dáil, if not the Saturday. I said I was going to get this legislation. We were two weeks ahead of them and by and large they copied what we did, if you look at it.'

He is still concerned that the only group yet to call a cease-fire, the Continuity IRA, may still be a threat. That grouping has links to Republican Sinn Féin and although some of the Continuity IRA leaders were arrested earlier in the year and it has gone through somewhat of a lull, Ahern refuses to rule out their threat.

'We still have the Continuity IRA,' he insists, 'and I won't rest. There is a crossover between the New ('Real') IRA and the Continuity. There was at the start, anyway, though I think there was a big change in the 32 Sovereignty with a new leadership. Omagh has done more to frighten them, thank God.

'But the Continuity are still there and I think the campaign still can't let up on the Continuity, for three reasons. One is that they can still do something terrible, and they have some capabilities, maybe not a lot, but they've some capabilities. Secondly, as long as there is somebody involved in the 'Armed Struggle' it means that all the security, militarisation stuff is required there. And thirdly, we have legislation which says that we will go after anyone involved in this and I feel dutybound to implement it wherever we can. Now there's a lot of intelligence on Omagh that's been formed. It's a huge operation: people from both sides of the border were involved in the bombing.

'It does cause concern. Over the years I had formulated a lot of information on these guys, so you know who you're dealing with.'

The human scale of the tragedy was brought into focus for Ahern when he went to Buncrana to meet the families of the three boys from the town who were killed and to attend their funeral, at which Unionist leader David Trimble, who was also present, was given a telling round of applause by the congregation for his role in the peace process.

'I went up to the three families in Buncrana,' Ahern remembers. 'I visited the three houses the night before the funeral. I felt terrible, absolutely terrible. They were three very different cases. Two of the kids only lived a few doors from each other – two Donegal families – and they were laid out. One of them was a United supporter [Sean McLaughlin, 12]. They had put a picture of Mary McAleese in his coffin. And then there was the other boy [Oran Doherty, 8] in his Celtic jersey.

'The father knew I was associated with Glasgow Celtic and asked me it I could get one of the players over the following day for the funeral.'

Ahern had attended the last game of the season at Celtic park, at which Celtic won the league for the first time in 10 years. Although caught up in controversy at the time about his treatment there, he was still respected well enough for Celtic to send over a jet with one of its players, Mark Rieper, and senior officials, to show that Omagh touched them too, and even more poignantly because Oran was a Celtic fanatic.

'The first house I went to was the English family [the Bakers] who had come over to get away from it all. [James Baker, 12, was also killed]. That was very sad. The wife was out collecting flowers in the field. She missed me, then followed me over to meet me in the other house and as devastated as they were, they were so nice. Then I went down to meet the Spanish kids. I met all the Spanish kids. Like any kids, they were sad, but up to their tricks and jokes. And I met their teachers.'

Spanish student Fernando Blasco Baseiga, 12, and his Spanish teacher, Rocio Abad Ramos, 23, also died. The Spanish Government sent over a military jet to bring their bodies home and those of the Spanish injured. Fernando's father had himself been the target of a terrorist attack, by ETA, several years ago, and despite the deep shame felt by Ireland at citizens from Spain had been killed by terrorists here, there were some comforting words from the Spanish that they too had suffered from the same affliction down through the years (later, ETA too announced a permanent cease-fire, modelling its aspirations on the Northern Ireland peace process).

The people in the town are now getting their lives back together, but no one, particularly Bertie Ahern, will ever forget the Omagh tragedy. The little boy, Sean McLaughlin, whose visible bomb-blasted remains he visited in Buncrana, had a reason for having a picture of him with President Mary McAleese in his coffin. He had earlier met her on a school trip to Aras an Uachtaráin. McAleese released the moving text of a poem Sean had written and which he presented her during his visit there.

It said:
'Orange and green, it doesn't matter,
United now, don't shatter our dream,
Scatter the seeds of peace over our land,
So we can travel across the bridge of hope.'

That bridge Sean so passionately wrote about, now appears to have been finally crossed.

Chapter 38

The Man with the Midas Touch

B ertie Ahern is the man with the Midas touch. Almost everything he has put his hand to in his political career has reaped golden political dividends. He brought industrial relations harmony to the country after decades of unrest; he practically single-handedly turned around the economy into the Celtic tiger it is today; and his astute negotiating skills with the Northern Ireland peace process have led to the first long-term hope of political and sectarian violence being eradicated for good from this island. Even though he is Ireland's youngest Taoiseach, his 21-year career in the Dáil has seen him traverse a couple of generations of politicians. He has been at the cutting edge of some of the most dramatic and exciting times in Irish politics, particularly those centreing around Charlie Haughey.

For a man who earns £96,000 a year, he now appears to earn every penny of it: his normal routine would be to get some sleep at 12.30 a.m., rise at 6.30 a.m., have breakfast and then go for a jog near his home. He'd then scan the morning papers, particularly the *Financial Times* and head to his office at Government Buildings in Merrion Street, where he'd spend the first several minutes discussing sporting matters with his senior staff. The rest of the day would see him busily toiling away, trying to sort out the country's troubles. He hardly has a minute to himself.

A deeply religious man, he has visited Lourdes with his late mother, Julia, and regularly attends Mass at the Pro-Cathedral in Dublin on Saturday evenings. He also seems to have time for everyone: on the wall in his constituency office in St Luke's he has prominently displayed a framed 'Missing' poster of Jo Jo Dollard, the 21-year-old from Callan, Co Kilkenny, who disappeared three years ago. He explains that Jo Jo's sister occasionally calls into his office and he has built up an interest in the case, as well as the other widely publicised cases of recently missing women. It was Ahern's sheer dedication to the Northern Ireland peace process for the good of the country, when he travelled up to the North for meetings and back down again for his mother's removal funeral, which endeared him to many.

Sundays are normally spent with his two daughters, Georgina and Cecilia. He likes to follow his beloved Dublin Gaelic football team when they're playing league matches and now and again jaunts over to Old Trafford to follow his favourite football team, Manchester United. He also keeps an avid eye out for Glasgow Celtic, and, bizarrely, Hull City. One of his few regrets is that when he first got elected to the Dáil in 1977, his football career had to end.

'I was playing extremely good soccer then and I neglected it over the next four or five years and missed out on a few medals,' he says.

Ahern was listening to the Beatles and the Stones during the '60s. He remembers hearing the news of the assassination of President Kennedy on the radio when listening to one of those pop shows. He is also a major Leonard Cohen fan.

When he got elected to Mayorality, the first thing he told his electors was 'just call me Bertie': and that's the funny thing about Ahern. Every man, woman and child in the street refers to him affectionately as just 'Bertie'. Indeed, a recent *Ireland on Sunday* opinion poll found that Ahern was the most popular Taoiseach of all time among those questioned. Ironically, in second place at 17 per cent to Ahern's 23 per cent was his own favourite politician and inspiration – Sean Lemass (Jack Lynch rated 11 per cent, Charlie Haughey 10 per cent and Eamon de Valera 9 per cent).

He enjoys his favourite tipple, a pint of Bass, in local haunts around his constituency area and the only major health problem – besides dieting! – is that he put his back out when lifting a cart on Moore Street in Dublin for a photo opportunity when he was Lord Mayor.

'It still gives me problems now and again,' he admits.

He has met practically every living world leader, including Colonel Gaddafi in his tent in Libya. Ahern and Haughey travelled to Libya in the early 1980s to seal a cattle deal.

'I am certainly one of the few who've met him in the tent; that was unique,' he laughs.

But surely he must have felt uncomfortable when he stood stoically beside Bill Clinton during his visit in Dublin when the President was asked probing questions about Monica Lewinski under the full glare of the world's media?

'I did not!' he chuckles. 'I found myself absolutely thrilled. I felt a bit sorry for him maybe, but I didn't feel uncomfortable under his barrage of questions. I really like Clinton. I've had a number of meetings, phone calls and discussions with him and he is a very charismatic guy, but he's a good fighter. Okay, he knows he got caught in these things – he knows – but it was an investigation into Whitewater and a planning issue and it ended up with a 455 page report. Okay, it's not very nice, but it's no grounds for impeachment.'

And what of his plans for the year ahead?

'This side of Christmas is the Budget, in which we have to try and help more on the lower paid and the social inclusion issues,' he enthuses.

'Agenda 2000 is going to be a huge thing in Europe; there's going to be a huge amount of negotiation in that. That's the whole structural funds, cohesion funds, capital funds. Then the North is going to be another slog, which it is every day.'

He feels empathy with young couples and others caught up in the housing crisis.

'It has to be tackled in a number of ways,' he explains. 'We've taken excellent action on the Bacon report, as far as getting investors out of the market, but the supply and demand issue still has to be there. Supply and demand means that we have to get more zoned land, we have to make sure that the land that is zoned is serviced and I think we have to get the next round of these rural designations up. I think the best thing we can do for rural Ireland, is start getting a lot of towns developed. There's an awful lot of people in Dublin who would be delighted to get out, a few miles out. '

He says he intends to run for another term as Taoiseach.

'I would like to do ten years. One thing I've learned in politics is that you don't start planning out your future. But I'd like to end up doing something different.

'From the time I started work in 1969 – jobs in the Mater, and so on – I've always been working at least a week and half more than the average person, so in terms of years, by next year, I'll have done 45 years work. I was never in a job that worked nine to five, or a journalist that works four days a week or something like that,' he laughs.

He has no ambitions to go into business when his political career has run its course.

'I'm not interested in wealth,' he scoffs. 'One thing about me, and anyone who knows me knows this is true, is that I'm not interested in wealth. I associate wealth with trouble and I don't really need that. Once I can walk that road over there, have a few jars, talk to the guys, go down to Tolka and Croker: that makes me happy.'

But he does reveal one wish.

'I wouldn't mind being back in administration, sport or something like that,' he confides. 'I'd love to get into something that I'd really like to be in 'til the end. I would love to be the president of some sporting organisation. Any sporting organisation. GAA, soccer, athletics. I love sport.'

This may be very fanciful stuff on Ahern's part. Ahern is the electorates' property now. They will decide what happens in the next 10 years.